T0092880

Developing Informed Intuition for Decision-Making

Data Analytics Applications

Series Editor

Jay Liebowitz

Developing Informed Intuition for Decision-Making

Edited by
Jay Liebowitz

CRC Press
Taylor & Francis Group
Boca Raton London New York

CRC Press is an imprint of the
Taylor & Francis Group, an **informa** business

AN AUERBACH BOOK

CRC Press
Taylor & Francis Group
6000 Broken Sound Parkway NW, Suite 300
Boca Raton, FL 33487-2742

© 2020 by Taylor & Francis Group, LLC
CRC Press is an imprint of Taylor & Francis Group, an Informa business

No claim to original U.S. Government works

Printed on acid-free paper

International Standard Book Number-13: 978-0-3672-5857-3 (Hardback)

This book contains information obtained from authentic and highly regarded sources. Reasonable efforts have been made to publish reliable data and information, but the author and publisher cannot assume responsibility for the validity of all materials or the consequences of their use. The authors and publishers have attempted to trace the copyright holders of all material reproduced in this publication and apologize to copyright holders if permission to publish in this form has not been obtained. If any copyright material has not been acknowledged please write and let us know so we may rectify in any future reprint.

Except as permitted under U.S. Copyright Law, no part of this book may be reprinted, reproduced, transmitted, or utilized in any form by any electronic, mechanical, or other means, now known or hereafter invented, including photocopying, microfilming, and recording, or in any information storage or retrieval system, without written permission from the publishers.

For permission to photocopy or use material electronically from this work, please access www.copyright.com (http://www.copyright.com/) or contact the Copyright Clearance Center, Inc. (CCC), 222 Rosewood Drive, Danvers, MA 01923, 978-750-8400. CCC is a not-for-profit organization that provides licenses and registration for a variety of users. For organizations that have been granted a photocopy license by the CCC, a separate system of payment has been arranged.

Trademark Notice: Product or corporate names may be trademarks or registered trademarks, and are used only for identification and explanation without intent to infringe.

Visit the Taylor & Francis Web site at
http://www.taylorandfrancis.com

and the CRC Press Web site at
http://www.crcpress.com

Printed and bound in Great Britain by
TJ International Ltd, Padstow, Cornwall

To all those decision makers who know that you
can't always rely strictly on the numbers

Contents

Preface

In these days of data-driven or data-informed decision-making, intuition seems to be lost in the discussion of how it can play a major role in everyday life, including executive decision-making. In some of my own recent research, however, we have found that directors and executives often trust and rely on their intuition for decision-making. Even Einstein has many quotes that stress the importance of "imagination" over "knowledge," particularly highlighting that the "really valuable thing is intuition."

Toward the goal of taking a "holistic" approach to decision-making and putting intuition into the equation of "analytics + intuition = success," this book provides different perspectives on intuition, intuitive awareness, and further developing informed intuition for decision-making. Various schools of thought, both in the U.S. and abroad, are represented in this book, including research and pragmatic issues and examples dealing with intuition.

Many analytics conferences discount the importance of intuition in decision-making. However, there are countless examples where the "intuitive mind" has played a critical component in making the correct decision. One of the main goals of this book is to create and stimulate a conversation on the importance of using intuition in the business context, or at least "informed intuition" or "rational intuition," as some people say.

We have tried to provide insight from many of the key individuals worldwide who look at intuition from different angles—whether through energy, meditation, practice, improvisation, medicine, or other perspectives. Some of this information may seem provoking, and you may not agree with all that is said. However, the chapters are filled with examples, tools, techniques, research, and vignettes to show how intuition is often a missing part of one's decision-making and there are ways to improve one's intuitive awareness.

I would like to first thank the well-recognized authors in this field who contributed their valuable insights in making this book a reality. My thanks also are extended to John Wyzalek and all his colleagues at Taylor & Francis Group, too numerous to mention here, for allowing me to carve an important stream of knowledge into the business and management literature. My gratitude is offered as well to my colleagues and students at Harrisburg University of Science and Technology for their many hours of discussions and thought-provoking ideas. Finally, and certainly not least, I am indebted to my family and parents for allowing me to be an "adventurer" and explore the great unknown!

Jay Liebowitz, D.Sc.
Washington, D.C./Philadelphia, PA

Editor

Jay Liebowitz is the distinguished chair of Applied Business and Finance at Harrisburg University of Science and Technology. He previously was the Orkand Endowed chair of Management and Technology in the Graduate School at the University of Maryland University College (UMUC). He served as a professor in the Carey Business School at Johns Hopkins University. He was ranked one of the top 10 knowledge management researchers/practitioners out of 11,000 worldwide, and was ranked #2 in KM Strategy worldwide according to the January 2010 *Journal of Knowledge Management*. At Johns Hopkins University, he was the founding program director for the Graduate Certificate in Competitive Intelligence and the Capstone Director of the MS-Information and Telecommunications Systems for Business Program, where he engaged over 30 organizations in industry, government, and not-for-profits in capstone projects.

Prior to joining Hopkins, Dr. Liebowitz was the first knowledge management officer at NASA Goddard Space Flight Center. Before NASA, Dr. Liebowitz was the Robert W. Deutsch Distinguished Professor of Information Systems at the University of Maryland–Baltimore County, professor of Management Science at George Washington University, and chair of Artificial Intelligence at the U.S. Army War College.

Dr. Liebowitz is the founding editor-in-chief of *Expert Systems with Applications: An International Journal* (published by Elsevier). He is a Fulbright Scholar, IEEE-USA Federal Communications Commission Executive Fellow, and Computer Educator of the Year (International Association for Computer Information Systems). He has published over 40 books and myriad journal articles on knowledge management, analytics, intelligent systems, and IT management. Dr. Liebowitz served as the editor-in-chief of Procedia-CS (Elsevier). He is also the series book editor of the new Data Analytics Applications book series (Taylor & Francis Group). In October 2011, the International Association for Computer Information Systems named the "Jay Liebowitz Outstanding Student Research Award" for the best student research paper at the IACIS Annual Conference. Dr. Liebowitz was the Fulbright Visiting Research Chair in Business at Queen's University for the Summer 2017 and a Fulbright Specialist at Dalarna University in Sweden in May 2019. He has lectured and consulted worldwide.

Contributing Authors

Jon Aarum Andersen holds a Master of Business Administration and a Master of Social Science from Norway. He has a Doctor of Economics (Ph.D.) from Lund University, Sweden. Dr. Andersen has written 13 university level textbooks and has more than 40 international research journal publications. He is a visiting professor at Ljubljana University, Slovenia. Professor Andersen is now affiliated with Örebro University School of Business, Örebro University, Sweden.

Puneet K. Bindlish is a practicing consultant and an academic in the area of Integrative Intelligence for organizations facing VUCA. He is also a co-founder of Integrative Intelligence. He teaches at the Indian Institute of Technology (BHU) in Varanasi, India. He has rich academic, consulting and entrepreneurial experience in the healthcare, telecom, technology, banking and insurance, education, sports, and public service sectors.

Kenneth Carling is a professor in Microdata Analysis at the School of Technology and Business Studies, Dalarna University, Sweden. He earned his PhD in statistics 1995 at Uppsala University, Sweden. Before arriving at Dalarna University in 2001, he worked with hospital productivity at the Swedish research institute SPRI, labor market policy at the research agency IFAU, financial stability at the Central Bank of Sweden, and served as senior lecturer at Yale University. Over the years he has been a member of *inter alia*, INFORMS, the American Statistical Association, and served as the president of the Swedish Statistical Society (the Cramér Society). He has taught and published in academic journals some 50 articles foremost in economics, operations research, and statistics. In recent years, his research interest has mostly focused on transportation, mobility of goods and humans, and environmental challenges that constitute important work programs in the European Commission's Horizon 2020.

Ozan Isler holds a Ph.D. (2009) in Economics from University of California, Riverside. He is an assistant professor at Dogus University, Istanbul and an external fellow of University of Nottingham's Centre for Decision Research and Experimental Economics (CeDEx). His research focuses on dual-process accounts of social and moral behavior. He received the European Union's Marie Curie Fellowship (2015–2017) and has published in leading academic journals.

Jessica Jagtiani pursues a multifaceted professional career in art, design, management, research, and teaching. Currently she is the Education Product Manager and Art Director at Embodied Philosophy, an online learning institute that offers educational experiences in Eastern philosophy, contemplative sciences, and consciousness studies. Jessica holds a Doctor of Education in Art and Art Education from Teachers College, Columbia University, a Master of Fine Arts in Studio Art from the School of the Museum of Fine Arts at Tufts University, and a Diploma in Visual Communications from the Universität der Künste Berlin. She teaches video art, photography, and digital media art courses in higher education and offers spiritual art workshops for professionals in leadership and education. Jessica's art practice involves diverse media, such as video, photography, performance art, sculpture, and installation. Her artwork has been exhibited nationally and internationally. Moreover, she has long-term experience as a manager and designer in the media production industry and is the co-founder of the post-production company rundblick.tv in Berlin. Her research interests include the experience of intuition, spirituality, identity constructions, art-based research, experiential learning, distance learning, and media education pedagogies. Jessica follows a personal spiritual path, which involves the practices of art, meditation, dance, and teaching.

Francesca McCartney holds a Ph.D. in Energy Medicine. Since 1976, Dr. McCartney has worked in the holistic health field as a medical intuitive in an integrative medicine clinic; she is also a spiritual counselor, educator, and author. In 1984, she founded the Academy of Intuition Medicine®, which offers vocational career training in the art and science of Intuition Medicine® and in 2017 founded the Academy of Intuition Medicine® Online. In 2006, she founded Energy Medicine University offering Ph.D. and M.A. degrees in Integrative Holistic Health. Dr. McCartney is author of *Intuition Medicine®: The Science of Energy* and *Body of Health: The New Science of Intuition Medicine® for Energy & Balance.*

Kirk Hurford first became involved with computers in 1978—thinking he would just build a word processor. Evolving from software developer to business manager and entrepreneur, Kirk is always in front of the wave. He has founded several technology-based companies, and provided technological direction for organizations and government agencies, including WordStar, Fujitsu of America, Link TV, the U.S. Navy, and the National Security Agency.

Gaëtan Mourmant is a visiting professor at IÉSEG, School of Management (Paris, France). He received his Ph.D. in information systems from Paris Dauphine University and Georgia State University. He worked 4 years as a Marketing Database Analyst in a global financial institution. As an entrepreneur, he managed more than

70 IT projects. Gaëtan's research interests include decision-making, entrepreneurship, and IT personnel turnover. He has published papers in the *European Journal of Information Systems, Grounded Theory Review*, and received the Magid Igbaria Outstanding Conference Paper at the 2012 SIGMIS Conference.

Sharda S. Nandram is a psychologist, economist, and professor at Vrije University Amsterdam and Nyenrode Business University, chair of the Buurtzorg OMRISE research group, and non-executive director at Buurtzorg India. She is also a consultant and a co-founder of Praan Group and co-founder of the concept of Integrative Intelligence. She has more than three decades of academic, consulting, and entrepreneurial experience in the healthcare, accountancy, banking and insurance, public service, education, and sports sectors.

She has earned two bachelors and two masters (one in psychology and the other in economics (both at the University of Amsterdam). She has also earned her Ph.D. in social sciences at the Vrije University at Amsterdam.

Asta Raami completed her Ph.D. thesis on the use and development of intuition in the Aalto University Media Lab in 2015, where she had worked beforehand for 15 years in teaching and research. After the dissertation, she has concentrated on making the potential of intuition known outside the scientific community.

In 2016, Dr. Raami published her first writings on the subject of utilizing the hidden potential of the human mind in her book, *Älykäs intuitio ja miten hyödynnämme sitä* (*Intelligent Intuition and How We Use It*, Schilds & Söderströms, 2016). In addition to this, she has worked as a co-writer in works concerning the new national level school curriculum *Ajattelun taidot ja oppiminen* (2016, PS-kustannus), since Finland is one of the first countries in the world where intuition is included in the national level school curriculum. Further, Dr. Raami has worked as a co-writer in a publication of Finland's Independence Fund SITRA titled *Sustainablity, Human Wellbeing and the Future of Education* (Pallgrave MacMillan, 2018) with her article *Towards Solving the Impossible Problems*. Dr. Raami's dissertation can be read online (*Intuition Unleashed: On the Application and Development of Intuition in the Creative Process*). Currently she works as a start-up entrepreneur in the Innerversity-program (www.innerversity.org).

David B. Resnik has an M.A. and Ph.D. in philosophy from the University of North Carolina at Chapel Hill and J.D. from Concord University School of Law. He received his B.A. in philosophy from Davidson College. Dr. Resnik was an Associate and Full Professor of Medical Humanities at the Brody School of Medicine at East Carolina University (ECU) from 1998–2004, and an associate director of the Bioethics Center at ECU and University Health Systems from 1998–2004. Dr. Resnik was assistant and associate professor of Philosophy at the University of Wyoming (UW) from 1990–1998, and director of the Center for the Advancement of Ethics at UW from 1995–1998. Dr. Resnik has published over

250 articles and 9 books on various topics in philosophy and bioethics and is a Fellow of the American Association for the Advancement of Science. He serves on several editorial boards and is an Associate Editor of the journal *Accountability in Research*. Dr. Resnik is also Chair of the NIEHS Institutional Review Board (IRB) and a Certified IRB Professional.

Danny Sandra is a transformation consultant and coach who assists leaders in guiding organizations through major transformations to realize integral growth. He has more than 20 years of international management experience with both start-ups and corporations, at each level in the organization, including C-level.

He holds an engineering degree, an MBA, and a diploma in craniosacral therapy. As part of his PhD, he is studying the phenomenon of entrainment in organizations at the Faculty of Business and Economics, University of Antwerp. He also regularly publishes in scientific journals about spiritual innovation, spiritual leadership, and consciousness development.

Eric W. Stein is associate professor of Management Science and Information Systems at The Pennsylvania State University. He is a full-time member of the graduate faculty in residence in the MBA program at the Penn State Great Valley campus (Malvern, PA), and is affiliated with the Smeal College of Business. Dr. Stein teaches behavioral science, knowledge-based systems, creativity and innovation in business, social entrepreneurship, and sustainability. For several years, he served as the Director of the New Ventures and Entrepreneurship program within the MBA program.

Dr. Stein has written on organizational memory and learning, strategic planning, human expertise, knowledge-based systems, creativity, and innovation. His works appear in several journals and books. Books include *Fostering Creativity in Self and the Organization* and *Designing Creative High Power Teams and Organizations*. His journal articles have appeared in the *Journal of Management Information Systems, Information Systems Research*, the *International Journal of Information Management, Journal of Business Ethics, Renewable and Sustainable Energy Reviews,* and *Expert Systems with Applications*, among others. Most recently, he has focused on the costs and benefits of running high tech vertical indoor farms. He is also is completing work on an instrument to assess creative strengths.

Dr. Stein holds an undergraduate degree in physics (with a minor in the humanities) from Amherst College. He received his Ph.D. in managerial science and systems from The Wharton School of the University of Pennsylvania.

Karen Storsteen is an executive coach, professional intuitive, organizational effectiveness consultant, and psychotherapist. She founded Performance By Design LLC in 1999, a company dedicated to individual and organizational brilliance, human performance improvement, innovation and profitable growth. She has taught hundreds of thousands in the intuitive, leadership, and management sciences to unleash everyday brilliance. Ms. Storsteen has been a regular on-air advisor on several FM/AM radio stations, developed several universities for large companies, been a contributing writer to *Inc.* and *TED Magazine*, and featured on NBC, CBS, and ABC. She has helped increase organizational productivity by 200 percent and radically improved performance. Storsteen is recognized by Mensa International, The Project Management Institute, higher education, and many Fortune 500 companies. She holds a Master of Science in Business Management and Organization and Master's Minor in Finance from the University of Colorado, Master of Arts Honors in Psychology from Regis University, and Bachelor of Science in Business Management from San Diego State University.

Dominique Surel is a Noetic scholar, dean of Faculty, and professor at Energy Medicine University (EMU, California), and holds M.B.A. and Ph.D. degrees. She lectures and conducts trainings worldwide about the human potential. Topics include controlled remote viewing (CRV), intuitive intelligence, and radiesthesia.

Onurcan Yilmaz is an assistant professor of psychology at Kadir Has University, Istanbul, Turkey. He currently leads the MINT lab (www.moralintuitionslab.com). His research focuses on dual-process accounts of morality and political cognition. He has published in leading academic journals such as *Cognition, Evolution and Human Behavior, Journal of Experimental Social Psychology, Social Psychological and Personality Science,* and *Judgment and Decision Making.*

Chapter 1

Intuitive Leadership: A Neurological, Psychological, and Quantum Approach to Heighten Intelligence, Innovation, and Performance

Karen Storsteen

Contents

Have you ever ignored your intuition and later regretted it? Conversely, have you ever listened to your intuition and thought, "That was a terrible idea … stupid intuition …"? Probably not! Why? Because you can rely on your intuition. You can count on this innate brilliance. Intuition is with you 100 percent of the time to ground you in the eye of the storm, tell you what to do in an emergency, and point you to your life's purpose. It allows you to envision the future and to take a bold leap of faith in the face of uncertainty. It is with you to help you make daily decisions with greater confidence and ease and to lead with courage, conviction, and compassion.

Whether you call intuition your inner voice, gut instinct, your higher self, or a sixth sense, it is your guide, consultant, and teacher—and it's free. Given that you are attracted to the subject matter of this book, you are likely aware of your intuitiveness and the value it plays in your work and life.

Neurologically, when you access your intuition, exponential intelligence emerges. You are accessing your highest level of intelligence as all of your intelligences kick in and line up at the same time: analytical, practical, social, emotional, and creative intelligences. Each of these intelligences strengthens as you develop your intuition. Intuitive decision-making enables exponential productivity improvement as well, as processing time can be reduced from years and months to minutes and seconds.

Over the last 10 years, one of the most extraordinary discoveries has been the understanding of neuroplasticity, dismantling the view that the brain is fixed and unchangeable. We now know definitively that the brain has the capacity to expand, reorganize, and rewire for heightened intelligence. Coupled with revolutionary findings in quantum physics, we are now in a better position to explain scientifically the mystery behind intuition and how to develop this brilliance!

A new, groundbreaking paradigm for human potential has emerged. We can envision what is possible and create the "impossible dream" when we uncover and consciously apply our intuitive intelligence in our lives and work. We can learn from the most significant leaders and scientists of our time who have used their intuitive intelligence to greatly benefit the world.

The information I will share with you in this chapter is grounded in science and decades of personal research ignited by a desire to understand my own extraordinary intuitive experiences. My curiosity grew from "common" and yet incredible experiences where I was able to perceive or know information with validity, without conscious reasoning or previous experience. I was compelled to understand this powerful "technology" and to explore the fascinating evidence behind our intuitiveness—to explain extraordinary intuitive phenomena that had been primarily inexplicable in years prior. Having worked in the fields of human and organizational development as an executive coach, management consultant, and later psychotherapist, I had developed several corporate universities for leaders teaching most every subject in the management and leadership sciences. Realizing the infinite power of intuitive intelligence, 16 years ago I took a leap of faith, faced my fears about challenging "traditional" thinking, and began teaching intuitive development to unleash everyday brilliance.

In this chapter, we explore the power of intuition. You will assess the degree to which you use your intuition today in business and life. We will discuss how stress diminishes intuition, effective decision-making, and brain functioning, as well as how to shift from stress to neurological power. In addition, you will learn several proven methods to develop and heighten your intuition. You will use a process at the end of the chapter to solve a problem or make a decision using your intuition. Lastly, you will reflect on your organization and the degree to which it supports an intuitively intelligent organization. Throughout the chapter, I shed light on the mechanics of intuition supported by sciences in psychology, neuroscience, and quantum physics.

Your Intuition in This Moment

You used your intuition when you picked up this book. In this moment, you are synthesizing information from your body, to include your gut and heart, with higher brain activity to create intuition. When your gut, heart, and head integrate, you are generating exponential intelligence and able to listen to your inner voice. In this moment, you have conscious perception and are also experiencing a physiological and emotional response to my words. Your analytical, rational, logical mind is also speaking, thinking about the reasons why you picked up this book. Perhaps you are looking for clarity, peace, and answers, or wanting to develop your leadership skills and intuitive abilities.

As a senior leader, you likely rose to your position due greatly to your intuitiveness and self-awareness. Intuitive people "read" their environment, people, and situations accurately, are aware of how they feel in the moment, integrate this information with higher brain function, and use this information wisely. If you describe yourself as a more left-brained, analytical type who bases most of your decisions on how you *think* about a situation, you probably are not noticing the degree to which your intuition is at work. Even if you think that you are not naturally wired intuitively, every one of us can develop and heighten our intuition, including you.

Intuition Is Your Greatest Asset

As you know, there have been many leadership and management practices to improve organizational performance over the years, such as scientific management, total quality management, change management, customer relationship management, project management, process re-engineering, Management by Objectives, Six Sigma, Scrum, quality circles, and situational leadership. I have taught and used many of these methods throughout my career as a management consultant identifying productivity gains across industries of up to 200 percent, while improving performance, employee satisfaction, and corporate value. These practices can be highly beneficial. And yet, developing intuition, our highest level of intelligence, has barely been on the radar. It is time for us to evolve to unprecedented levels of human functioning wherein we will utilize the capabilities that already reside within us.

The lack of focus and importance with respect to our intuitive intelligence in business is counter-intuitive. We need to rethink the way we think. In U.S. business, we have created cultures that support the rational, logical mind and inadvertently neglect the whole brain. We will not get to where we need to go by relying solely on intellect and logic, as they are not intelligence and wisdom. Relying solely on intellect and our "mental" mind, we ignore the instinctive and intelligent senses of the body, heart, and gut and the way we process this information emotionally. We cut ourselves off from our "whole self" and are therefore unable to perceive the entire picture. Intuitive decision-making embodies both linear (left brain) and nonlinear (right brain) processing. Albert Einstein said, "The intuitive mind is a sacred gift and the rational mind a sacred servant; we have created a society that honors the servant and has forgotten the gift." In addition, Einstein stated, "The intellect has little to do on the road to discovery. There comes a leap in consciousness—call it intuition or what you will—and the solution comes to you and you don't know how or why."

Overrationalizing and overintellectualizing minimize creativity, risk-taking, empathy, imagination, inspiration, ingenuity, teamwork, happiness, self-worth, efficient and effective decision-making, and perception, as well as profits and growth. Making practical decisions can even be thwarted as common sense and street smarts are overridden by overwhelming amounts of data, facts, and figures. Fear often pervades as these environments tend to be more critical, judgmental, opinionated, and risk-averse. The heart of the organization is minimized, and the egoic mind is in charge. The critical intelligence of empathy is undervalued. Stress impedes kindness. So, what's wrong with this picture? Neurologically, these environments dumb people down, and optimal performance is unattainable.

Leaders who consciously develop their own intuitive intelligence and the intuitive acumen within their organization will surpass the competition. Intuition is the neurocompetitive advantage. Where can intuition be practiced within your organization? Everywhere. Is there any industry where intuition would not be applicable? No. In my work with corporate clients, we have applied intuitive decision-making processes to strategic planning, product development, marketing, business development, project management, operations, and support functions such as human resources and IT. You use your intuition in developing your mission and vision, scanning your organization's environment for opportunities and threats, envisioning future products and services, and being attuned to unstated customer needs to increase sales, and to improve morale and motivate employees. Even the accounting staff, a role more generally defined by accounting rules and procedures, can benefit by developing their intuition as it will improve the accuracy of their work and efficiency.

According to a 2006 Annual CEO Survey of 252 U.S. CEOs, 62 percent indicated they are more likely to rely on their intuition than on data-driven analyses and quantitative information when making decisions. Where would you put yourself on this spectrum? In today's fast-paced environment, the need to make quick decisions in the face of uncertainty is pressing. Organizations do not have time for analysis paralysis. The ability to prioritize projects and resources, quickly get to the root of systemic issues, and identify patterns through volumes of data requires us to turn up the volume on our intuition. Dr. James Watson, Nobel laureate and co-discoverer of DNA, stated, "Intuition isn't mystical. It's a sort of background sense of how things should work, its facts hidden in the brain. Intuition is logic."

Are You Listening to Your Intuition? Are You on the Right Path?

Below is a checklist to begin to assess the degree to which you listen to your intuition in life and work and are on the "right" path. The list below is not all-inclusive. Signs that you are listening to your intuition and are on the "right" path are when you:

☐ Are in alignment with what you value	☐ Are using your greatest strengths and talents
☐ Do work that is fulfilling, has meaning, and is enjoyable	☐ Feel valued
☐ Follow your intuition over the opinions and expectations of others	☐ Are in tune with the signs your body is delivering to you
☐ Trust, in the face of uncertainty, that everything will work out okay	☐ Listen to your gut and heart
☐ Are self-aware	☐ Have confidence in yourself and abilities
☐ Are open to feedback	☐ Look forward to your day
☐ Feel empathy and compassion for others	☐ Enjoy your home life
☐ Experience doors opening easily for you	☐ Feel positive about the future
☐ Are often in the right place at the right time (experience synchronicity)	☐ Have restful sleep
☐ Can change direction with ease when something isn't working	☐ Are peaceful
☐ Feel creative	☐ Enjoy your colleagues and friendships
☐ Can resolve problems and make decisions with ease	☐ Experience life as an adventure; you are curious and enjoy challenges
	☐ Are playful
	☐ Are energetic
	☐ Laugh often and are happy

You are also intuitive when you:

☐ Can sense when someone is lying, cheating, or manipulating
☐ Can sense danger and a potential threat
☐ Can read past another's words and body language to understand their inner world
☐ See patterns in large amounts of data and can quickly identify root causes to problems and solutions
☐ Are often able to foresee events with validity
☐ Have insights come to you when you are relaxing or sleeping
☐ Feel connected with nature, the world around you, the Divine, and/or higher intelligence(s)

Conversely, you may not be listening to your intuition and may be ready for a change when you:

☐ Have difficulty making decisions — overanalyze decisions or put decisions off	☐ Are tired often
	☐ Feel numb with loss of heart
	☐ Have a difficult time sleeping or sleep too much
☐ Have stress and anxiety	☐ Are unhealthy and/or sick a lot
☐ Avoid problems, people, and situations	☐ Are sad or depressed
☐ Are in a rut, bored, and lackluster	☐ Don't know where you are headed and have an unclear direction
☐ Feel confused, disoriented, and out of balance	

As you reflect upon both lists, which list describes your experience in the last three to six months (or more), greater than the other? When we follow our intuition, we are in integrity and at peace with ourselves. We trust ourselves, which invites others to trust us in return. You cannot lead if you don't know where you are going, and you can't know where you are going unless you know who you are. Intuition allows you to listen to your higher self and reminds you of who you are and why you exist. When your thoughts, behaviors, and decisions align with your higher self and core values, you can experience peace and joy. When you are true to yourself, self-consciousness gives way and leadership emerges. In the expression and celebration of your true essence, you rise above the judgments of others as the source of your happiness lies within.

As you are a human being, ups and downs are to be expected, and there are times in life when our intuition is more fully awake than others. There are also times when your intuition may be speaking to you but you are not following it. Listen to your intuition now. What is it telling you about the truth of a situation you are now facing? The great majority of the time, it's the pain and struggle rather than a compelling vision of the future that is the impetus to change. It's often the cognitive dissonance, the mental discomfort and stress that is triggered by a situation that contradicts a belief or value, that provides the catalyst to change. To eliminate the pain, people find ways to resolve the contradiction to find peace. For example, if you value being with your family and yet you are putting too many hours in at work, you will experience cognitive dissonance.

If you checked many of the boxes on the second list, perhaps it's a wake-up call to bring you back into alignment to what is truly important to you. Your intuition may be prompting you to follow your dreams and make decisions that will put the life you desire into motion. Steve Jobs said, "Have the courage to follow your heart and intuition. They somehow already know what you truly want to become."

Your intuition is the gateway to your spirit. When you listen to your spirit, you are inspired. The word *inspire*, according to the Merriam-Webster dictionary, means to breathe life into and shares a connection with *spirit*, which comes from the Latin word for breath. If you checked most of the boxes on the first self-assessment list, you probably use the energy of your inspiration to create and manifest what you desire quite easily. As you well know, leaders must create the environment for people to be inspired. This requires that you search and lead from within, to continue to develop your own leadership potential. Employees want to unleash their spirit at work. They want to self-actualize and realize their greatest potential. The correlation between employee satisfaction and performance is well-documented.

Stress Diminishes Intuition and Intelligence

If you answered "yes" to many of the behavioral indicators on the second list on the above self-assessment and are having difficulty listening to or following your intuition, you may be stressed or depressed. Under significant stress, it's difficult to listen to our intuition and find our direction. On a scale of 1 to 10, 1 being little to no stress and 10 being very high stress, where would you put yourself on this scale in the last several months?

The World Health Organization calls stress a "worldwide epidemic." "Stress is a major health problem," warns the American Psychological Association. Numerous studies show that job stress is far and away the major source of stress for American adults and that it has escalated progressively over the past few decades. According to the American Medical Association and American Psychological Association, in the U.S., on a team of 10, four will describe themselves as extremely stressed, another four say they are one stressor away from extreme stress, and only two will state they are not stressed. According to a 2018 study by the American Institute of Stress, 80 percent of workers feel stress on the job and nearly half say they need help in learning how to manage stress. Forty-two percent say their coworkers need such help. Stress is a risk factor for depression. "Depression is among the leading causes of disability worldwide," the WHO says (2018).

As an introduction to the neurological issues associated with stress and recent scientific discoveries to extinguish it, allow me to serve as an example. Roughly 16 years ago, I had become single and was supporting two children, my father died suddenly, my mother died 11 months later, and I moved three times. During this time, I was getting my second master's degree, had my own management-consulting practice where I was reorganizing several large corporate clients, and started my private counseling practice. Whew ... all in one year! To say the least, I was stressed! Further, I had suffered from post-traumatic stress disorder my entire life. I had become accustomed to living with the discomfort and "overfunctioning" through it. During this period of great loss and change, I had been called to traffic school. I had three traffic tickets, the highest number of traffic tickets in the class that year. The instructor wisely correlated each student's number of traffic tickets with the life changes and stressors they experienced that year. Obviously, I had difficulty concentrating and focusing and was making errors. I had always had a high level of resilience, but this time it was too much; I felt overwhelmed. We experience stress when we feel our circumstances outweigh our ability to handle them. I needed to regain clarity and my sense of peace. I needed to feel grounded in the eye of the storm. I had to dig deep to uncover all aspects of myself and to recognize my greatest strengths along with my perceived limitations. Along this arduous but wondrous and transformational journey, however, I found great inner resources, intuitive resources, that were beyond extraordinary. Without being fully aware of it at the time, I had rewired my brain from stress to neurological power and extraordinary intuition.

I had always been intuitive, as it runs in my family, but now I was operating at an entirely new level. Executives, law enforcement, higher education, the media, and people from all walks of life started hearing about my abilities and coming to see me as a professional intuitive. I was asked to speak around the country and was a regular on several radio shows, providing intuitive, psychological, and business insights to callers. It was during this time, many years ago, that I met Don Joseph Goewey, who had heard about my work. President of ProAttitude and author of the 2009 book *Mystic Cool*, Goewey had been the lead executive officer in the Department of Psychiatry at Stanford Medical School earlier in his career and shared the book he was writing with me. He taught me the mechanics of how I had rewired my brain through new findings in neuroscience called neuroplasticity. I found the missing piece to my puzzle. Much of what I share about stress and the brain is a summary of his research and findings.

Our thoughts and feelings influence the chemistry that regulates much of our health. "Chronic stress floods the brain with stress hormones and is neurotoxic to the brain," states Goewey. "Chronic stress literally shrinks higher brain function and the prefrontal cortex, leaving the primitive brain, which is in charge of a fight, flight or freeze response. Under stress, we can become aggressive and angry, be passive and avoidant, and/or have difficulty taking action or making decisions." Notice PET scans of a brain from the Mayo Foundation for Medical Education and Research that compare brain activity during periods of depression (left) with normal brain activity (right). The scans show diminished brain activity due to depression.

We could exchange the word *depressed* for the word *stressed* and the brain would look similar. The brain on the left is not getting as much oxygen or blood flow.

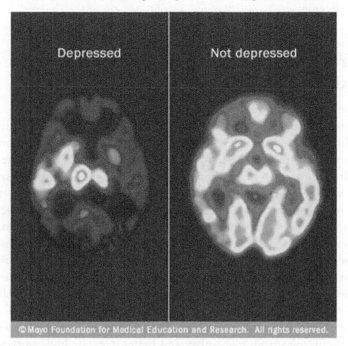

©Mayo Foundation for Medical Education and Research. All rights reserved.

The primitive brain plays an important role as, among other things, it assesses our environment and responds rapidly when we are in danger. It can also give us amazing physical strength in times of an emergency. The problem, however, is that the primitive brain reacts with a fear response whether the fear is imagined or warranted. Goewey states, "The brain makes up emergencies that the mind thinks are real." The acronym *FEAR* stands for Future Expectations Appearing Real. Psychological fear is based on stored memories from the past, projected forward. Often our perception is distorted, causing us to react inappropriately. We can be impulsive and make risky decisions, for example.

As Goewey states, "Chronic stress is an individual and company losing its brain power." In contrast to the antiquated theory that believes fear is a motivator, he says, "a brain chronically under stress starts to shut down and work less, not harder. Stress, biologically, is fear. Stress hormones dampen the brain's executive function. Imbalances in brain chemistry make people uninspired and unmotivated. Adrenaline and cortisol drain energy. Stress hormones impair memory, attention span, and decision-making. Executive brain functions in charge of planning, troubleshooting, learning, cooperation, attuned communication, and emotional regulation are compromised." As a result, intuition and insight are thwarted.

The effects of stress on employee health, productivity, turnover, and absenteeism is staggering. A survey of thousands of U.S. workers across all industries by

Mental Health America in 2017 found that nearly three-quarters of all employees are either actively seeking a new job or are thinking about doing so, with the cost of replacing an employee being 20 percent to 50 percent of their salary.

Shift from Stress to Neurological Power and Extraordinary Intuition

Neuroscience used to think that our brain structure, and the genetic blueprint that determined our traits, behaviors, and health, was fixed by the age of 6. Genetics and early-childhood experiences developed a brain that was hardwired, limiting a person's potential. Neuroscience used to believe, for example, that if you were born with a gene wired for stress or depression, your wiring was fixed and thus psychological therapies would likely be ineffective. We now know however, through epigenetics, that we can turn genes on and off. It appears that DNA is more of a genetic switchboard than a blueprint. If you were born with a gene predisposed to stress or depression, for example, the good news is that you can turn this gene off. Conversely, we also know that if you were not born with this unfortunate gene expression, environmental and life experiences such as trauma can trigger this gene on. We can influence gene activity and expression to change health outcomes and our brain.

We have a new understanding of how the brain works. We can shift from stress to neurological power through neuroplasticity. Neuroplasticity is the capacity of the brain to expand, reorganize, and better integrate higher brain function. Goewey states, "Neuroplasticity is a process that rewires the brain, shifting control away from the amygdala, the primitive network that triggers stress reactions and fight or flight, to the prefrontal cortex, where the brain generates the intellectual, creative, emotional, and intuitive intelligence people need to succeed. If we have a problem with stress, as most people do, it's because of the way our brain is wired, so the solution is to change the wiring." Through specific practices and processes, an individual can rewire their brain in eight weeks.

You may be asking, with all the stress-management training over the years, why has stress continually been on the rise? "Because stress reduction has focused on behavioral changes," says Goewey. "The new science focuses on attitudinal changes. This new approach focuses on learning processes that literally rewire the brain through a specific shift in attitude. A positively peaceful attitude literally rewires the brain. We can reshape our brain to create a new mind."

The Heart and Gut Are Intuitive, Precognitive, and Intelligent

A positively peaceful attitude not only rewires the brain but creates coherence with the heart and body. Positive emotions, such as love and appreciation, decrease heart-rate variability and lead to smooth, sine-wave-like patterns in heart rhythms. According to the HeartMath Institute, "Heart signals have a significant effect on brain function—influencing emotional processing as well as higher cognitive faculties such as attention, perception, memory, and problem-solving." The HeartMath Institute states further that,

> During stress and the feeling of negative emotions such as anger and frustration, our heart-rhythm pattern is erratic and disordered, and the corresponding pattern of neural signals traveling from the heart to the brain inhibits higher cognitive functions. This limits our ability to think clearly, remember, learn, reason, and make effective decisions. In contrast, the more ordered and stable pattern of the heart's input to the brain during positive emotional states has the opposite effect—it facilitates cognitive function and reinforces positive feelings and emotional stability. This means that learning to generate increased heart-rhythm coherence, by sustaining positive emotions, not only benefits the entire body but also profoundly affects how we perceive, think, feel, and perform.

The HeartMath Institute and other researchers found that the heart is far more than a simple pump. "The heart is, in fact, a highly complex, self-organized information-processing center with its own functional *brain* that communicates with and influences the cranial brain via the nervous system, hormonal system and other pathways," the institute says. "The idea that we can think with our hearts," states Joseph Chilton Pearce, author of the 2012 book *HeartMind Matrix: How the Heart Can Teach the Brain New Ways to Think*, "is no longer just a metaphor but is, in fact, a very real phenomenon." This research confirms what many cultures have believed for centuries: that we can trust our heart. "When the electrical patterns of the brain synchronize with the far more powerful electrical rhythms of the heart, there is a coherence that is achieved among the heart, brain, and entire body, allowing for greater access to our intuition and the clarity to make better choices," states the HeartMath Institute.

Consider a romantic relationship that was successful and one that wasn't. What signs were there at the beginning? What did your heart tell you when you first met this person? What other physiological signs did you notice (for example, loss of energy, fatigue, warm, calm, or agitated)? What did your gut tell you? Did you have butterflies?

The gut, which extends from the esophagus to the anus, is often nicknamed by scientists as our "second brain." The second brain is not in charge of conscious thought, of course, but research is revealing that it does much more than merely handle digestion. Michael Gershon, chairman of the Department of Anatomy and Cell Biology at New York–Presbyterian Hospital/Columbia University Medical Center and author of the 1998 book *The Second Brain*, states that the second brain contains some 100 million neurons, more than in either the spinal cord or the peripheral nervous system. This multitude of neurons enables us to "feel" the inner world of our gut and its contents. Equipped with its own reflexes and senses, the second brain can control gut behavior independently of the brain, Gershon says. "The system is way too complicated to have evolved only to make sure things move out of your colon," says Emeran Mayer, professor of Physiology, Psychiatry, and Biobehavioral Sciences at the David Geffen School of Medicine at the University of California, Los Angeles. For example, scientists were shocked to learn that about 90 percent of the fibers in the primary visceral nerve, the vagus, carry information from the gut to the brain and not the other way around. "A big part of our emotions are probably influenced by the nerves in our gut," Mayer says. "Butterflies in the stomach—signaling in the gut as part of our physiological stress response—is but one example. Although gastrointestinal turmoil can sour one's moods, everyday emotional well-being may rely on messages from the brain below to the brain above. For example, electrical stimulation of the vagus nerve—a useful treatment for depression—may mimic these signals," Gershon says.

Goewey states, "In one fluid motion, we register a sensation in our gut, internally feel and interpret what we sense, correlate what it tells us with what we know from memory, filter our possible choices, mobilize our skill, and then act from what feels right."

Serendipitously and sadly, while writing this paragraph about heart and gut intelligence, I received a call from a distressed client. She expressed that she was having a panic attack—I could feel it. She said that out of the blue, her heart was racing, she couldn't get a deep breath, couldn't stop vomiting, and had severe diarrhea. As she cried in panic, she couldn't pinpoint why she had suddenly had such a strong reaction and become so violently ill. It didn't make sense to her. She was on a business trip, and work seemed to be going fine. By the end of our call, she had relaxed and her body had responded in kind. The next day, she received a call from a distant relative that her estranged mother, who lived in another state, had died early that morning.

Foresight

Consider times in your past when you felt something was going to happen before it happened. How many times have you thought about a friend you haven't spoken to for quite some time and they call you? Many people say they felt in their heart and gut that something was "off" before the tragedy of 9/11. On one occasion, while teaching my class on Intuitive Leadership to the Project Management Institute, one student, who had been in military combat years earlier, shared that one night as he lay down to rest, he heard in his mind's ear an intuitive message say, "Turn your body in the opposite direction." He listened to the message. A few hours later, he awoke to a near-miss bullet to his feet. If he hadn't listened and turned his body around, he would have been shot in the head.

In my practice, I use foresight daily to assist my clients. For example, one client, a CEO, quickly read me the names (without any other information) of companies he considered acquiring. I had never heard of any of these companies. Of the 30 companies he named, I intuited that two of these companies could be good acquisition opportunities and that one of the two companies would be calling him soon to discuss the possibility of my client buying their company. The next day, I received a call from my client that the company I had identified did indeed call to discuss being acquired. In his company, we blended intuitive intelligence with strategic planning, process redesign, job enrichment, management training, and organizational restructuring to save his company from a takeover and doubled the value of the company in six months.

To understand the science behind these precognitive experiences, years ago I found a study by the HeartMath Institute. In this study, 30 calm and 15 emotionally arousing pictures were presented to 26 participants. The study used skin conductance, EEG, and ECG measures with each participant to identify where and when in the brain and body intuitive information is processed. They found that the heart receives and responds to intuitive information as the heart was responding prior to the pictures being shown, during a 6-second blank-screen interval. The researchers also found that heart-rate acceleration occurred prior to future emotional stimuli (such as a picture of a bloody knife) compared with calm stimuli (a cute dog). They found that prestimulus information was communicated from the heart to the brain. They also found that females were more attuned to intuitive information from the heart. Both genders can greatly develop their intuition, however.

Precognition and foresight are natural and instrumental for visionary leaders. The examples I presented above can be explained through energy and non-local communication or quantum entanglement.

Living in the Quantum Field—Intuitive "Weirdness" Explained through Quantum Entanglement

Let's start with the basics. The universe was created by energy. Scientists agree that everything is energy. The human body is energy. Your thoughts and emotions are energy. Consciousness is energy. Author Ervin Laszlo in his 2008 book *Quantum Shift in the Global Brain* expresses it this way: "Although what we perceive with our senses is solid matter moving about in empty space, in reality the material universe, including particles, stars, planets, rocks, and living organisms, is not material: Matterlike things are standing, propagating, and interacting waves in a subtending medium." We are non-local beings. David Bohm, a physicist, authored a central thesis that says what we perceive as separate parts—you, me, the trees, and the stars in the next galaxy—are all part of a seamless whole that is pulsing with life and intelligence (the holomovement). We inhabit a universe where every point is interpenetrated by every other point. Our outer limits aren't confined to our body; we have expandable, permeable boundaries and can pick up all sorts of information from the outside world. A sea of energy exists to allow for instantaneous information. Imagine each one of us as a whitecap within an ocean of energy, interconnected but having our own individual expression.

Many writers and researchers speak about intuitive judgment as developed by experience, training, and knowledge, even if some of this knowledge is unconscious to us. The premise is that we can make effective decisions spontaneously based on our ability to use very limited information from a very narrow period of experience and arrive at a conclusion. The writers use the example of our instinctive ability to mind-read, which they say is how a person can get to know another person's emotions just by looking at his or her face. This is one level of intuition, localized intuition, and is extremely useful.

On another, deeper and more expansive level is non-localized intuition or quantum entanglement, which is based on energy and is not limited to the physical, time or space, or prior experience. We are all capable of this level of intuition. Reading body language, for example, would not explain how I am able to answer a caller question and pick up and provide valid information about someone I have never met and can't see, who lives in another state, and who gives me a fake name or no name, in a moment's notice live on FM radio. Sometimes, listeners write their questions and send them in, so I don't have a voice to go on, either. It would not explain how my daughter and I are able to provide specific information about crimes for families of Citizens Against Homicide or other crime bureaus impromptu without knowing information about the victim, murderer, or case. While doing an interview for the staff and faculty at the University of Denver on intuitive development, the interviewer recalled a time when I was on his radio show. Although his show was geared toward leaders in business, he reminded me of when a grieving father called to seek my help in finding his missing young daughter. I "tuned in" energetically to his daughter and to the higher intelligence of the quantum field, and apparently, the information I supplied led to his finding his daughter in another country. In business, I use these intuitive skills to help executives better understand their customers, employees, and board, and to aid in negotiations, for example.

I hear in my "mind's ear" specific words, phrases, and thoughts related to the area of focus, as well as see images in my mind's eye. Intuitively, I can feel into the inner world of another. I relax while raising my vibration, send love to those I am helping, and create a resonance that commingles with another's energy. Think of yourself as a radio receiver picking up a radio wave. This energetic connection is not limited to people. The HeartMath Institute conducted a study and found that when a human sent loving thoughts to his or her dog, not only would the heart-rate variability of the human decrease, but the dog's heart rhythms would match the electromagnetic rhythms of the person sending the love!

Heighten Your Energy

As you raise your energy, you raise your intuition. Likewise, as your intuition heightens, you will have an increase in energy. You already know of ways to raise your energy—exercise, eat healthy, sleep, and hold positive thoughts.

We have discussed some of the benefits of positive emotions. Positive emotions also correlate with higher levels of energy and vibration. Consider your emotional state over the past three months. Circle the words that describe you: anger, guilt, love, apathy, sadness, desire, willingness, courage, fear, enlightenment, peace, reason, grief, shame, and acceptance. What emotional states do you think primarily describe your team? Your organization?

Grounded in quantum physics and nonlinear dynamics, Nobel laureate David R. Hawkins, M.D., Ph.D., and author of the 1995 book *Power vs. Force*, developed a scale of consciousness. As one's level of consciousness heightens, one's energy and vibration rise as well. We say, for example, "I like that guy's vibes!" The higher our energy, the greater our power. Individuals and organizations who have higher levels of consciousness and power have a stronger electromagnetic attractor pattern, which energetically pulls people, opportunities, resources, and customers to them. Individuals who have higher levels of energy and power can manifest more easily and bring into their reality that which they desire. Manifesting is supported by quantum duality: Thoughts affect matter, and the nature of particles can be altered. Having a clear thought and vision is not enough; individuals and organizations require higher levels of energy to create, produce, and succeed.

With respect to the list of emotional states above, as a human, it is normal and healthy to have a full range of experience. If you had never felt anger, for example, I would be concerned. Having said that, we don't want to live in low-energetic-feeling states. Which emotion on my list above would you guess has the lowest energy associated with it? You are right if you chose shame. Grief, sadness, and anger also have low levels of energy, and Hawkins stated that these levels of consciousness do not allow for productivity. The highest levels of consciousness, according to Hawkins, include unconditional love, joy, peace, and enlightenment. Unfortunately, when I ask teams and organizations to think about their company's collective mindset and to circle the words that describe how most people are feeling, I typically hear the words "fear," "apathy," "desire," and "anger," with a sprinkle of "courage," "willingness," and "reason." Productivity, performance, and intuition are impaired.

Uncover Your Blind Spots, and Embrace Your Whole Self

This book is about helping you make informed decisions. Your ability to make conscious decisions is based on the degree to which you are self-aware. You can perceive others and situations only as clearly as you perceive yourself. As is true for all of us, there are parts of you that are in your conscious awareness and parts of you that are in your unconscious. A lot of the research says roughly 85 percent of our thoughts are subconscious and unconscious. Some of what is unconscious to you includes what Carl Jung, renowned psychiatrist and psychologist, referred to as our shadow side. Our shadow side includes the traits we dislike about ourselves or ignore. Our shadow side is on the other side of our persona, the roles we play in response to how we believe we need to "show up" in the world, whether as a parent, son, leader, educator, or counselor, for example. Starting in infancy and as you grew up, you learned to show up in the world in a way that would ensure your security, enable you to gain continuous love and approval, and diminish what you believed to be unacceptable. Over time, you learned to disown these parts of you and cut yourself off from your "whole self." Although unconscious to you, these disowned aspects of you continue to drive your thoughts, feelings, and behaviors as if on autopilot. It is important to note that the aspects you learned to deny are not necessarily right or wrong. They are an underdeveloped side of you. For example, if you are typically in charge, direct people, assert your thoughts and ideas, and drive quickly toward results, your shadow side may be to follow, listen, gain more input, ask for help, and have greater patience. Often under stress, we act from our *default setting* and turn up the volume on our strengths. Caution is advised, as our strengths when overutilized become a weakness. In addition, in striving for perfection, we can become incongruent with our "real self" and "whole self," as we cannot be perfect. In wearing a mask of perfection, we lose ourselves and the gift of others being able to know, receive, and trust us. Leaders aren't perfect; they are authentic; they exemplify the truth.

To lead, we must know who we are, which requires us to know where we have been. Counseling is an excellent way to gain insights into unconscious patterns and to learn to honor all sides of you. It allows us to understand why we do what we do, accept ourselves, and lovingly let go of what no longer serves us. For example, I coached and counseled the president of a financial institution. She grew up poor and didn't feel she was able to rely on her parents for her security needs. She was "self-made" and responsible for her parents at an early age. She never wanted others to feel the way that she had and dedicated her career to helping people ensure their financial security. Her direct reports and organization felt that she was very bright but overly controlling, micromanaging, and distrusting. Morale was low. In her unconscious attempt to "rescue" people and her belief that she was responsible for taking care of others, she inadvertently disempowered her direct reports. Her team misinterpreted her kind intentions as her not believing in them. Once she understood the correlation between her past and current behaviors and how she was being perceived, she had insight that led to behavior change.

What does this have to do with developing your intuition? Your intuition awakens when you come to know your true self and love yourself. In your journey of self-discovery, you learn self-acceptance. With self-acceptance are power and transformation. You embrace rather than resist your feelings. You use your feelings to intuitively understand yourself in relationship to your inner and outer world.

Empathy starts with self, and when you are coherent within yourself—body, mind, and spirit—you realize you are connected to the totality of everything else that exists. Rather than seeing the parts, you see and experience the whole, as you are no longer cut off from yourself. You realize that your separateness is an illusion. You approach life with an open heart. Empathy and love allow for the commingling of energy and resonance, where you feel into the inner world of another. It allows for the capacity of instantaneous understanding through connectedness to what may be referred to as universal intelligence, the Divine Mind, the Collective Unconscious, or God. Hawkins stated,

> The individual human mind is like a computer terminal connected to a giant database. The database is human consciousness itself, of which our own cognizance is merely an individual expression but with its roots in the common consciousness of all mankind. This database is the realm of genius; because to be human is to participate in the database. Everyone, by virtue of his birth, has access to genius. The unlimited information contained in the database has now been shown to be readily available to anyone in a few seconds, at any time and in any place.

Mindfulness

How many times have you gone around and around an issue, struggling to find the solution to a problem, only to have the answer present itself when you weren't expecting it, such as in the shower or at the driving range, for example? Perhaps the answer came to you in your sleep! In an awake beta brain-wave state, we can be tense and stressed, and in this state it's difficult for our intuition to speak and to access our unconscious. Relax, and the solutions comes to you, through intuition.

As a professional intuitive, I had to learn how to quickly shift my brain waves from beta to the slower brain-wave states of alpha and theta where I could listen to my intuition, often under significant pressure and sometimes with a lot of background noise (such as on radio or film). I had to learn how to center myself quickly, relax, be open, trust in the present moment, and focus my attention. Athletes call this state as being in the "zone," and musicians, artists, and writers may use the term *flow*. You have had times where you have been in the zone and flow, where hours feel like minutes and you experience an alert, mellow high. You are in a state of peak performance and know just what to do easily and almost effortlessly.

Developing your intuitive muscle takes practice. You cannot "tune in" when you are "tuned out." You cannot listen to your inner voice if it is quieted by the ego's incessant mind chatter or drowned by the constant noise of your environment. Turn off your TV, computer, and phone for a while. Practice mindfulness, which is maintaining a nonjudgmental state of heightened or complete awareness of your thoughts, emotions, or experiences on a moment-to-moment basis. Twenty minutes a day of meditation can rewire your brain and make you more intelligent. It also has tremendous health benefits. Meditation is the exercise of singular, mindful attention in a relaxed way. There are many forms of meditation. Find the ones that work best for you. Walking in nature, yoga, gardening, praying (to include a two-way dialogue), and artwork are forms of meditation. Focused attention alters brain-wave patterns and releases serotonin into the bloodstream, leading to a quieting down of ego activity—those executive functions of the brain that include worrying, analyzing, assessing. Once ego activity quiets down, the subtler inner cues of intuition can become more prominent. Many organizations, such as Google, are now providing areas for relaxation and meditation in their work environment. When you sleep, your brain waves are in a delta brain-wave state. Ask your intuition a question before you go to sleep, and awaken with the answer. Dreams wake us up!

The Intuitive Process

In this moment, think of a problem you are trying to solve or a decision you are trying to make. You are going to use your intuition to find clarity through an intuitive process. First: Prepare. Find a quiet place where you won't be interrupted. Relax and close your eyes. Take deep breaths, and with each breath go further into relaxation. Focus on your heart, and remember a time that gives you great joy and peace or something you appreciate. Be open to receiving. Believe and trust that you will receive your answer. Second: Ask the question you want to answer. For example, should I hire this person? What do I need to know to resolve this conflict? What is getting in the way of me moving forward? Third: Accept all the information and impressions you receive, and don't discount any of it. You may not know what some of the impressions mean, as they may come in the form of a metaphor. You can drill down intuitively by asking more questions if an impression isn't clear. Fourth: Record your impressions, and integrate them with what you think and know about the situation. When you are ready, follow the process, ask your question, and await the answer(s).

You may have heard the answer in your mind's ear, seen the answers metaphorically or literally in your mind's eye, or felt the answer in your body (maybe you felt calm, tingles, or heaviness in your gut). You will receive information typically based on your predominant learning style. If you had trouble tapping into your intuition, don't worry about it! It takes practice and time to relax and quiet the mind chatter that often accompanies stress. Heightening your intuition is like an exercise program for the brain.

Your Organization's Intuitive Intelligence

Imagine yourself operating from your highest level of intelligence—your intuitive intelligence. How would you go through your day? How would you feel? How would you impact your organization, customers, and industry? How would you show up in your personal life?

Envision your organization attaining and sustaining peak performance. What would be possible if leaders and employees joyfully brought the best of who they are to the forefront—living and breathing from their gifts? How would a positive and peaceful mindset reshape the mind of your organization and impact stakeholders? If people were using their intuitive intelligence, and thereby optimizing creative, practical, analytical, social, and emotional intelligence toward a shared vision, what would your organization create?

What changes would have to be made organizationally to unleash everyday brilliance? Just as there must be coherence within our body and brain to access intuition, there must also be alignment and structure within the organization to enable it. What beliefs would need to change? How would leaders need to lead? How would the mission, vision, and values drive this new mindset? How would processes, job designs, and the organization need to be structured to heighten intuitive intelligence? How could IT enhance it? How might you select and hire differently? How would training, performance management, and reward systems develop and enable genius? What could you do to start the process?

Conclusion

To optimize intuition requires a belief in its power and the courage to trust it. It requires self-awareness, an inner calm, and an open-hearted approach to life. It requires that you take care of yourself, heighten your energy, and develop a regular mindfulness practice. In sum, to access your highest level of intelligence—your intuitive intelligence—the key is bliss! Who knew? Your intuition.

References

Business Wire (2013). *CEOs More Likely to Rely on Intuition Than Metrics When Making Business Decisions*, November 6, 2006. Retrieved from www.businesswire.com/news/home/20061106005268/en/CEOs-Rely-Intuition-Metrics-Making-Business-Decisions

Gershon, M.D. (1998). *The Second Brain*. New York: Harper Collins.

Goewey, D.J. (2009). *Mystic Cool: A Proven Approach to Transcend Stress, Achieve Optimal Brain Function, and Maximize Your Creative Intelligence*. New York: Beyond Words.

Hawkins, D.R. (1995). *Power vs. Force: The Hidden Determinants of Human Behavior*. Sedona, AZ: Veritas Publishing.

HeartMath (2013). *Science and Research*, December 9, 2013. Retrieved from www.heartmath.com/about/research-information.html

HeartMath (2018). Scientific Foundation of the HeartMath System. Retrieved from www.h eartmath.org/science/?utm_source=googlesearchutm_medium=cpc&utm_campaig n=1331864764&utm_content=293478074551&utm_term=heartmath%20institut e&gid=58844866448&device=c&model=&position=1t1&placement=&gclid=EA IaIQobChMIspiBseib3wIVEb7ACh3rKQ7iEAAYASAAEgK33_D_BwE

Laszlo, E. (2008). *Quantum Shift in the Global Brain: How the New Scientific Reality Can Change Us and Our World*. Rochester, VT: Inner Traditions.

Mayo Clinic (2018a). PET Scan of the Brain for Depression. Retrieved from www.mayoclinic. org/tests-procedures/pet-scan/multimedia/-pet-scan-of-the-brain-for-depression/ img-20007400

Mayo Clinic (2018b). Stress Symptoms: Effects on Your Body and Behavior. Retrieved from www.mayoclinic.org/healthy-lifestyle/stress-management/in-depth/stress-symptoms/ art-20050987

McCraty, R., Atkinson, M., and Bradley, R.T. (2004). Electrophysiological evidence of intuition: part 1. The surprising role of the heart. *Journal of Alternative and Complementary Medicine* 10, 133–143.

Mental Health America (2018). 2017 State of Mental Health in America—Report Overview Historical Data. Retrieved from www.mentalhealthamerica.net/issues/2017-state -mental-health-america-report-overview-historical-data

Pearce, J.C. (2012). *The Heart-Mind Matrix: How the Heart Can Teach the Mind New Ways to Think*. Rochester, VT: Park Street Press.

Chapter 2

Thinking Outside the Brain™: For Accurate Intuition

Dominique Surel

Contents

> The growing interest in decoding intuition is a result of the globalizing socio-economic environment generating an increasingly complex context, creating scenarios of uncertainty and divergence of value systems in which we must make decisions at a much faster pace. The quest for developing decision-making skills opens doors to explore the more ephemeral human qualities such as intuition.
>
> **(Surel, 2007)**

Introduction

As a professional trainer of intuition, I have found that the success in developing one's accurate intuition is directly related to understanding what it is, and how it functions. This chapter will therefore address scientific research findings that explain how intuition is an underdeveloped but natural cognitive skill. The focus is on accuracy which is attained in a normal awake state. Intuition is a normal cognitive skill and no meditation is necessary; on the contrary, as you will discover, meditation could trigger your imagination to contribute false information. Distinguishing between wishful thinking and imagination is critical in eliciting accurate and valuable intuitive insights. In this chapter, I introduce the effective intuition Energetic Imprints©, a methodology I created as a complementary tool to decision-making and for accurate assessment of situations and future trends. There are also five other simple but powerful intuition-building tools. What is important to remember is that you need to practice and develop intuition in your everyday life so that it becomes a natural and normal component of your decision-making process in your professional and personal life, as well as if you are ever in a crisis situation. Many people receive accurate intuitive information without even understanding what it is or having been trained in this science. Imagine if we were able to understand how and why this information comes to us, and that we could practice some exercises to develop it further? Our decision-making process would be different as well as the outcomes.

Intuition Saves Lives

The following are two real examples of how powerful accurate intuition can be.

It was a four-way stop intersection. There were no oncoming cars from any direction. I put my foot on the accelerator and the car starts moving but, to my surprise, my foot all of a sudden is on the brake. Why? Am I losing control of my body? I quickly look again; no traffic and for the second time place my foot on the accelerator and the car starts to move when, in a flash of a second, my foot is back on the brake and a red Jeep going about 50 mph runs through the intersection. Major accident avoided.

Was this a random coincidence that for some reason my foot hit the brake? Twice? It could conceivably have been a strange random phenomenon were it not for the fact that these types of events happen quite often in my life and in many other people's lives.

Here's another example of how intuition can save lives in the law enforcement environment:

Officer Bill Tyler, from Colorado, was called to a home for a domestic disturbance. Upon hearing the call Bill felt rather uneasy about the situation and immediately called for a cover car to assist in the possible arrest of the suspect (first intuition information). When they arrived, the wife stated that her husband was in the bedroom. Bill felt that if the officers present went into the room and announced themselves, the suspect was going to shoot at them (second intuition information). Although they knew there was a gun in the house, they had no idea where it was. The wife went into the bedroom first to tell the husband the police were there and she was escorted out. The suspect was under the blankets pretending to sleep. Bill instructed the suspect to get out of bed so he could be interviewed. At that point the officers still did not know if he had a gun or not. When the suspect started to move slowly, Bill's intuition kicked in again: he immediately yelled that if he was going for the gun his head was going to be put all over the headboard. Bill then told one of the cover officers to get the gun that was underneath the pillow, even though he had not seen the gun. That officer indeed recovered a loaded .380 semi-automatic pistol, hidden under the covers, that the suspect was trying to get to. Bill's three intuitive insights most probably saved lives.

The stories above are examples of life-saving situations but intuition also happens in everyday normal decision-making situations. Intuition is often described as a knowing, an idea out of the blue, a feeling, a twitch in the body, a feeling from the gut, and other types of gestalts. It often appears unsolicited or as an answer to a direct question.

INTUITION AND COMPLEX ISSUES
IN DECISION-MAKING

Intuition can be a missing piece of information or even a solution. One of the more valuable aspects of intuition is that it can oftentimes offer a piece of information that you do not even know you are missing. Part of the problem when we are confronted with difficult decision-making is that we are not sure if we have 100 percent of the accurate information. Even if we think we have 90 percent of the information the following questions arise:

How sure are we that we are only missing 10 percent?

How sure are we that what we do have is all accurate?

In the 10 percent or even 1 percent of the information we are missing, there may be a critical piece that would totally change our perception of the problem and how we make the decision.

How do we know, what it is we don't know?
Intuition Can Illuminate the Decision-Making Process

HOW INTUITION IS USED
IN DECISION-MAKING

Problem-solving—finding a solution
Assessing complex situations—clarity
Forecasting—identifying new trends, predicting directions
Creativity—disruptive innovation, novel ideas
Extra information you don't know you are missing
Futuristic scenarios—strategic planning

INTUITION: A POWERFUL EDGE

Thinking process
Decision-making
Strategic Planning
Negotiation, mediation
Forecasting
Creativity

Tool #1: Benchmarking Your Accurate Intuition©

The purpose of this tool is to establish a type of baseline, and acknowledge that you have had many intuitive insights. The focus in this chapter is on accuracy, therefore it is important to acknowledge false intuitive information and recognize accurate information so that we can learn how to discern between the two. One of the issues about intuition is that it is not fully understood and unfortunately not enough attention is put on proof of accuracy. Another misunderstood aspect of intuition is that men don't have it as much as women. This is not true. What might be true is that our society expects men to be more pragmatic and less emotional than women. Since intuition is not understood by the mainstream, it is considered more ethereal and assumed men are not subject to this type of phenomenon.

Following a methodology to develop intuition that is not based on accuracy is not only misleading but can be detrimental to the outcome of your decision. The following table allows you to record past intuitive experiences that you had in either your personal life or your professional life. Sometimes intuition in one's professional decision-making situations is more subtle and can go unrecognized. Therefore you can begin by recording the more obvious intuitive experiences. Eventually, with practice, you will be able to more clearly identify intuition in your assessment and decision-making process.

Describe an intuitive insight from the past	Outcome? Accurate?
I was out doing errands when all of a sudden I felt I should go home sooner than later. Part of me thought that was silly; I was not ready to go home. Yet as I started driving, I made a turn toward home.	I got home and discovered my toilet was leaking. The water had filled the bathroom floor and was just about to go into the carpeted hallway. Had I gotten home later, the damage would have been much worse. Accurate

Intuition: Conscious Mind vs. Unconscious
Why Intuitive Information Can Be Elusive

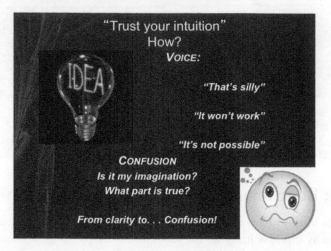

People say you should trust your intuition. This is easy to say but in reality it is a tricky situation. Here's what usually happens. You are working on a project, trying to evaluate a specific database with quantitative data. Your mind is going in one direction when all of a sudden, out of the blue, you think/hear: *I should focus more on the data from Department X.* It's a clear statement that you can accept but just as you start thinking about it, another voice/thought comes through and says: *Really? Why? That's silly. No reason to look there.* In a few seconds you have gone from clarity to confusion. Where did that idea come from in the first place? Was it my imagination? I feel it could be true and valuable information but I'm not sure anymore.

First, let's go over a few definitions so that we are all on the same page when referring to these labels. Let's assume the brain consists of three areas: the conscious, the subconscious, and the unconscious. The conscious mind is the part that thinks. It's the intellect that analyzes rationally, logically, and derives conclusions. The subconscious is more or less a hiding place for any type of suppressed emotions, programming, etc. The unconscious we shall define as the portal into the non-local realm. It is the function through which we receive intuitive information. The problem is that our Western educational system and social models do not address the unconscious. It is ignored.

The result is that our conscious mind has taken over and is in charge of our thinking process to include decision-making and assessment of situations. It takes into account our life experiences and data to analyze, to make deductions, even to imagine when needed, and all the other processing functions involved in intelligence. The question is: where does intuitive insight fit in? Have we trained our mind to integrate intuitive information into our thinking process? For most, the answer is no. Educational systems do not offer such courses or training. On the contrary, we are often told as children to ignore anything that is not logical or rational as per the mainstream norms.

Our conscious mind has been trained to be what I call The Big Boss in our thinking process, and usually does a very good job. So what happens when a piece of information comes into the picture, out of the blue, from the usually silent unconscious? The conscious has a strong reaction. First it might try to ignore it. Who is this unconscious who, out of the blue, thinks it has some valuable element to contribute? If, however, the unconscious insists on pushing forth the information then two things can happen: if we have learned about intuition, we recognize it as such and accept it; or if we are not careful, the conscious will accept the intuitive information but will build a story around it using the imagination. We are then left with a story that contains both accurate and imagined information. What is true? What is not?

The nature of the conscious mind is to deliver complete stories to answer any queries we may have. It has been trained through our educational system to be very creative and imaginative but never to acknowledge and integrate intuitive information. That being said, when developing creative thinking, intuition does come in but we are never trained to discern between accurate intuition and imagination. This is the essence of the problem in integrating accurate information into our thinking process without creating pollution from our imagination.

This battle between the conscious and unconscious was discovered in the Controlled Remote Viewing (CRV) research funded by the U.S. military. In the quest to discover how the human mind can retrieve non-local information and develop precognitive skills, over a 20-year period the military invested about $20 million in R&D in the 1970s. Some of my understanding about intuition was acquired by being trained to the advanced level in CRV by Lyn Buchanan, one of the best military CRV viewers. Asked to describe the result of the R&D efforts for this chapter, Lyn Buchanan explains: "The result was a powerful protocol that trains a person to have the conscious mind work as an accurate recorder of the exact non-local information the unconscious mind is perceiving, not as a governor over it. Sort of like having the two waltz, with the unconscious mind doing the leading. In that way, it suppresses the conscious mind's tendency to force logic and imagination into the process" (personal communication, Dec. 1, 2018). The expected result of following the protocol is to obtain accurate and detailed information about a specific place or activity, anywhere on the planet, and in the past, present, or future.

The question remains: how can we manage the conscious mind interfering with an intuitive thought? The exercises introduced in this chapter address this issue. Although they are simple, they are effective if practiced regularly. Tracking for acurate intuition is a good way to start evaluating your accurate intuition.

Tool #2: Tracking Accurate Intuition©

INTUITIVE INSIGHTS	OUTCOME	INTUITION?	FEELINGS
Leaving for appointment: July 5, 2018 When it came time to leave the house, I kept getting distracted and had to double-check the windows were shut, then the back door was locked. I left 5mns later than planned	There was a major crash on the highway that had just happened. Had I left the house 5mns later, I might have been involved.	YES	I wasn't thinking about things to check. It just came to me very strongly but I was not asking or triggering these thoughts. Thinking back, I felt some odd pressure in my arms
Finished writing the report and checked it as usual. Something told me to check it again. I did not want to waste any more time on it – decided to hand it in. Each time I went to press on Send button, something stopped me. I took another quick look through it and found that I had inverted one of the numbers	Next time I feel some type of odd resistance to executing something, I will pause and recheck things.	YES	Again, I did not ask myself: is there something I should verify? The resistance came from outside my brain or mind. It was as if my hand was being physically held back from pushing Send button
Before attending the staff meeting on Tuesday, I kept thinking I was going to be reprimanded for something. I thought about all the reasons why it would happen and I was really nervous going into the meeting.	I was not reprimanded for anything. Meeting went very well and I felt acknowledged for my work. Next time my mind talks to me, I will recognize that it is not intuition.	NO	When I think back, I was emotionally worried and actively thinking about reasons why the meeting could go badly. My imagination was also involved. It all came from my emotions and my mind

Record your intuitive insight in the first column and then state the outcome of the situation. You might have to wait a few days to fill it out, until you have the outcome information. Then evaluate whether or not your intuitive insight was correct. The last column (Feelings) is very important as this is where you will begin to discern between your personal signals of accurate intuition and your conscious mind or imagination.

Building Accuracy

Unfortunately, most people, to include many intuition practitioners, do not have a grounded knowledge about what intuition is and is not. Although scientific findings are explaining this phenomenon, not many individuals are willing to make the effort to learn about the findings as it is much easier to operate within one's own belief system. The outcome of this paradigm is that there is now a lot of disinformation about intuition, and instead of recognizing a "false intuition" practitioners tend to justify the inaccurate information in some way.

Once you understand that the conscious mind and imagination can, and will, interfere, then it becomes very clear that we need to acknowledge false intuition as much as the clearly correct one in order to learn how to discern between the two. As you will learn later in this chapter, intuition is not an emotion; it is purely information, which may manifest by a physical gestalt or just an idea. To begin discerning between all these subtleties and false intuition, ask yourself questions:

Do I feel any different when I received accurate intuition versus imagination?
Does the information come in more quickly when it is accurate?
Do I feel my thinking mind engaged when it is not accurate?
Did I feel emotional when it is not accurate?
Do I feel any physical twitches when it is accurate?
Does the accurate information come through as a thought? A picture? A
   knowing?
Does the imagined/false information come through differently? If so, how?
Any other gestalts you are discovering?

Tool #3: Your Intuition Receptors©

Intuition is information, and information comes in via signals. It has been demonstrated that the human being can receive intuitive signals through our sensories such as a gut feeling. As everyone is different, intuitive receptors will also
be different. Some individuals never have a gut feeling, but might feel a sort of
pinch in their heart or maybe in the neck, while other individuals might pick
up smells.

The purpose of this exercise is to give meaning to your physical intuitive signals and discover others you may not be noticing. This will increase your intuitive
insights and the accuracy of the meaning. Directions: Each time you feel a possible
intuitive insight or information signal, record it below, and fill out the table. Every
few weeks, go back and read the table to identify any trends. Keep a journal. See
examples below.

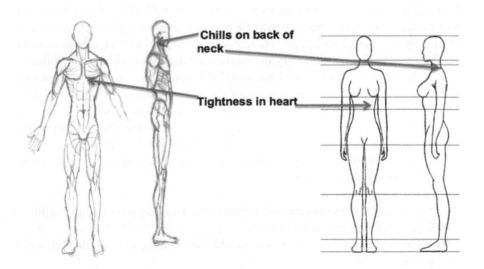

Example of Journal

SENSORY	COMMENTS	CONCLUSIONS
Chills back of neck	As I was writing up the report, when I got to the Communications section, I felt chills on the back of my neck.	Two days later, as I reviewed my final report I discovered I had not fully understood one of the situations I described. Next time I get chills on my neck. I'll stop and verify what I'm doing
Tightness in chest	As I was evaluating the financials of our 5 subsidiaries, I felt a tightness in my chest each time the name of Y-subsidiary came up. All signs had been pointing that it was the most successful subsidiary, and I was not worried about that one.	I could not ignore this strong tightness in the chest and switched to review company-Y and discovered some serious but deeply buried discrepancies.

Research: Intuition Is a Powerful Tool in Decision-Making Process

One of the reasons that intuition is not taken as seriously as it should be is because there is the false notion that there is no scientific evidence to prove that it even exists. It might be true that we cannot totally understand the mechanics of intuition, but in the last 15 years this topic has generated a lot of compelling findings from the academic and scientific communities. For example, in their research on the use of intuition, Luo & Cheng (2006) contended executives would be more interested in identifying and using their intuition if they had a better explanation and understanding of the concept, rather than referring to it as a "gut feeling."

In a 2004 research paper, Cartwright points out: "Effective decision makers use rational and analytical cognitive processes but they also appear to use skills described as *instinct and intrinsic gifts*. The special skills are difficult to define and are often referred to as intuition, which is linked to sharper forecasting skills" (Cartwright, 2004). The problem, as researcher Patton (2003) points out, is that most decision makers do not question their decision-making pattern and tend to rely mostly on rational skills, and yet, according to Hayashi (2001), if leaders could recognize and apply intuition, they would increase decision-making capabilities.

Another study by Carlson and Kaiser (1999) reports that in companies whose profits doubled in five years, 80 percent of these organizations were led by CEOs with higher than average intuitive abilities. Did you know that 82 of the 93 winners of the Nobel Prize over a 16-year period agreed that intuition plays an important role in creative and scientific discoveries (Cooper & Sawaf, 1997)?

Here are some more research findings that highlight the value of using intuition in the decision-making process:

- **Faster and more accurate evaluation** of data and decision-making skills
- **Clarity of thought** in decision-making
- Ability to make decisions **more quickly** than using only rational thought process

■ Enhances **creativity**—innovation
■ Feel for future—better **forecasting** skills

One of the more interesting scientific studies about the value of intuition was conducted in 2003 at the R&D department of AstraZeneca. At the time, the R&D department was managing a budget of €2.4 million. The research question was: Is intuition helpful in the development of new products? The conclusion of the study states: "This study suggests that *intuition is an intrinsic* part of the creative process in drug discovery" (Sundgren & Styhre, 2004). Research studies about the value of intuition abound and they all point to many valuable attributes of intuition in the decision-making process.

Perhaps one of the most compelling comments about the value of intuition was made in 2004 by Ket de Vries, Chaired Professor at the INSEAD Business School, who stated that he believes intuition enhances leadership skills but that unfortunately the part of the brain responsible for more intuitive processes is not stimulated in business schools (Coutu, 2004).

A Historical Perspective

The concept of intuition was identified and acknowledged going back to the ancient times. The Romans and Greeks believed that intuition comes from outside the human body and mind. They believed intuitive insights and information came from the Divine, or the Universe itself. What we call intuition today, the Romans and Greeks attributed to information communicated by the gods. They used their human energy, and unconscious to establish connection with this source in the Universe, or with the Divine. They believed that this communication connection was a channel to God (Langan-Fox & Shirley, 2003), and called it *Noûs*. Aristotle, Plutarch, Plato, and Heraclitus all believed in the *Noûs* connection and defined it as a faculty of a higher mind. Intuition was deemed to be property of the Cosmos, and rules the Universe.

What is interesting to note is that the ancients' understanding of intuition did not include the modern versions of: tacit knowledge, experience, right brain function, emotions, mediation, etc. They defined intuition simply as the direct connection to the Divine, which explains why intuitive insights, when they are truly intuitive, are always accurate. The information is received straight from the source without any human interpretation from the conscious mind. There is no intermediary (Baltussen, 2007). Plutarch and Plato believed that the soul is more divine than the body but *Noûs* is more divine than the soul (Menn, 1998). *Noûs* is always accurate, it cannot be wrong because it is Truth itself.

What is particularly interesting is that the concept of intuition can be found throughout the ages in different cultures, in most worldwide belief systems, and follows the one defined by the ancient Greeks and Romans. In ancient Indian philosophy this "higher mind" was also considered to be a property of the Cosmos. It is only in modern times that we have forgotten this concept and attribute it to some kind of intellectual or emotional function and thus accuracy has become an issue.

How Was the Concept of Noûs Forgotten?

The Scientific Revolution in the 17th century led to the Industrial Revolution, which in turn changed humanity's understanding of the world. We witnessed the birth of mechanization, industry, technology, factories, and faster, effective production methods. In general, the human aspect of our societal development became lost and ignored. We forgot the *Noûs*. The new mechanistic way of advancing and thinking created even more mechanistic solutions culminating in the creation of robots replicating human functions and thinking but without intuition. This direction not only ignores the power of intuitive thinking but it also completely ignores the possibility of a human spirit or soul and even the development of the human potential itself.

Modern Science Supports the Concept of Noûs

One of the groundbreaking research studies on intuition was conducted in 2014 by Rezaei, Mirzaei, & Zali. They concluded that: Intuition is *accessing information from outside of our brain from the non-local world*. This research was followed by other studies with the same conclusions. Today, scientists refer to intuition as "non-local intuition" because it does not emanate from inside the human brain or body. It is the brain and body that receives information signals from the external environment. Scientists now refer to intuition as "the knowledge or sense of something that cannot be explained by past or forgotten knowledge." Perhaps without knowing it, scientists have rediscovered the ancient concept of connection to the non-local realm, or the Divine, which the ancients labeled as *Noûs*.

Further findings demonstrate that researchers overwhelmingly agree that: intuition is not from any kind of knowledge, experience, emotion. It is something separate that takes place in the unconscious (Hoose, 2006; Jolij & Lamme, 2005; Korthagen, 2005; Miller & Ireland, 2005; Radin & Schlitz, 2005; Sinclair & Ashkanasy, 2005). More specifically Dane & Pratt (2004) point out that "intuition is ... as a completed thought. Furthermore, Sadler-Smith & Shefy (2004) explain that "intuition is a ... inference."

What is most important to note is that both the ancient definition of *Noûs* and modern scientific findings refute the mainstream beliefs that intuition is a function of creativity, tacit knowledge, pattern recognition, life experiences, meditation, memory, etc. Intuition is information that comes from outside the brain or mind. This brings us to the next question: where does it come from? There is only so much information one can communicate in a chapter. Suffice it to say that scientific research on human consciousness and non-local information has made great progress in searching for explanations. By moving away from the Newtonian-Cartesian and materialistic-reductionistic paradigms, scientists are exploring different aspects of holographic systems. In the case of intuition, a holographic type of network might contain all information from the world, or universe, and can be accessed by our human body, or instrument, by connecting into the network. Neuroscientists are also exploring the fact that our brain is a holographic system. Intention is very powerful and we use it to accomplish our everyday thinking and activities but intention is also the way to connect into this holographic type of paradigm, if we know that it exists. If we do not know or believe it exists, then we will never be able to tap into it.

Advanced Research on Human Consciousness

It is thanks to modern technology that researchers have been able to detect how intuition works in the brain as well as in the heart. Developments in the fields of neuroscience, using neuroimaging, have made considerable progress in terms of identifying specific brain functions in relation to human emotions, feelings, and thought processes (Farah & Wolpe, 2004). For example, it is now possible to identify what parts of the brain are operating when an individual is using memory about a specific topic. fMRI technology, for example, is so precise it can determine that a person can know something about themselves without having to retrieve the information from the part of the brain that supposedly stores autobiographical data (Lieberman, Jarcho, & Satpute, 2004).

As mentioned earlier, the brain is now believed to function as a holographic type of system. Ede Frecska, MD, PhD, Chief of Department at the National Institute of Psychiatry and Neurology in Budapest, Hungary, explains how the interface or connection into the non-local intuition information might happen: "The proposed subcellular medium is not restricted to the brain tissue, it spreads across the whole body, and provides a space-and-time-independent holographic image of the Universe inside the body via non-local connections" (Frecska, 2012). This supports other research specifically on intuition that says our human sensory system functions as an antenna to receive the non-local information—thus the term "gut feeling" for those who receive it through the gut.

In 2011, Professor Michael Persinger from Laurentian University in Canada claimed that not only is the brain a holographic type of system but also that the earth's magnetic field can contain the information of 7 million human brains. Using sophisticated EEG and PET scan instruments, he estimated that for the brain to diffuse one event into this magnetic field takes about 10 minutes. He has also demonstrated that brains can tap into this realm of information. This might explain some of the intuition information that we can access (Persinger, 2011).

Intuition—Information from the Future?

Many replicated scientific experiments using EEG demonstrate the human body responds to intuitive stimulus and it can do so up to seven seconds or more before the individual experiences the activity. As was pointed out in Bill Tyler's story earlier in the chapter, seven seconds in a crisis situation is a significant amount of time. To be notified by a specific feeling that something unknown is about to happen can totally change the decision-making and potentially avert disaster to include saving lives.

In 2004, McCraty, Atkinson, and Bradley conducted an experiment using intuition and the outcome of investment and found that

> . . . physiological measures . . . show that informational input was received by the autonomic system some 6 to 7 seconds before the outcome of the investment choice was known. This is consistent with previous findings from a rigorous experiment, . . . where it was found that the heart receives pre-stimulus information approximately 6 seconds prior to a future event (McCraty, Atkinson, & Bradley 2004).

Another study, focusing on the evidence of intuition using the electroencephalogram (EEG), demonstrated "compelling evidence that the body's perceptual apparatus is continuously scanning the future" (McCraty, Atkinson, & Bradley, 2004). The findings are aligned with the theory that intuitive thinkers appear to be more skilled in forecasting.

When we understand that accurate and critical intuition information can appear when most needed and in a matter of seconds, it makes sense to start developing this skill during our everyday life so that it can kick in when necessary, and in crisis situations.

The Heart: Headquarters for Reception of Intuition

Throughout the ages, the heart has been considered as one of the most powerful organs of the human being. Aristotle claimed that the heart is not only intelligent but also is the most important organ, while the brain and lungs are there to cool and protect the heart. He asserted that educating the mind without educating the heart is no education at all. However, by the 16th century it was believed that the role of the heart was to pump blood. The focus was on the vessels and the flow of blood throughout the body. The concept of the heart's function as an intelligent organ was forgotten, until the early 1990s.

In 1991, Dr. J. Andrew Armour (MD, PhD), Center of Research, University of Montreal, claimed that actually the heart is not just a pump. It is an organ complete with "an intricate network of several types of neurons, neurotransmitters, proteins and support cells, like those found in the brain proper" (Armour, 2007). Armour continued to describe the heart as an elaborate circuitry that acts independently from the brain. The heart can learn, remember, feel, and sense. There are several direct pathways to the brain into the medulla. The signals from the heart to the medulla influence perception, decision-making, and other cognitive processes. From these findings the field of neurocardiology was born, and Dr. Armour coined the term "heart brain." Further research findings from the HeartMath Institute reveal that the heart generates the strongest magnetic field by the body, and is an important carrier of information. It sends extensive emotional and intuitive signals to the brain. The heart emits more electrical activity than the brain. The heart's electrical field is 60 times greater in amplitude than the activity in the brain, and its electromagnetic field is 5,000 times stronger than the brain's field.

Once again, after thousands of years, modern science appears to rediscover some of the ancient beliefs related to intuition. Dr. Paul Pearsall, a researcher in psychoneuroimmunology, describes the heart function in more eloquent terms by stating: "The heart is more than just a pump. It conducts the cellular symphony that is the very essence of our being" (Pearsall, 1998).

Heart Brain and Conscious Mind: Integration

Dr. Paul Pearsall (1998) states: "The idea that the heart may also be able to think is met by anger and mockery from the brain that believes that the heart, even if it does think, must be thinking much too slowly, sentimentally to be of immediate use in its daily wars for self-preservation and enhancement." McCraty et al. (2004) from the HeartMath Institute states that although the heart is in a constant two-way dialogue with the brain and the heart is sending far more signals to the brain than the brain is sending to the heart, the brain insists on keeping control of this communication system by blocking and/or destroying any information not generated by itself. Again, this explains the accuracy issue discussed earlier. A piece of intuitive data enters through our heart and is sent upstairs to our conscious mind which immediately has a negative reaction: where is this coming from? I did not retrieve it myself, therefore it must not have any value and I reject it.

The nature of the human mind is such that it has a strong need to explain things. It has also been programmed to take any facts and immediately link them together to create a story, to satisfy its agenda, belief system, or wishful thinking. Furthermore, the conscious mind cannot tolerate the unknown. If the accurate information appears incomplete, it will quickly and easily create, or imagine, what the missing piece is to complete the story and feel that it has done its job. This might explain the explosion of diverse conspiracy theories in the 21st century. With the appearance of the Internet we now have access to so much more information and disinformation that the conscious mind is having a field day taking any data and constructing a story to satisfy our need to explain everything and to fix the discomfort we have with the unknown. In an article published in *Scientific American*, Hsu (2008) states that the mind's nature will make up stories in our heads for every action and conversation. It appears as if the brain has a big ego, and needs to show off.

> ## INTUITIVE INTELLIGENCE = INTEGRATION
>
> The **BRAIN** is in control and on the defensive for physical survival and physical comfort. It thinks it has all the answers and knowledge. It has a big ego.
>
> The **HEART** needs to have a bond and create loving relationships and spiritual connections.
>
> Thinking through the heart will enhance intuitive insights and perhaps even lead to more compassionate and sustainable decision-making.

Tool #4: Think Through Your Heart©

How do you know if you are consciously connected to your heart? Below is a simple exercise that you can do any time during the day. This modified exercise is based on heart information from Rollin McCraty, PhD, head of HeartMath Research.

THINK THROUGH YOUR HEART

The heart is the reception headquarters of information signals. When you integrate the heart function with your thinking, you will be more sensitive to incoming intuitive insights as well as be more connected into other individuals. When you combine thinking through your heart with critical thinking, you begin to be more synchronized with colleagues who are also practicing this method. It creates operational synergy whereby individuals begin to correctly guessing what others are thinking. Individuals begin to think beyond the boundaries of an organizational structure. Synchronicity happens and you "read each other's mind". The result is that collaborative decision-making occurs harmoniously and quickly, with more accuracy because it contains the common elements of the heart, intuition and critical thinking.

INCREASE YOUR ACCURATE INTUITION

1. Focus your mind on your physical body

2. Imagine (a picture of) your heart.

3. Your heart is located in the middle toward the left side

4. Place your hand to feel the location of your heart. Feel the heartbeats

5. Breathe deeply and feel the air traveling inside your body to include through the heart

6. Take smooth breaths counting slowly to five as you breathe in and slowly to five as you breathe out

7. Think of a loving thought. Something that evokes appreciation and love. Think of a person or a pet Feel the warmth in your heart

Benefits of this heart exercise
Increase your intuitive insights
Prevent and relieve stress
Provide emotional balance and mental clarity
Ward off emotional negativity
Recharge your energy reserves

© Dominique Surel

Tool #5: Energetic Imprints©—Recording Intuitive Information

Energetic Imprints© is a method that I invented in the late 1990s, while practicing radiesthésie. Radiesthésie is the ancient science based on the principle that everything emits an energy field. The human body is compared to an instrument that can be developed to tune into the non-local realm, or the holographic universe. Its roots go back to alchemy. The concept is that a human being is an instrument that can be trained to access information signals from the non-local realm. Vibrational physics is another name it has been given because there are very strong correlations with quantum physics. In a paper published in 2012, neurologist Dr. Frecska discusses how humans can receive non-local information through sensory signals that are processed with the use of "a holographic form of storage."

Although there are books written about radiesthésie, they are mostly in French and the essence and application of the principles are still passed on by word of mouth. While living in Paris, I had the privilege of being privately trained in radiesthésie by a radiesthésiste who was also a physician with an engineering degree. While practicing I noticed that non-local information does not always come through in human language. Information comes through in the form of signals. The data sometimes come in as impressions or gestalts, not in words. Furthermore the information is sometimes overwhelming because there is so much of it that it is difficult to record all of it in the moment. There is also a risk that if you try to remember what you could not write down, you are inviting the conscious mind to help out and as we know, it will do everything it can to cater to our invitation to give us the whole story or picture, thus the high risk of imagination polluting the intuitive data.

Since data manifests in energetic frequencies (for lack of a better term) can we record it in its "raw" form, in the moment that we receive it, without inviting the conscious mind to find the words? In my experience of trying to record every piece of intuitive information, I often noticed feeling strange subtle impulses in my body and my hand making odd movements on the paper while I tried to write down words while keeping up with the high-speed incoming information. Finally, I tried something that I thought seemed ridiculous: what would happen if I just let my hand do what it wants to do? Perhaps it might draw or sketch the image of the information that I am not able to see. I let my hand go free. Although nothing visually revealing appeared, only a bunch of squiggles with spaces in between them, while my hand was creating these, I felt distinct and clear gestalts of information; but of course I was not able to record them in words because I was too busy making more squiggles!

I had an "Aha" moment when I decided to touch the squiggles with my hand and discovered they emanated distinct gestalts, or signals of information that I was able to record into words without inviting the conscious mind.

Business Example of Energetic Imprints©

A major manufacturer of paintballs once asked me to look into an R&D problem. They had come up with a new design but the paintball gun was not working properly and they could not figure out the problem. There was something wrong inside the gun. Would I look into it, using my intuitive method? I knew nothing about paintball guns but accepted the challenge. Following my protocol my hand drew the following scribbles or Energetic Imprints©:

As you can see, there is no visual representation. They are just squiggles that my hand wanted to draw. I numbered each one as a separate event or motion. Using my finger, I retraced over each one, recording the impressions that came to my mind, without thinking or analyzing why this word came up. For number 1, the following impressions came up: This is the basic part. Feels like there is no problem there. I then moved on to 2a and got the following impressions: This is another piece. It is separate from the main part. Feels like there is a problem outside the basic part. At that point I questioned these impressions as they did not make any sense. In my mind there was only one part and I was to discover the problem in that part. I moved on to 2b with these impressions: Something here is not fitting (in this other part)—there is a ring-like part that is leaking. Moving to the impressions of 3: The top—something on the top of the basic part is not right.

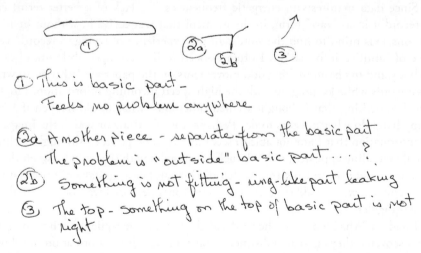

These intuitive findings did not make sense. I felt that I had failed to find the problem in the basic part of the gun and did not give my thoughts to my client for a couple of days, hoping that I might get some additional insight. But each time I tried to elicit more information, nothing else came up. Finally, with disappointment, I sent my short summary to the client and waited. I did not hear back for about three days. My conscious mind told me that he was probably so disappointed that I had not found the problem that he was not even going to get back to me. Finally, I received an email thanking me for finding the root of the problem. Thanks to my report, they discovered that the problem was not in the gun itself (the basic part) but in the fixture of the CO_2 tank that locks on the top of the gun. There was a problem with the gasket. They had been so sure the problem was in the design of the gun itself that they had focused only on that.

This Energetic Imprint© technique is applicable in any industry and for any type of problem-solving or assessment scenario. A very important element in using this method is to ask precise questions and to keep the conscious mind completely objective and neutral. As the intuitive information comes in, it is imperative not to be tempted to ask questions or to judge the incoming information. The conscious mind will insist on making comments and judgments because it feels it is losing control of the thinking process and will consequently interrupt the flow of intuitive insights. There are two ways to train yourself to become neutral while receiving intuitive information. One is practice, the second is to exercise critical thinking in everyday life. Training the conscious mind to manage reactive biases and opinions when evaluating situations in everyday life will minimize the resistance to incoming flow of intuitive information.

How to Use Energetic Imprints© in Your Decision-Making Process

Usually the best time to use this method is after you have considered all data as well as all rational and logical possibilities. At this point, your brain has processed all the presently available information concerning the issue. It's now time to actively solicit any unknown piece of information, or solution from your unconscious mind. At this point, you let your hand discharge the information-energy onto paper. Once you are done, you go over each imprint with your fingers. The rule to record accurately is not to think. Just write down, without judgment or critical comments, what comes to you. This is the most difficult part of the process because the conscious mind will want to offer its opinion. Once you feel there is no more information, then you can derive meaning from the string of impressions.

Another example: A client asked for my intuitive advice for an acquisition. He gave me the names of three different companies of which I knew nothing about. After drawing Energetic Imprints© and deciphering them, I found that company A had a healthy financial situation with a dynamic organizational culture. A summary of the Energetic Imprints© for Company B revealed some sort of darkness, something that did not seem true. Company C seemed to be losing steam. I indicated to the client that Company A seemed the best match for what he was looking for. The client was surprised and informed me that Company A was not even in the running, but he felt he had to give me three names not two. His choice had been leaning for Company B. After a few weeks the client got back to me to say that after further due diligence he had found that Company B was fudging their sales numbers and that key employees were leaving Company C. After investigating Company A, he decided to acquire that one. In the long run, Company A proved to be the correct one. What is interesting is that the client, after having chosen two companies, felt himself that maybe there was a third one, and included it, Company A.

TOOL #6: PRACTICE YOUR INTUITION©

Test and practice your intuition by doing the following exercises. Then come up with your own—make them fun. Levity keeps the ego at bay!

PRACTICE YOUR INTUITION—HAVE FUN!

Below are a few simple, yet powerful exercises to develop your intuition.

Do not let your conscious mind judge whether or not these are silly, simple, too difficult, ridiculous, etc. … Just DO them! The judgments are your conscious voice complaining that you are developing a competing skill and its ego is not happy!

The Telephone Rings

Is it for you or someone else?

A male or female caller?

Routine or from someone you haven't heard from for a long time?

Long distance or local?

Next call?

Who might it be? Male, Female? Department? Topic?

In the Office—Who Will Walk by Next?

Male or female? Color clothes?
From which department?
Will they have a business question or just a friendly hello?

Your Next Meeting

What will be the mood, possible issues, dress, questions ?

Parking

Turn on your *mental radar* and try to map-out where there is a free space

Invent Your Own Exercises—Have Fun !

Fun is an important component: keeps the ego at bay
© *Copyright: Dominique Surel*

Conclusion

The model below illustrates how Intuitive Intelligence is manifested by the complete integration of the conscious mind, the unconscious mind, and the physical sensories, in order to connect into the non-local realm.

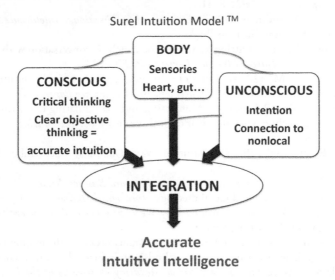

Surel Intuition Model ™

As we journey through the 21st century, we are faced with increasingly difficult decision-making. With the advent of the Internet, the volume of information and disinformation has exploded into uncontrollable levels while the time available to make decisions has decreased. The result is we are often feeling overwhelmed in correctly assessing situations and predictive scenarios. Meanwhile, automation and artificial intelligence are quickly progressing in trying to emulate the human being. On the global level, there is an increase in violence and human suffering. Even the ecology of our planet is threatened. We know that Intuitive Intelligence is enhanced by thinking through our heart, and that the heart is programmed with compassion and bonding with other heart energies. I would like to end this chapter by suggesting that thinking through the heart not only benefits our decision-making process in our personal and professional lives, but also that the quality of our decisions might be more evolved and offer sustainable solutions for the global issues we face and for the relief of human suffering.

References

Agor, W. H. (1986). The logic of intuition: How top executives make important decisions. *Organizational Dynamics, 14*(3), 5–18.

Armour, J. A. (2007). The little brain on the heart. *Cleveland Clinic Journal of Medicine, 74*(1), S48–S51.

Baltussen, H. (2007). Did Aristotle have a concept of 'intuition'? Some thoughts on translating 'nous'. In E. Close, M. Tsianikas and G. Couvalis (eds.) *Greek Research in Australia: Proceedings of the Sixth Biennial International Conference of Greek Studies,* Adelaide, Australia, 53–62.

Cartwright, T. (2004). Feeling your way: Enhancing leadership through intuition. *Leadership in Action, 24*(2), 8–11.

Cooper, R. K., & Sawaf, A. (1997). *Executive EQ: Emotional Intelligence in Business.* London, UK: Orion Business Books.

Coutu, D. (2004, January). Putting leaders on the couch: A conversation with Manfred F. R. Kets de Vries. *Harvard Business Review, 82,* 270–273.

Dane, E. & Pratt, M. (2004). Intuition: Its boundaries and role in organizational decision-making. *Academy of Management Best Conference Paper.*

Farah, M. J., & Wolpe, P. R. (2004). Monitoring and manipulating brain function: New neuroscience technologies and their ethical implications. *The Hastings Center Report, 34*(3), 35–45.

Frecska, E. (2012). Nonlocality and intuition, *NeuroQuantology,* September 2012, 10(3), 537–546.

Hayashi, A. M. (2001). When to trust your gut. *Harvard Business Review, 79*(2), 59–65.

Hoose, B. (2006). Intuition and moral theology. *Theological Studies, 67,* 602–624.

Hsu, J. (2008). *The Secrets of Storytelling: Why We Love a Good Yarn, Scientific American, Mind & Brain,* August/September.

Jolij, J., & Lamme, V. A. F. (2005). Repression of unconscious information by conscious processing: Evidence from affective blindsight induced by transcranial magnetic stimulation. *Proceedings of the National Academy of Sciences of the United States of America, 102,* 10747–10751.

Kopeikina, L. (2006). The elements of a clear decision. *MIT Sloan Management Review, 47*(2), 19–34.

Korthagen, F. A. J. (2005). The organization in balance: Reflection and intuition as complementary processes. *Management Learning, 36,* 371–388.

Langan-Fox, J., & Shirley, D. A. (2003). The nature and measurement of intuition: Cognitive and behavioral interests, personality, and behavioral interests, personality, and experiences. *Creativity Research Journal, 15,* 207–222.

Lieberman, M. D., Jarcho, J. M., & Satpute, J. B. (2004). Evidence-based and intuition based self-knowledge: An MRI study. *Journal of Personality and Social Psychology, 87,* 421–435.

Luo, C. M., & Cheng, B. W. (2006). Applying even-swap method to structurally enhance the process of intuition decision-making. *Systemic Practice and Action Research, 19,* 45–59.

Maani, K. E., & Maharaj, V. (2006). Links between systems thinking and complex decision making. *System Dynamics Review, 20,* 21–48. Retrieved December 14, 2006, from EBSCOhost database.

McCraty, R., Atkinson, M., & Bradley, R. T. (2004). Electrophysiological evidence of intuition: Part 1. The surprising role of the heart. *The Journal of Alternative and Complementary Medicine, 10,* 133–143.

Menn, S. (1998). *Descartes and Augustine.* Cambridge University Press, New York, NY.

Miller, C., & Ireland, D. H. (2005). Intuition in strategic decision making: Friend or foe in the fast-paced 21st century? *Academy of Management Executive, 19,* 19–30.

Patton, J. R. (2003). Intuition in decisions. *Management Decision, 41,* 989–996.

Pearsall, P. (1998). *The Heart's Code.* Broadway Books, New York.

Persinger (2011). https://www.youtube.com/watch?time_continue=11&v=9l6VPpDublg. Published on Mar 30, 2011.

Radin, D. I., & Schlitz, M. J. (2005). Gut feelings, intuition, and emotions: An exploratory study. *The Journal of Alternative and Complementary Medicine, 11*, 85–91. Retrieved September 24, 2005, from ProQuest database.

Rezaei, S., Mirzaei, M., & Zali, M.R. (2014). Nonlocal intuition: Replication and paired-subjects enhancement effects. *Global Advances in Health and Medicine, 3*(2), 5–15.

Sadler-Smith, E., & Shefy, E. (2004). The intuitive executive: Understanding and applying "gut feel" in decision-making. *Academy of Management Executive, 18*(4), 46–51.

Sinclair, M., & Ashkanasy, N. M. (2005). Intuition: Myth or a decision-making tool? *Management Learning, 36*, 353–371.

Sundgren, M., & Styhre, A. (2004). Intuition and pharmaceutical research: The case of AstraZeneca. *European Journal of Innovation Management, 7*(4), 267–279.

Surel, D. (2007). *Identifying Intuition in the Decision-Making Process: A Phenomenological Research Study* (Doctoral dissertation). Available from ProQuest Dissertations and Theses database. (UMI No. 3333908).

Chapter 3

Establishing Intuitive Faculties: Receptivity, Awareness, and Interpretation

Jessica Jagtiani

Contents

In this chapter, I would like to offer insight into what looking at the emergence of intuition in the practice of art has to offer professionals in business as well as in other fields. What can one learn about faculties of intuition and the ability to intuit by exploring qualities of art practice? While I make an example by applying the practice of visual art here, the features described in this chapter may be found in any artistic practice, such as dance, music, poetry, etc.

Both artists and business executives state the importance of intuition in their professional practice. However, exploring and comparing intuition in both fields shows significant differences in the emergence of intuition in the practices. My dissertation research, which was published in 2018, is a qualitative-phenomenological study that explores the experience of intuition in the professional practices of business and art, in order to show comparability and extend the base of intuition, while at the same time revealing what is unique about its emergence in art practice. At the heart of the research, intuition was examined as a form of knowledge-making—direct knowing, and its characteristics regarding the two professions, art practice and business practice, were investigated and compared. The findings of the study suggested that both, artists and business executives, are aware of intuitive perceptions. However, the participating artists seemed to experience intuition more often, were able to talk about intuitive experiences more clearly, seemed to have more awareness and control over the ability, and experienced heightened levels of intuition that the business executives did not. So why is that?

Data indicated that experiences of intuition are enhanced through methods such as contemplative practices that quiet the mind. Notions of quieting the mind may widely be found in Eastern philosophies and ancient practices that show similarities to processes in art practice, such as transcendence, focus, non-attachment, visualization, a body-mind-spirit connection, and applying intention. These distinct qualities allow for alternative knowledge-making methods that can create preferable conditions for intuition to flourish, such as increasing self-awareness, processing emotions, developing focus, refining the senses, and fostering ethicality, all of which may awaken and strengthen abilities of intuition.

What Is Intuition?

Intuition is challenging to define because of its many dimensions, abstract qualities, and the varying definitions that are used in the research literature. It is a form of experience that is subjective in nature and therefore hard to be evaluated, scientifically probed, or described with our common language system. The elusive and subjective nature of intuition limits the objectivity of what to call intuitive because what is counter-intuitive for one may be intuitive for another. An intuitive perception manifests through intensities in the body, or by feeling sudden surges or depletion of energy (Damasio, 1999; Fisher, 2007). As described here, it relates simultaneously to both embodied perception and to awareness that goes beyond the five common senses and involves extrasensory perception (Fisher, 2007). How intuition is perceived and understood is not only defined by the perspective of the professional field the research is conducted in but also influenced by culture, education, geography, expertise, belief system, memory, experience, and general exposure. Given these limitations, a synthesis of definitions is necessary to clarify the nature of the term *intuition* used. In this chapter, *intuition* is defined in its broadest sense and most original way as "direct knowing," which presents an opportunity to reconcile conflicting interpretations by focusing on their intersections and interrelations instead of their differences (Sinclair, 2011).

The Integration of Intuition in Cognition

The most distinctive aspect of Western thought is logic and its outcome of evidence. Eastern philosophy, in contrast, does not focus on the elaboration of facts for a full grasp of the whole; it comprehends intuitively. Therefore, the Eastern mind is essentially vague and indefinite (Li, 2014). Peter Ping Li (2014), professor of Chinese Business Studies at the Copenhagen Business School in Denmark, describes the Eastern notion of intuition as "exploratory" in nature and as the core of the Eastern paradigm of cognition, while the Western notion of intuition is "exploitative" and perceived as irrelevant to the Western paradigm of cognition, which has logical analysis at its core. The Western notion of intuition mainly refers to fast and frugal decision-making based on a heuristic routine rooted in System 1 (experiential system) (Kahneman, 2013), while the Eastern notion of intuition is not limited to System 1, as it arises from both System 1 (experiential) and System 2 (deliberate), as an equilibrium beyond the dual-processing model (Evans, 2008; Li, 2014). Li suggests that many practitioners of the West have tacitly applied the Eastern philosophy of wisdom in their practice without being conscious of it. Yet, research in the Western world is mainly conducted from a Western viewpoint that essentially disregards perspectives on intuition that do not quite fit into rigid Western philosophy. Identifying and studying every noticed aspect of intuition, exploring its ambiguous notion and unfamiliar characteristics, are important in order to obtain a holistic view on the experience of the phenomenon, which could lead us to a greater understanding of cognitive processes.

Eastern Views on Intuition

In Eastern philosophy, intuition is mostly linked with religion and spirituality and has various meanings according to different spiritual texts (Leaman, 2000). The here offered views on intuition are broad perspectives of two main Eastern branches of philosophy. In Hinduism, intuition is far more important than intellect itself and understood as an ability that can be achieved through self-realization. Devoted self-purifying Yogic practices including meditation will remove modifications, such as desires, anxiety, greed, and fear, and guide one to a path of self-realization. Intuition in Sanskrit is called "Buddhi" (derived from *budh*: to be awake, to understand, to know), which is a higher intelligence, in which one's senses, observation, listening, awareness, and visualizing abilities are heightened and unique. In order to reach intuition one needs to attain a calm mind that is receptive, attentive, nonjudgmental, and no longer limited by sensory experiences and personal biases, but capable of seeing beyond fragmented and divisive appearances. Non-dual schools of Hinduism take intuition to be an experience through which one can come in contact with and experience Brahman, the ultimate metaphysical reality (Indich, 2000; Sharma, 2006; Brodd, 2009). In Buddhism, intuition is understood as a faculty in the mind of immediate knowledge. It places the term *intuition* beyond the mental process of conscious thinking, as the conscious intellect cannot necessarily access subconscious information, or render such information into a communicable form. Intuitive insight, termed "seeing Dhamma," or the truth taught by the Buddha, is not by any means the same thing as rational thinking. Intuitive insight can only be gained by means of a true inner realization (Sumedho, 2013, 2014).

Receptivity

Certain views of the various Eastern philosophies differ radically, yet, most Eastern philosophies share a specific conception of God and the cosmos. This shared position, unlike in Western monotheistic religious traditions views God not external to the cosmos, but as residing within it. This outlook is often called *pantheism*, a term literally meaning "all-God" (Fieser, 2017). Schools of Eastern mysticism all emphasize the basic unity of the universe, which is the central feature of their teachings: to become aware of the unity and mutual interrelation of all things, to transcend the notion of an isolated individual self and to identify themselves with the ultimate reality (Radin, 2006; Capra, 2010). Classical Hindu writings, such as the Upanishads and the Bhagavad Gita, involve the pantheistic idea of God at the core of one's true identity and discovering the Self-God through yoga practices such as meditation. The theme of pantheism in Buddhism emerged first with the notion of nirvana, the idea that one should free oneself from all desire and components of our ordinary consciousness in order to subdue the individual self and experience the oneness of everything. This shared viewpoint appears to be a significant aspect in the experience of intuition not only in ancient Eastern views but also in current Western observation. In the study of artists and business executives, I found that in a heightened level of intuition, the artists perceived a notion of unity in all.

> It was like seeing the inter-connectivity of everything and it was like
> a tiny opening into a window and it was amazing and I remember

thinking that day like, "Oh. Is this what people talk about when they say spiritual awakening?"

(Artist participant, personal communication, 2016)

Renowned scientists, such as Albert Einstein, Niels Bohr, Max Planck, Werner Heisenberg, and J. Robert Oppenheimer, pioneered in revealing that the universe is not an assembly of physical parts but instead is an entanglement of immaterial energy waves that form a vibratory field. The concept of matter in subatomic physics utterly differs from the traditional idea of material substance in classical physics. This is also true for concepts of space, time, or cause and effect underscored by modern quantum physics. Yet, the concepts of classical physics are still fundamental to our perspective on the world, and with their radical transformation our whole worldview is beginning to change (Capra, 2010). This change of perception, an awareness of the interconnection of all things, appears significant for the receptivity of higher levels of intuition.

Awareness

Psychologist Frances Vaughan (1973) states that intuitive experiences include mystical apprehension of absolute truth, insight into the nature of reality, unitive consciousness, creative problem-solving, holistic decision-making, artistic inspiration, and scientific discovery and invention, which can be attained through notions of patterns and possibilities, extrasensory perception, clairvoyance, telepathy, precognition, retrocognition, feelings of attraction and aversion, picking up "vibes," bodily sensations, hunches, and premonitions. Robin M. Hogarth (2001), former president of the Society for Judgment and Decision Making and the European Association for Decision Making, notes that many psychologists working within the scientific tradition may not accept versions of Vaughan's statements about intuition as an extrasensory phenomenon. Yet, much of the information offered by Vaughan appears reasonable (Hogarth, 2001) and is reflected in the participants' accounts of the research study. The participants in the study, both business executives and artists, experienced intuition in various forms. However, the artists reported more experiences of intuition with further variations, were able to talk about the experiences more clearly, and seemed more aligned and familiar with the experience (Jagtiani, 2018). Vaughan (1979) describes four levels of intuition: physical, emotional, mental, and spiritual. Although any given experience may have elements of more than one level, experiences can usually be categorized according to the level at which they are consciously perceived. It appeared that the business executive participants in the study experienced the first three of the following four levels of intuition, while the artist participants indicated to experience all four levels of intuition.

The physical level: Intuitive experiences frequently depend on physical and emotional cues that bring them to conscious awareness (Harris, 2000). At the physical level, intuition is characterized by a strong body response that may be experienced in a situation where there is no reason to think that anything unusual is going on. For example, the business executives in the study frequently described experiences of intuition perceived as an empty feeling in their stomach or a feeling in their gut. The artists added the experience of a feeling in the spine, the heart, the shoulders, the throat, and activity in the mind's eye when experiencing intuition.

The gut: Intuitions at the physical level are related to the body-mind connection, especially when considering sensations in the gut. When "going with the gut" to make a decision or feeling "butterflies in the stomach" when nervous, one is likely receiving signals from an unexpected source often called "the second brain." This "brain in the gut" is altering medicine's understanding of the links between digestion, mood, health, and even the way we think (Wang & Wang, 2016). Scientists call this brain the enteric nervous system (ENS). For decades, researchers have known of the connection between the brain and the gut, but scientists thought communication was traveling one way: from the brain to the gut. However, today it is well recognized that gut microbiota affects the brain's physiological, behavioral, and cognitive functions and that emotional well-being may rely on messages from the gut to the brain (Hadhazy, 2010), though its precise mechanism has not been fully understood yet (Wang & Wang, 2016).

The spine: The experience of sensation in the spine also appears significant. The spine is the first element that is formed in a mother's womb. The spinal column is part of the central nervous system and is an important channel for all the bodily stimuli that are transferred via the nerves to the brain. From a spiritual perspective, the spine and intuitive experience may be interpreted through the concept of the chakra system. Chakras (Sanskrit *cakra*—"wheel of energy"), often interpreted as a whirling, vortex-like energy aligned along the spinal axis, are considered to funnel universal energy into the human energy system. Particularly found in tantric traditions, chakras are believed to be psychic-energy centers. In the ancient Upanishads (ca. 7th century BCE) references are made to an esoteric human anatomy composed of subtle life energy or "prana." This anatomy involves 72,000 nadis (Sanskrit, "tube," "pipe," "channel") along which prana travels. Nadis are subtler than the nerves referred to in modern physiology and are closely associated with the nervous system, stemming from and intertwining with the chakras (O'Sullivan, 2014; Wallis, 2016). The critical aspect in the participants' accounts of intuitive perception that links the experience of intuition to the yoga chakra system is the location of the perceived bodily sensations, such as the stomach, the heart, the throat, and the mind's eye. In various chakra systems of tantric lineages, these locations are associated with chakra centers in the body.

The emotional level: At the emotional level, intuition comes into consciousness through feelings. Awareness of intuition at this level typically involves knowing how to react to one's feelings in interpersonal situations. Sensitivity to other people's "vibes" or "vibrations of energy," instances of immediate liking or disliking with no apparent justification, or a vague sense that one is inexplicably supposed to do something, can be instances of intuition operating on the emotional level (Vaughan, 1979). All participants of the study, artists and business executives, reported the experience of this level. The emotional level of intuition appeared especially important in the practice of the business executives as the professional practice in business highly depends on interpersonal relationships, such as reading the sincerity of people's intention or responding to people in appropriate ways. Described by the artists, the experience of being drawn to things, subjects, places, activities, and actions may also be placed within the emotional level of intuition.

The mental level: Intuition on the mental level often comes into awareness through images or words in the mind, or what is called "inner vision." Patterns of order may be perceived where everything at first appears chaotic, or patterns of change may be apprehended intuitively long before the verification process of careful observation is completed. This type of intuition implies an ability to reach accurate conclusions on the basis of limited information (Vaughan, 1979). All participants of the study experienced this level of intuition, for example seeing the future by extrapolating through connecting data information, hearing an inner voice, receiving images in the mind's eye through visualizations, or dreams. Both artists and business executives in the study experienced intuitive perceptions led by dreams and visualization, yet, only the artists consciously implemented the method into their practice (Jagtiani, 2018).

The spiritual level: At the spiritual level, intuition is independent from feeling, thoughts, and sensations. At this level, intuition does not depend on sensing, feeling, or thinking. It is not associated with the body, emotions, or pattern perception relating to specific problems or situations. Paradoxically, the cues on which intuition depends on the other levels are regarded as interference at this level. However, an awareness of how intuition can function on the other levels, the levels of sensation, feeling, and thinking, helps to dispel the misconception of intuition as a way of knowing as an all-or-nothing proposition (Vaughan, 1979). The notion of the spiritual level is consistent with the broader concept of intuition typical of Eastern views. This level of intuition appears to be experienced only by the artists in the study, who described that the experience of intuition may come with the perception of a unity of everything existing. An ancient relationship between art and spirituality can be tracked in the chronicle of art. Art appears more suitable to be practiced in a spiritual way than business practice, thus access to higher-level intuitive experiences may likely be found more often in artists than business executives (Jagtiani, 2018).

The collective (un)conscious: The artist participants experienced intuition at times as a form of collectiveness and consider information attained through intuition to come from the collective (un)conscious. The study's artists suggested that artists oftentimes tap in to the collective (un)conscious on different levels to bring things forward. Artists are mirrors for the greater world, creating spaces for transition, possibility, and vision (Jagtiani, 2018).

Data collected over 15 years suggest an emerging noosphere or the unifying field of consciousness described by sages in all cultures (Global Consciousness Project, 2015). This concept of a collective consciousness and conscious universe, including associated notions, is deeply integrated in Eastern philosophies but also recognized by Western scholars and scientists, such as Ken Wilber (1982), David Bohm (2002), Dean Radin (2006), Rupert Sheldrake (2009), Fritjof Capra (2010), and many more. It has been given numerous names such as the ether, the Akashic field, quantum vacuum, a unified quantum field, morphic field, the one mind, the cosmic mind, the universal mind, the holographic universe, and the collective unconscious. In traditional Hindu belief the Akashic field is considered to be the basic reality of the cosmos. Tuned into the Akashic field, one can access abilities that appear to be supernatural, but are in fact completely natural. People who practice meditation have reported this kind of experience. In Vedic tradition it was the basis for the affirmation that consciousness is not an emergent property that originates through material structures such as the brain and the nervous system, but a vast field of consciousness that constitutes the primary reality of the universe. The artists in the study appeared to experience this field by reaching heightened levels of intuition (Laszlo, 2006).

Where Consciousness Resides

The relationship between the mind and the brain is a mystery that is central to how we understand our very existence as conscious beings. Some scholars understand the mind as strictly a function of the brain, and consciousness as the product of firing neurons; others, however, strive to scientifically understand the existence of a mind independent of, and separate from, the brain. In their article, "Consciousness in the Universe Is Scale Invariant and Implies an Event Horizon of the Human Brain," Meijer and Geesink (2017) bring together neuroscience and quantum physics and posit that the "mind" is a field that exists around the brain. This field lies and operates in a fourth spatial dimension (hyper-sphere), and shares information with the brain possibly through quantum wave resonance, which is a mechanism of extremely rapid information processing in the brain. This means, instead of signals being sent between neurons in the brain, a wave pattern that encompasses all neurons as well as the mental field transmits the information instantaneously. The "mind," thus, may be able to pick up information from the earth's magnetic field, dark energy, and other sources, and transmits wave information into the brain tissue that is instrumental in high-speed conscious and subconscious information processing (Meijer & Geesink, 2017). The theory suggests that the "mind" or mental field is both non-material and, at the same time, physically part of the brain; it entertains a non-dual wave/particle relation according to quantum physical principles which is directly dependent on the brain physiology but not reducible to it. Meijer (2017) describes the "mind" alternately as "a holographic structured field," a "receptive mental workspace," a "meta-cognitive domain," and the "global memory space of the individual." Meijer and Geesink (2017) imply that the theory may directly contribute to answering philosopher and cognitive scientist David Chalmers's (2010) famous question, "[h]ow can something immaterial like subjective experience and self-consciousness arise from a material brain?" (p. 70). If the "mind" truly interacts with the brain this way, as conceived by Meijer and Geesink, it could be a step toward explaining phenomena, such as ultra-fast subconscious mental processes, extrasensory perception, and intuition.

Differences between Art Practice and Business Practice

The business executive participants in the study mainly see the purpose of intuition as its ability to protect and make sense of things. The artists furthermore define intuition as an instrument for and of connectivity, considering intuition as a method of connecting with something beyond themselves, such as their higher selves and the universe. There is a spiritual aspect to the way the artists describe the source of their intuition. In contrast, the business executives suggest that experience, external clues, and individual beliefs are the core source of their intuition—there needs to be a rational connection between intuition's information and its source, such as something you have experienced, read, or thought about. Yet, when further asked about the source of intuition, their answers slightly changed, and they also referred to terms that have a more spiritual essence, such as "an energy force, the sixth sense, and a source larger than oneself" (Jagtiani, 2018). The different views on the purpose of intuition may originate in the distinctive motivations of the two professions. Running a business comes with certain risks, such as strategic risk, compliance risk, operational risk, and reputational risk. Therefore, a main aspect for business executives to be concerned about is protection; consequently, intuition may be experienced as preparation and protection. Art practice, on the other hand, values the ability and desire to connect (Jagtiani, 2018). Through art, people find connections with themselves, with each other, with nature, and with the universe. Art has the power to integrate and reveal the wholeness of things, and therefore has always been central in human life (Ikeda, 2010). For this reason, the artists may understand the experience of intuition as a form of connecting. On the other hand, however, the exact opposite of this claim can also be argued: art is full of risk—through putting yourself out there, risking failure, economical struggle, and rejection—and business is all about connectivity—via employees, clients, the company's network, the way a company's systems relates to other systems, or even just the sum of data links. The difference, however, lies in the core intention of the practices, in which case I would argue that most art practice has the core intention to express, share, and connect while most business practice has the core intention to expand, profit, and protect.

Working conditions: Inhibiting factors for intuitive experiences in the business profession can be attributed to the working conditions which are often busy, dealing with a multitude of people and having to meet deadlines and fixed goals. According to Eastern wisdom and the findings of my research, the optimum alignment for an experience of intuition is a quiet mind. In business, little time and place is given to turn inward and quiet the mind and preference is set to rational thought, speed, data, and quantitative analysis over intuition. Art practice, in contrast, gives great importance to intuitive thought, emotions, feelings, and qualitative analysis. While intuition strives in a state of non-attachments, business executives are usually bound to a specific goal or business plan. In art making, on the other hand, there are no set rules or goals other than to create; there might be a theme or a vision but the methods to get to the outcome are undefined and open-ended. A further factor is that usually in business, one works with a number of other people, which means that decisions are often not made individually, several people have to be on board. This can be extra difficult when wanting to make a decision based on intuition. The findings indicate that conditions to intuit are more difficult in business than in art practice. This likely is, in part, the reason for a greater development of intuitive faculties in the study's artist participants (Jagtiani, 2018).

Intuition in Art Practice

Art is one of very few accepted practices in the Western world that allows one or even demands one to listen to intuition; it makes one aware of its presence. Not all artists may claim to be guided by intuitive processes in their practice, but I argue that most are. Artists often develop the conscious ability to "engage intuitive insight and affective cognition to open themselves to extra-rational modes of thought and states of bodily awareness" (Piha, 2005, p. 32; see also Fisher, 2007). While many artists develop highly individualistic semiotic vocabularies, they simultaneously decode visionary experience to the social, economic, and cultural relations that concern their context of practice. Art embraces aspects such as ambiguity, ambivalence, openness, variation, reform, and complexity. Artists may sometimes feel they have to defend the reality of their experiences and the certainty of their insights because they appear uncommonly retrieved. Simultaneously, they may disrupt notions of established boundaries that appear essential within the rational Western philosophy (Piha, 2005; Fisher, 2007).

The study's data indicates that experiencing and processing intuition can be enhanced through quieting the mind. Methods to quiet the mind can be found in Eastern practices, which show similarities to processes performed in art practice that carry factors and attributes beneficial to the experience of intuition, such as:

1. **Transcendence**—Attained through attention toward the non-material world and the unity of all
2. **Focus**—Attained through a quiet mind by passive or active meditation
3. **Non-attachment**—Attained through letting go of predeterminations
4. **Visualization**—Attained through focused imagination
5. **A body-mind-spirit connection**—Attained through awareness of relationships between emotions, feelings, thoughts, and energy flow
6. **Intention**—Attained through curiosity, exploration, and aiming in a direction

Artists usually desire to stabilize their attention in a state where the artwork appears before their thinking is leading. Artists are interested in a specific shift of attention, where they can apply their mind toward their artwork and focus their attention, so the artwork is produced from a state of mind that is separated from the thinking itself—from an instrument of alternate intelligence (Palmer, 2011; Jagtiani, 2018). In art making one is often caught in the flow of creative expression, which is a meditative state. In Eastern traditions, art is regularly practiced as a form of meditation, such as with mandala, yantra, or calligraphic works.

Quieting the Mind

Achieving a quiet mind might be more difficult than it sounds. Other functions of the mind, such as the intellect or sensations, cannot be easily forced either, yet one can pay attention to them. One can think about thinking, pay attention to one's feelings, or can ignore them; the same is valid for intuition.

Being in the present: The mind, more often than not, is reliving and rewriting events of the past, or imagining, rehearsing, and planning for the future. This becomes a habit of mind and a habit of attention, which may hinder the ability to intuit. Intuition accesses information that is beyond the mind, fed from the stream of pure perception. One's intuition can only be accessed in the present moment. Consequently, one's access increases when one stabilizes the relationship to the present which quiets the mind. Vice versa, practices that quiet the mind help to come more fully into the present, increasing access to intuitive wisdom (Birchfield, 2015).

Emotional attentiveness: Degrees of intuitive awareness may be affected by factors such as time, place, mood, attitude, state of consciousness, and innumerable idiosyncratic variables. For example, any attempt to apprehend the totality of another person through intuition involves quieting the mind as well as dissociation from personal emotions. Only when one can free oneself from one's own personal attentions or ego involvement, one can achieve the level of transpersonal experience, in which one knows another person through empathetic identification with the totality of the energy field (Vaughan, 1973). Releasing emotions that might interfere, letting go of the past, silencing any exterior distractions, and turning quiet inside are contributing factors to enabling intuition to come through. The biggest obstacle to developing intuition may be self-deception. Being aware of one's emotions is useful when starting any kind of self-observation, because one begins to sort out what are emotional reactions from what are accurate perceptions, particularly in interpersonal intuitions (Vaughan, 2011; Jagtiani, 2018).

Observing the mind: When one looks within, one discovers the ways in which the mind obstructs our capacity to access intuition. We notice its stream of commentary, judgment, and habit. Through observing the mind with an attitude of inquiry and without judgment, one may develop an ability to discern the difference between the intellect and pure awareness. By placing one's awareness on awareness itself, the mind eventually quiets, and intuitive wisdom becomes more accessible (Birchfield, 2015; Jagtiani, 2018).

Paying attention: If one begins to pay attention to intuition, one can recognize it as a way of knowing, which transcends reason, but it is not a substitute or in opposition to reason––it is an addition to reason (Vaughan, 2011). Intuiting is being present in the moment to how one feels and putting oneself in situations where one can test their intuitive sense by asking does this feel right. The challenge is to keep exploring potential methods to quiet the mind that could work for one. This will lead to understanding one's own workings with intuition. As we become more intuitive we also become less fearful, which helps to provide a sense of being in the world in a way that we can trust ourselves and trust each other (Vaughan, 2011). Trust is a significant aspect in becoming aware of and interpreting intuition. It is also part of a larger sense of wanting to experience each other more fully and as who we really are, with less fear and less defensiveness, in order to be more open and more receptive to a genuine exchange of ideas and communication. Ajahn Sumhedo, senior Western representative of the Thai forest tradition of Theravada Buddhism, suggests:

> Intuitive awareness is frustrating to an analytical person whose faith is in thought, reason, and logic. Awareness is right now. It's not a matter of thinking about it but being aware of thinking about it. How do you do that?... Trusting is relaxing into it; it's just attentiveness, which is an act of faith (saddhā), a "trustingness."

> **(Sumedho, 2014)**

Methods to Quiet the Mind

Before one can pay attention to intuition, one has to be able to hear it amid the cacophony of one's busy life. One has to slow down and listen, which often requires solitude.

Meditation: In meditation one uses a technique, such as focusing the mind on a particular object, mantra, or activity, to achieve a mentally clear and emotionally calm state. There are many different ways to meditate. A common technique to prepare for a meditative state is to focus on the breath, a technique the participants of the study describe as beneficial to intuition. The exercise of connecting mind and breath appears in many Eastern manuals as a fundamental practice used for clearing the mind and is traditionally proposed as a resolution to the tendency of the mind to become distracted and scattered. Meditation generates awareness. Intuition is inseparable from developing self-awareness; this is why any discipline or practice that requires self-observation is helpful to improve the ability to intuit. The process of meditation involves becoming in touch with more and more subtle levels of thought, as you quiet the mind heavy desires and aggressive thoughts evaporate and more delicate thoughts can come to mind opening the realm in which intuition operates (Vaughan, 2011). One could think that intuition only works in situations of a quiet mind. However, benefits of quieting the mind through regular practice of meditation lie in learning and memory processes, emotion regulation, self-referential processing, and perspective taking (Hölzel et al., 2011), which may result in one being more patient and tolerant, focusing on the present, increasing self-awareness, reducing negative emotions, and increasing imagination and creativity. Attaining these abilities can make typical stressful situations or moments of crisis easier to handle and accessible for intuition to emerge.

Physical activity: One technique to quiet the analytic mind, mentioned by the artist in the study, is physical activity, such as walking, dancing, jogging, physical yoga, etc. Exercise calms our mind, improves our mood, and instills confidence and self-esteem (Jordan, 2017). Therefore, physical exercise is a suitable form of creating a condition for intuition. Extraordinary proficiency made possible by focusing mind, body, and spirit toward one task is no longer a controversial idea. However, it does require self-discipline. If one allows the mind to race around while exercising, or if one exercises while listening to a broadcast or chatting with friends, then it is just physical exercise. Yet, a concerted focus on the activity and, for the most part, to do it in a receptive state of mind may turn any ordinary activity into an opportunity to intuit.

Focusing: Another form of meditation is focusing on images or objects, either in one's own mind or in the exterior world. Mental imagery can be a very useful tool for bringing intuitive perceptions into some kind of tangible form. Expressions such as "I got the message from the clouds in the sky" stand for a specific focusing of internal intelligence, an internal attention that focuses on the problem and the inner stream of reverie. The inner stream of impressions is played out on the object surface with your eyes open. The clouds in the sky are a nice pointed focusing surface. These external objects or surfaces lend themselves as devices to focus the inner mind. It is not really the trees or the rock or the clouds in the sky, but it is the quality of attention that one brings to one's problem and one uses the external object as a device to focus one's attention (Palmer, 2011).

Distraction: Giving the mind a distracting task to do is another method for entering an intuitive state of mind, such as the Zen Buddhist technique of kōan, a paradox to be meditated upon that is used to train Zen Buddhist monks to abandon ultimate dependence on reason and to force them into gaining sudden intuitive enlightenment (Conners, 2011). A number of recent studies have reported that decision quality is enhanced under conditions of inattention or distraction (Dijksterhuis, 2004; Dijksterhuis et al., 2006; Dijksterhuis & Nordgren, 2006). Often described as the unconscious thought effect, this was then interpreted to support the unconscious thought theory (UTT), which claims that unconscious incubation processes during the distraction interval are responsible for the enhanced performance compared to the conscious deliberation, which is subject to severe capacity limitations (Dijksterhuis & Nordgren, 2006). UTT, which proposes that under complex conditions unconscious thought leads to more accurate choices than conscious thought, explores the combination of or alternation between active searches for information on a problem, in which the individual searcher is goaloriented, and incubation periods, in which the individual stops any active attention and engages in a period of "distraction." "Distraction" is a phase of diverted attention that leads to listening to inner feelings (Gigerenzer, 2008). Even if intuition may seem instant at the "Aha!" moment, it is not always instantaneous: an extended phase of development may be necessary.

Dreaming: For many people paying attention to dreams can enhance their intuitive abilities (Vaughan, 2011). In a dream state one has all of the necessary elements to enter an altered state, in which attention moves away from the thinking state. After one's attention has moved from thoughts and has gone empty to no thinking, the dream occurs spontaneously. It is not directed by the thinking self, yet there is a state of awareness. There is an observer, and in the morning the dream may be recalled. The observer was awake enough to remember the dream and when the attention shifts back to the thoughts, the dream is recovered and submitted for analysis (Palmer, 2011). Carl Jung's theories of dream interpretation and dream consciousness is offered as a way of tapping into "unconscious wisdom" (SadlerSmith, 2012), and suggests that most dreams operate on the level of stories, myths, and archetypes—making them a source for ideas and inspiration (Gregoire, 2013). Anecdotes from the history of the creative arts and scientific discovery add credence to this claim. For example, Salvador Dali's painting *The Persistence of Memory* is said to have been inspired by a dream. "Dreams-as-intuitions" have generative (creative) and mental rehearsal (simulation) functions (Sadler-Smith, 2012), which appears significant to both art practice and business practice.

Interpreting Intuition

Interpretation of intuition is difficult because signals may be ignored, obscured, or misunderstood. There may be a lack of awareness or too much emphasis on analysis. It takes time, focus, and awareness to hear intuition. Most people in Western culture spend years trying to improve their analytical or System 2 abilities, yet their intuitive abilities are neglected. For instance, educational systems throughout the world, with rare exceptions such as in Waldorf or Montessori schools, tend to favor empirical learning over experiential learning. The specificity that the empirical state of consciousness demands, however, happens to be the very thing that obscures intuition. Instead, intuition thrives, as do all of the senses, in an environment of first, receptivity, and then, and only then, specificity. Furthermore, there might be a lack of interpretive skill. Even if people pay attention to their intuition and savor the sensations it provides, the difficult task of translation remains. Artists are skilled at translating their abstract sensations into a recognizable and transmittable form, which may be why the artists in the study reported more and varied experiences of intuition. But for most the ability to translate remote and abstract sensations remains very difficult. Consequently, intuitive sensation is misinterpreted, leading to inaccurate judgments. However, translation of intuitive sensations is a skill that can be learned (Voss, 2014).

Staying on center: The difficulty of determining when a perception is truly intuitive, in the sense that it apprehends reality, or when it is imaginary, or simply a result of personal projection, is a means of intellectual discrimination. A nonjudgmental approach aids the experience of intuition. A reorientation from outer to inner reality is central to turn the mind toward nondiscriminating awareness (Sangharakshita, 1998). The elusive nature of intuitive perception, however, makes it challenging to study because lack of discrimination can lead to incorrect assumptions with no basis in reality. Each individual pursuing to develop and nurture the cognitive function of their own intuition must be willing to learn by trial and error. Paying attention to intuitive perceptions and learning to trust them are important factors in functional development and requires a willingness to test the validity of the perceptions. Personal striving or the desire to be right interferes with the process itself; the ego needs to stand aside in order to permit the experience. Interpretation and evaluation must be temporarily held in suspension, yet they are essential to the process of development and integration. To have a clear perception into the nature of reality, one needs to stay centered between the two poles of fear and desire that tend to be in the way of seeing clearly (Vaughan, 2011, 1973).

An undeniable feeling of confirmation: "Intuition is true by definition. If a seemingly intuitive insight turns out to be wrong, it did not spring from intuition, but from self-deception or wishful thinking" (Vaughan, 1979, p. 45). The way that the participants of the research study understood perceptions to be "accurately" intuitive was described through the quality of feeling that came with the experience. When intuition comes through, there appears to be a feeling of "rightness" accompanied with it that cannot be negated.

> You know when you're swimming under water and you're like, "this is cool, there are nice things about this," and then you get above the water and you can breathe again and you're like, "phew, this feels right"…It's

> more like that. Like coming into a place where I'm like, "oh this is the
> right place for me," I feel comfortable. …like I belong in this place.

(Artist participant, personal communication, 2017)

> I realize sometimes like, "Oh, no that's not intuitive." Like it's not
> that I really know, it's I really want this and then there are different
> moments when I'm like, "I really have this feeling that this is right." So
> there is a difference between these two.

(Business executive participant, personal communication, 2017)

Interpreting intuition is an ability that can only be learned through practice. As with other skills, the more one practices the better one will get. It is not something that can be learned in textbooks but arises through combined effects of experiential and formal learning—especially because of its subjective aspect. A continuous, focused, and active involvement in the experience through observation, repetition, tracking, and reflection on the experience is needed. Journaling or diary keeping can be beneficial in this endeavor. Talking about intuitive experiences may also be helpful; however, the subject often appears off-limits in Western cultures.

The Interconnection of the Deliberate and the Intuitive Mind

A main problem of developing intuition in the Western world is that it usually understands the intuitive and the rational mind as separated and does not realize their interconnection. Intuition is not a process that operates independently of analysis; rather, the two processes are essential complementary components of effective decision-making systems (Simon, 1987). Confident decision makers blend logic and intuition (Patton, 2003). From an integrated perspective of "direct knowing" intuition can employ experiential or deliberative processing systems; it can be of a holistic or inferential type in various degrees of complexity. Philosopher Henri Bergson (1999) suggests that intuition and the discursive activity of our intellect are not different organs yet two sides of the same thinking activity—an activity driven by the spirit. The thinking activity stirs in one direction when it takes a discursive, conceptual, quantitative, analytic, and external perspective and in the opposite direction when it intuitively sympathizes with the metaphysical and psychological reality (Henden, 2004). Recent research has moved away from the split view between experience-based intuition with its cognitive component and affect-based intuition with its emotional and sensory aspects and tends to acknowledge the importance of both (Sinclair, 2011). Expositor of Tibetan Buddhism and Buddhist meditation Lama Anagarika Govinda (1959), proposes:

> Whatever there is of feeling, perception, and mental formations, it is mutually connected, not disconnected; and it is impossible to separate the one from the other and to show up their difference. Because what one feels, that one perceives, and what one perceives, that one is conscious of.

This is in accordance with, author on intuition Tony Bastick's (2003) views, who suggests:

> The intuitive process is dependent upon the interaction of emotional states and cognitive processes. It is evident from the feeling of satisfaction and reductions in tensions that accompany an insight that emotional involvement plays a part in intuitive processes. A whole-body unifying theory is needed to describe intuitive processes.

Both artists and business executives in the study agree that the deliberative mind does not function separately from the intuitive mind. The mind, while intuiting, is a responsive listener, becomes aware of intuition in the process, translates feelings and sensations, keeps track, separates out interferences, tests assumptions, and interprets the experience.

Conclusion

The research study revealed once more that intuition is complex, particularly through its close relationships with other elusive phenomena such as emotions, feelings, spirituality, and consciousness. However, the complexity of intuition might just be a perception caused by our current lack of sufficient knowledge in the field of energy. New understandings in science aligned with a reemerging interest in ancient knowledge unlock novel and exciting headways to follow and investigate. It is a matter of being receptive to uncommon and new (or actually ancient) approaches to knowledge-making and cognition.

Regarding the development of intuition in business practice, it is important to realize that the approach to the experience of intuition plays a significant role. In business practice and when training professionals in the field of business, it is beneficial to recognize that processes that may not seem relevant to business practice, for example implementing distracting activities, creating visualizations in the mind, focusing on the breath or external objects, or engaging in attentive physical activity, may be beneficial exercises to the development of intuition and holistic decision-making. There are numerous methods to quiet the mind and different methods have different effects on people. Seeking approaches and techniques for the development of intuition, art practice may serve as an exemplary in the Western world. Artists and their openness to intuition become a model for educational practitioners offering a way to think outside rational linearity, a way of opening minds to new possibilities in thought engaging the kinds of insights crucial to shaping a caring and insightful society. Central for the development of intuition is awareness achieved by the focused exploration of self in regard to everything else. The greater the development of intuitive ability in a person the more likely are experiences of heightened levels of intuition, such as the spiritual level. In developing intuition and self-awareness ethicality in a person may also increase. This notion, to me, appears as the most significant beneficial result offered by the development of intuition. Especially considering the countless decisions made in the field of business and other leading fields that are often purely profit driven and disregard harmful and damaging consequences to living beings and the environment. Developing intuition may help us all in making mindful, holistic decisions and creating a better world for the future.

References

Bastick, T. (2003). *Intuition: Evaluating the Construct and Its Impact on Creative Thinking.* Kingston, Jamaica: Stoneman & Lang.

Bergson, H. (1999). *An Introduction to Metaphysics.* Indianapolis, IN: Hackett.

Birchfield, J. (2015, January 8). When the intellect serves intuition: A portal to innovation. *Huffington Post.* Retrieved August 29, 2017, from http://www.huffingtonpost.com/jan-birchfield-phd/when-the-intellect-serves_b_6437524.html

Bohm, D. (2002). *Wholeness and the Implicate Order* (1st ed.). New York: Routledge.

Brodd, J. (2009). *World Religions: A Voyage of Discovery* (3rd ed.). Saint Mary's Press, pp. 43–47.

Capra, F. (2010). *The Tao of Physics: An Exploration of the Parallels between Modern Physics and Eastern Mysticism* (5th ed.). Boston, MA: Shambhala.

Chalmers, D. J. (2010). *The Character of Consciousness.* Oxford: Oxford University Press. doi:10.1093/acprof:oso/9780195311105.001.0001

Conners, S. (2011). *Zen Buddhism: The Path to Enlightenment* (special ed.). (B. Williams, Trans.). El Paso, TX: Norte Press.

Damasio, A. R. (1999). *The Feeling of What Happens: Body and Emotion in the Making of Consciousness.* New York: Houghton Mifflin Harcourt.

Dijksterhuis, A. (2004). Think different: The merits of unconscious thought in preference development and decision making. *Journal of Personality and Social Psychology, 87*(5), 586–598. doi:10.1037/0022-3514.87.5.586

Dijksterhuis, A., & Nordgren, L. F. (2006). A theory of unconscious thought. *Perspectives on Psychological Science, 1*(2), 95–109.

Dijksterhuis, A., Bos, M. W., Nordgren, L. F., & van Baaren, R. B. (2006). On making the right choice: The deliberation-without-attention effect. *Science, 311*(5763), 1005–1007. doi:10.1126/science.1121629

Evans, J. S. B. T. (2008). Dual-processing accounts of reasoning, judgment, and social cognition. *Annual Review of Psychology, 59*(1), 255–278. doi:10.1146/annurev.psych.59.103006.093629

Fieser, J. (2017, September 1). Chapter 4: Classical Eastern philosophy. *The History of Philosophy: A Short Survey*. Retrieved from https://www.utm.edu/staff/jfieser/class/110/4-eastern.htm

Fisher, J. (2007). *Technologies of Intuition*. Toronto, Canada: YYZ Books.

Gigerenzer, G. (2008). *Gut Feelings: The Intelligence of the Unconscious* (reprint ed.). New York: Penguin Books.

Global Consciousness Project. (2015, July 29). Retrieved December 8, 2018, from https://noetic.org/research/projects/global-consciousness-project

Govinda, L. A. (1959). *Foundations of Tibetan Mysticism*. Retrieved from http://archive.org/details/in.ernet.dli.2015.505725

Gregoire, C. (2013, November 16). 8 famous ideas that came from dreams (literally). *Huffington Post*. Retrieved from https://www.huffingtonpost.com/2013/11/16/famous-ideas-from-dreams_n_4276838.html

Hadhazy, A. (2010) Think twice: How the gut's "second brain" influences mood and well-being. *Scientific American*. Retrieved August 10, 2017, from https://www.scientificamerican.com/ article/gut-second-brain/

Harris, J. (2000). *Jung and Yoga: The Psyche-Body Connection*. Toronto, Canada: Inner City Books.

Henden, G. (2004). *Intuition and Its Role in Strategic Thinking* (Dissertation). Oslo: BI Norwegian School of Management.

Hölzel, B. K., Carmody, J., Vangel, M., Congleton, C., Yerramsetti, S. M., Gard, T., & Lazar, S. W. (2011). Mindfulness practice leads to increases in regional brain gray matter density. *Psychiatry Research*, *191*(1), 36–43. doi:10.1016/j.pscychresns.2010.08.006

Hogarth, R. M. (2001). *Educating Intuition*. Chicago, IL: University of Chicago Press.

Ikeda, D. (2010). *A New Humanism: The University Addresses of Daisaku Ikeda*. London: I.B. Tauris.

Indich, W. M. (2000). *Consciousness in Advaita Vedanta* (1st ed.). Delhi, India: Varanasi: Motilal Banarsidass.

Jagtiani, J. (2018). *The Natural Power of Intuition: Exploring the Formative Dimensions of Intuition in the Practices of Three Visual Artists and Three Business Executives*. Columbia University. doi:10.7916/D8PZ6S88

Jordan, B. J. (2017). *Live 1,000 Years: The Amazing New Science of Happiness, Health, Money, and Love: Discover Who You Are? Where You Came from Before Birth? Where You're Going after Death?* Morrisville, NC: Lulu Publishing Services.

Jung, C. G. (2010). *Dreams* (R. F. C. Hull, Trans.). Princeton, NJ: Princeton University Press.

Kahneman, D. (2013). *Thinking, Fast and Slow* (Reprint ed.). New York: Farrar, Straus and Giroux.

Laszlo, E. (2006). *Science and the Reenchantment of the Cosmos: The Rise of the Integral Vision of Reality*. Rochester, VT: Inner Traditions/Bear.

Leaman, O. (2000). *Eastern Philosophy: Key Readings*. Abingdon, England: Routledge

Li, P. P. (2014). Toward the geocentric framework of intuition: The yin-yang balancing between Eastern and Western perspectives on intuition. In M. Sinclair (Ed.), *Handbook of Research Methods on Intuition* (pp. 28–41). Cheltenham, England: Edward Elgar.

Meijer, D. K. F., & Geesink, H. J. H. (2017). Consciousness in the universe is scale invariant and implies an event horizon of the human brain. *NeuroQuantology, 15*(3). doi:10.14704/nq.2017.15.3.1079

O'Sullivan, T. (2014). Chakras. In D. A. Leeming (Ed.), *Encyclopedia of Psychology and Religion* (pp. 294–297). Boston, MA: Springer US. doi:10.1007/978-1-4614-6086-2

Palmer, H. (2011). *Cultivating and Applying Intuition* [electronic resource].

Patton, J. R. (2003). Intuition in decisions. *Management Decision, 41*(10), 989–996. doi:10.1108/00251740310509517

Piha, H. (2005). Intuition: A bridge to the coenesthetic world of experience. *Journal of the American Psychoanalytic Association, 53*(1), 23–49. doi:10.1177/00030651050530011601

Radin, D. (2006). *Entangled Minds: Extrasensory Experiences in a Quantum Reality* (4th ed.). New York: Paraview Pocket Books.

Sadler-Smith, E. (2012). *Inside Intuition*. Abingdon, England: Routledge.

Sangharakshita. (1998). *Know Your Mind: Psychological Dimension of Ethics in Buddhism*. Cambridge, England: Windhorse Publications.

Sharma, R. N. (2006). *Wisdom of Hindus*. Gurgaon, India: Shubhi Publications.

Sheldrake, R. (2009). *Morphic Resonance: The Nature of Formative Causation* (4th ed.). Rochester, VT: Park Street Press.

Simon, H. A. (1987). Making management decisions: The role of intuition and emotion. *Academy of Management Executive (1987–1989)*, 57–64.

Sinclair, M. (Ed.). (2011). *Handbook of Intuition Research*. Cheltenham, England: Edward Elgar.

Sumedho, A. (2013, August 7). *Buddha*. Retrieved October 17, 2017, from https://buddhismnow.com/2013/08/07/buddha-by-ajahn-sumedho/

Sumedho, A. (2014). *The Ajahn Sumedho Anthology—The Sound of Silence* (Vol. 4). Hertfordshire, England: Amaravati Buddhist Monastery.

Vaughan, F. (1973). Exploring intuition: Prospects and possibilities. *Journal of Transpersonal Psychology, 5*(2), 156.

Vaughan, F. (1979). *Awakening Intuition* (1st Anchor Books ed.). Garden City, NY: Anchor.

Vaughan, F. (2011). *Awakening Intuition* [electronic resource].

Voss, J. (2014, July 22). *The intuitive investor: A simple model of intuition*. Retrieved August 29, 2017, from https://blogs.cfainstitute.org/investor/2014/07/22/the-intuitive-investor-a-simple-model-of-intuition/

Wallis, C. (2016, February 5). *The real story on the Chakras*. Retrieved August 3, 2018, from http://hareesh.org/blog/2016/2/5/the-real-story-on-the-chakras

Wang, H.-X., & Wang, Y.-P. (2016). Gut microbiota-brain axis. *Chinese Medical Journal, 129*(19), 2373–2380. doi:10.4103/0366-6999.190667

Wilber, K. (1982). *Holographic Paradigm* (1st ed.). Boulder, CO: Shambhala.

Chapter 4

Intuitive Managers across Organizations and Gender

Jon Aarum Andersen

Contents

Personality and Leadership Research

The very first problem that leadership researchers tried to solve was related to personality traits. Did leaders emerge owing to their personality? What traits made other people perceive a person to be a leader? Several reviews of the extensive research on leadership and personality have been presented. A comparative review of 124 published studies by Stogdill (1948) compelled him to conclude that persons who were leaders in some situations may not necessarily be leaders in others. While there were positive correlations between a number of traits and emergent leadership, these correlations were weak.

Gibb (1969) concluded that personality traits could not be isolated to determine leadership emergence. His summary showed that it was neither possible to find one specific personality trait that characterized leaders nor possible to isolate a number of traits, when combined, which could explain leadership. The research failed to find a relationship—even a modest one—between personality and leadership. Gibb (1969, p. 227) wrote that "research showed no scientific basis for a relationship between traits and leading positions." He did point out, however, that personality traits—including intuition—could not be excluded in leadership because they were probably not completely without consequences.

Stogdill (1974) concluded that personality research had limited value when predicting an individual's leadership potential. There were, however, indications that traits work with other factors in a position of leadership. After Stogdill's (1969) dismissal of five decades of research dedicated to developing a trait-based theory of leadership, theories on managers' behavior emerged. In the case of intuition, the focus has changed from intuition as a personality trait to intuition in terms of an explanation of a behavioral pattern or as a decision-making style.

Robbins and Judge (2007) wrote that intuitive decision-making is an unconscious process created out of distilled experience. They added that intuition does not operate independent of rational analysis as these two components complement each other. Intuition can be a powerful force in decision-making (ibid.).

Leadership Theory

Several hundred definitions of leadership have been presented over the years. This indicates a strong link between leadership and organization. In management and organization theory leadership is tied to an organization or a group. Sociologists and political scientists, however, also study leadership in social and political movements, which have not (yet) become organizations.

Blake and Mouton (1985, p. 198) defined leadership as follows: "Processes of leadership are involved in achieving results with and through others." Blake and Mouton (1985) stressed that goal attainment can only be achieved with or through other people inside as well as outside the organization. By doing so they have pinpointed what may be seen as the dilemma of leadership. The formal leader (manager) is responsible for results in accordance with organizational goals. No leader or manager can achieve the goals of the organization by their own efforts alone. If that were possible, there would be no need for an organization, or for a leader.

A problem when dealing with leadership comes from different ideas about *what* to lead and *whom* to lead. In psychology, the premise is often that it is a group to lead. It is also usually assumed that those to lead (and the leader) pursue a common goal (e.g., Hogan et al., 1994). Leadership is related to groups, which are based on common goals. Wallis (2002) claimed that a wide range of definitions converge toward the concept that leadership is a social influence process through which members of a group are steered toward a common goal. It is not so in management. Organizations and groups (departments, etc.) are *not* based on common goals. Organizations are established to solve tasks in order to achieve goals. The major goals are decided by the founders (owners and principals) of the organizations. Those who are employed by business enterprises or who work for public agencies do not always share the goals of their companies or institutions. Those people, who constitute the majority of the working population in the world, work in order to achieve the goals of the shareholders/owners of companies or the citizens of their country. The employees may, however, support the goals of the group or organization more or less sincerely. In most cases private enterprises and public agencies are studied. The issue is leadership in organizations (Yukl, 2010).

In this chapter, leadership is defined as the behavior in which one individual in a group, organizational unit, or organization engages in aiming at systematically influencing other people so that the group or organization can solve specific tasks and attain given goals. No distinction is made here between the terms *leader* and *manager* (*leadership* and *management*) as the study only concerns formal leaders, that is, managers in private and public organizations.

The statement that "leadership is an influence game" is often attributed to McClelland and Burnham (1976, p. 105), but in fact they wrote: "After all, management is an influence game." It is only by acting or refraining from taking action that subordinates, superiors, owners, financiers, customers, and other parties can be influenced. It is thus imperative in leadership research to address the *reasons* for actions as well as different kinds of actions. Leadership style theories (e.g., Blake & Mouton, 1964) regard leadership styles to depend on leaders' attitudes and assumptions. Motivation profiles (e.g., McClelland, 1990) are consequences of leaders' needs. When it comes to decision-making styles or behavioral patterns some theories are not based on personality theory, e.g., Rowe et al. (1986) and Driver et al. (1990).

The Concept of Intuition

Introduction

In psychology, intuition is regarded as a personality trait. It is an inborn, stable characteristic. Probably the most influential contribution to the subject of intuition is Carl Jung's work *Psychological Types* (1921/1971). Quinn and Hall (1983) have used Jung's typology as a social science meta-theoretical framework. Jung's typology has proven qualities in defining and predicting behavior (Keegan, 1984). Morgan (1986) shows how Jung's theories have influenced organizational thinking. Research on the composition of leadership groups has been based on typologies (e.g., Belbin, 1987). Bass (2008) has two references to Jung. It appears that Jung's typology has been revived in recent years—especially in the field of leadership and management.

Jung (1971) pointed out that in real life the types are not found in the pure forms. The typology rests on two elements (attitudes and functions) and is often presented by using three dimensions in the human psyche: (1) attitudes—extrovert and introvert, (2) perception functions—sensing and intuition; and (3) judgment functions—thinking and feeling.

The Three Dimensions

Introversion and extroversion are attitudes. The second dimension is the perceptive functions. These functions describe how we perceive the world, the problem, or the task. The third dimension—the judging functions—concerns how we judge the problem (once it is perceived). Sensing is the function that tells us that something exists. Thinking is the function that tells us what this something is. Intuition is the function which reveals the possibilities which may exist in what we have perceived. Feeling is the function that tells us how to relate to what we have perceived based on our own subjective value system. Attitudes and functions are conscious (Stevens, 1990).

Definition of Attitudes

Jung distinguishes between two different attitudes to life, that is, two ways of reacting in given situations. These he found sufficiently significant and generally evident to enable him to describe them as typical (Fordham, 1964). Extrovert people have a tendency to react quickly. They are more inclined toward action than consideration and reflection. Introverts are more inclined to slower reactions to events that occur and to demands from other people. They need more time to incorporate, integrate, and absorb impressions from outside. The extrovert experiences loneliness as something awkward while the introvert is energized by periods of loneliness. The extrovert person often agrees with the standpoint of the majority while the introvert opposes the same standpoint just because it is a popular one (Jung, 1964).

Extroversion and introversion indicate in which direction the human energy flows (Jung, 1971). An extrovert person is oriented toward the outer environment while the introvert is driven by an inner world of conviction, memories, and thoughts. For both attitudes the case is the same—the outer and inner worlds are linked together, but the flow of energy is in opposite directions.

Definition of Function

Jung (1992, p. 134) defined function as "a certain psychic action form which under different conditions in principle remains the same." He claimed that there are four functions, which we apply to orient ourselves in the world: sensing, which is a perception through our senses; thinking, which gives us meaning and understanding; feeling, which judges and assesses; intuition, which tells us about the possibilities in the future and enlightens us on the atmosphere that surrounds all experiences (ibid.). With function we mean a way of perceiving the reality as well as judging and assessing the reality which we perceived in the first place.

In only one place Jung used the term decisions ("important decisions") when referring to the functions (Jung, 1933/1992, p. 103). Carlyn (1977, p. 461) argued that "thinking/feeling has to do with the decision-making style which is preferred by a person." Myers and McCaulley (1985) described the functions in terms of decisions. Jung applied the concept of function to designate specific forms of psychic activity and behavior in people generally which remain the same regardless of circumstances (Benfari, 1991). Jung described the psychological functions as adoption or orientation mechanisms. Jung (1992, pp. 121–45) defined the four functions as follows:

> (1) *Sensing*. The sensing types perceive things as they are. They show great respect for facts and information. Sensers have a great ability to register details and seldom fail when facts and details are part of the situation.
>
> (2) *Intuition*. The intuitive person concentrates on the possibilities and is less concerned with details. He often finds the solutions directly without basing them on facts.
>
> (3) *Thinking*. Thinkers are analytical, particular, precise and logical. They see things from an intellectual angle and often miss the emotional sides of the problem.
>
> (4) *Feeling*. The feeling types are interested in other people's feelings and dislike analysis. They stick to their own values and dislikes. They enjoy and prefer to work together with other people.

All people prefer one of the four functions. The preferred one is called the "dominant" or "superior" function. The opposite of the dominant function (which is the strength of that person) is called the inferior function (which is the weakness of that person). If, for instance, the dominant function is thinking, the weakest function will then be feeling. If the dominant function is sensing, the inferior function will be intuition. An essential point in the theory of types is that all functions are equally good. This does not imply that all thinkers are equally good at logical thinking or that all sensing types are equally good at perceiving things. Nor does it imply that the person who has thinking as his or her dominant function is better at logical analysis or is more intelligent than those with other functions as the dominant ones. Functions are only relative to the individual person. Jung's typology can be interpreted as affirming that there are only four ways of solving problems. There are only two ways in which we can perceive problems, namely by the use of the functions sensing and intuition. Once we realize that we have a problem there are only two ways to solve the problem, for instance when choosing between alternatives, that is by use of the thinking or feeling functions. The functions are in opposition to each other. All humans have one function which is applied the most—the dominant one—and an auxiliary function. When these two functions are revealed we have a description of an individual's decision-making style.

Differences between the types can also be clarified by the time orientations which characterize each type. Individuals with dominant sensing function are oriented toward the present while the intuitive persons are oriented toward the future. The thinking types see time as a line. The feeling types, however, have their time orientation in the past.

The personality type theory distinguishes between the types in terms of time orientations where the intuitive ones have the longest time horizons. According to Jaques (1990) the hierarchical levels in organizations are reflections of the planning time span of the managers and supervisors. The level of responsibility in any organizational position, whether a manager's or a foreman's, can be objectively measured in terms of the target completion time of the longest task, project, or program assigned to that role (ibid.). The more distant the target completion date of the longest task or program, the higher position the individual ought to have. Bass (2008) refers to research on the planning time span of managers which supports this argument. When work groups are established all personality types need to be represented in order to fully define the problem and to choose the best way to solve it (Belbin, 1987).

People solve problems and make decisions in a variety of ways. This is due to the fact that humans apply different functions. Problems can only be solved and decisions made by the use of intuition, sensing, thinking, and feeling. Which functions are dominant and preferred depends on the personality of the individual. Effective problem-solving and effective decisions are made when the person in question applies the function most appropriate to the problem, situation, or task at hand. To what extent Jung's typology and especially the four functions are relevant for the understanding of managers' decision-making behavior will be addressed.

The Contribution of Myers–Briggs

Isabel Myers must be credited with bringing Jung's typology to life (Keirsey & Bates, 1978). Isabel B. Myers and Katharina Cook Briggs studied Jung's theory and tested it for more than 20 years before constructing their instrument (MBTI) in 1941. The Myers–Briggs instrument measures the 16 types (eight combinations of function and two attitudes) (Briggs-Myers & McCaulley, 1985). The Myers–Briggs Type Indicator is a questionnaire developed to make it possible to test Jung's theory and put it to practical use (McCaulley, 1990). Jung's typology and Myers's contribution are not identical theories.

Keegan's Contribution—Intuition as Decision-Making

Introduction

In the Western world great emphasis is placed on the analytical way of solving problems (Fordham, 1964). By and large we overestimate the thinkers and underestimate the intuitive, feeling, and sensing types in the Western culture. Too much management technique overemphasizes thinking while individual values, commitment, and motivation are often ignored (Keegan, 1984). However, only one-fourth of what managers do requires the logical capabilities. Other aspects of managerial work like supervision of daily activities, motivating subordinates, and being creative require quite other ways of reacting (ibid.). Thinking refers only to one of the steps of the managerial problem-solving process, namely to evaluate alternatives and select solutions.

In reviewing the plethora of planning and decision-making models that are currently available, one realizes that, while each has value, each is incomplete. The typology theory of Jung is almost complete in the sense that it touches on both functions of perception and both functions of judgment and their relationship to each other (Keegan, 1984). Jung's theory has stood the test of time in the fields of psychology and psychiatry, according to Keegan. Keegan's ambition was to make the theory available to more professionals and primarily to managers. In the field of management development the typology presented by Jung gives a genuine insight into the question why persons succeed or fail in their decision-making, and how they do it (Keegan, 1984). Keegan has based his work on the original works of Jung and developed the theory further and adapted it to the field of management and organization theory.

The main point is the following. Intuition is a personality trait and traits may influence behavior in different degrees. In Keegan's work the main contribution is the description of decision-making behavior (how managers perceive when becoming aware of a problem or possibility and how they solve the problem or utilize the possibility). A personality theory has then become a basis for a behavioral leadership theory.

Decision-Making Styles

Keegan's focus is on decisions, implying that the attitudes are of less relevance. This is based on the four functions and Jung's claim that there is one dominant, one auxiliary, one underdeveloped, and one unconscious function for all humans. Keegan (1984, p. 34) presents eight decision-making styles:

> (1) intuition with thinking (as auxiliary function), (2) intuition with feeling, (3) thinking with intuition, (4) thinking with sensing, (5) sensing with thinking, (6) sensing with feeling, (7) feeling with sensing, and (8) sensing with intuition.

Sensing and intuition are denoted perception functions. Thinking and feeling are called judgment or decision-making functions (Keegan, 1984). The fact that all humans in addition to perceiving a problem (by the use of sensing and intuition) also must judge and chose by the use of thinking and feeling makes Jung's typology a genuine individual decision-making theory. The term *decision-making function* refers to one of the four functions as defined in the Jungian typology. The term *decision-making style* refers to one of the eight combinations of one dominant and one auxiliary function.

From the concepts established here regarding problem-solving and decision-making we may return to the problem-solving process. The first four steps in the process can now be directly linked to these concepts. In order to "find and define the problem" the perceiving functions of sensing and intuition are needed. In order to "generate alternative solutions" and "evaluate alternatives and select solution" the judging functions of thinking and feeling are used. In order to "conduct ethics double-check" the feeling function is needed. Jung's functions cover all the four steps of the problem-solving and decision-making process (Keegan, 1984). Can intuition be measured?

The Measurements of Intuition

Myers–Briggs Type Indicator (MBTI)

The Myers–Briggs Type Indicator (MBTI) is a questionnaire developed to enable testing for Jung's theory and using it in practice (Briggs-Myers & McCaulley, 1985). Isabel Myers and Katharina Cook Briggs studied Jung's theory and tested it for more than 20 years before constructing the instrument MBTI in 1941. However, it was not until 1962 that the MBTI was launched as a research instrument (Briggs-Myers, 1962). It is now one of the most common tests for normal people and is used worldwide (McCaulley, 1990). The test has become very popular for measuring how managers make decisions and solve problems (Bass, 2008). The Myers–Briggs instrument measures the 16 types (eight combinations of function and two attitudes) as described above (Briggs-Myers & McCaulley, 1985).

"The MBTI has become so widespread that it has almost lost its roots in the Jungian theory" (Stoknes, 1992, p. 103).

Keegan's Type Indicator (KTI)

The instrument "Keegan Type Indicator Form B" measures the variables extroversion and introversion as well as sensation, intuition, thinking, and feeling by 44 statements/questions (Keegan, 1982). Twelve items concern the attitudes, and 16 items refer to the functions sensing and intuition and 16 items to the functions thinking and feeling. The items concerning the attitudes are bipolar. Of the 32 items aiming at measuring the functions, 24 are bipolar statements and 8 items are statements to be ranked on a scale from 1 to 4.

Keegan (1980) contains a description of the instrument and guidelines on the scoring. It is important to stress that the instrument is an open one and its merits will not be reduced if the respondents have knowledge of Jung's theory. This being so, no score from the test is better or worse than any other. The reliability has not been tested separately. The face validity can easily be established as Jung's typology has very clear descriptions of the concepts and terms applied enabling the formulation of valid statements and questions. The content validity has been tested and the correlation between the scores and the assessment of the respondents was high (Keegan, 1980).

Are Managers Intuitive Types?

The purpose of Jung's typology has not been to label people in terms of their personality type, but to *understand* their behavior. The theory does not, however, predict any relationship between type-based behavior and specific consequences of the behavior. In the instrumental leadership tradition the focus is on the relationship between leadership behavior or behavioral patterns and organizational outcomes.

A hypothesis has been launched that managers with a decision-making behavior based on intuition and supported by the thinking function would be more frequently found than those with other combinations. A study by Andersen (1994) found—when data was collected from the decision-making styles of 222 managers in eight Swedish corporations using the Keegan Type Indicator—that the majority of the managers (32 percent) were, indeed, intuitive types.

Managers' Intuition and Organizational Effectiveness

Introduction

The burning issue in leadership theory on decision-making is the following: Is there one best way to make decisions? In this case the problem is: Are intuitive managers more effective than other managers when the relationship between intuitive managers and the degree of organizational goal attainment is tested empirically?

The research into decision-making behavior is basically descriptive. For management research this kind of research is less relevant because the explanatory elements are weakly developed. There are hardly any theoretical contributions which contain a hypothesis regarding a relationship between specific decision-making styles and "situations" and effectiveness. These putative relationships have not been tested empirically because the concept of situation has not been operationalized.

Many theories can be described by the terms *phenomenon, cause,* and *effect.* The *phenomenon* is behavior, that is, decision-making behavior of managers. It is specific behavioral patterns that Jung described by the use of the function terms of sensing, intuition, thinking, and feeling. The *cause* of distinct type (dominant function) is the personality of the individual. Type is a congenital personality trait (Jung, 1971). Jung's theory describes types and type-related behavior and holds that type is caused by personality.

The term *effectiveness* implies a ratio. Effectiveness embraces two entities, and is very often in the field of management perceived to mean the degree of goal attainment. Definitions, which we find in business administration and management, will have at least one financial (economical) entity or a ratio.

There is but a weak basis for assuming a direct relationship between decision functions (decision-making styles) and effectiveness. Keegan (1984) argued that the four functions are effective in different situations, that is, in relation to the different types of problems and tasks to be addressed. These arguments are not precise regarding the concepts of situation, problem, and task.

Another track that may be followed is taken from McCaulley (1990). She claimed that the intuitive and thinking types are those who most likely are successful. Eccles and Nohria (1992) introduced the concept of *robust action.* Robust actions are characterized by moves that managers make which preserve their flexibility in circumstances of uncertainty. They (ibid.) suggested some principles of robust actions, among them "judging the situation at hand." To make decisions and act at the right time depends on being able to judge the situation. The ability to see opportunities and threats when in a managerial position is crucial. This may well be a characteristic of intuitive managers. Andersen (2000) suggested that intuition as a decision-making style appeared to be related to organizational goal attainment. Based on these arguments a hypothesis on the connection between intuition in managers and organizational effectiveness was presented.

When testing leadership hypotheses empirically and quantitatively the variables must be measured. The assumed independent variable (decision-making style) was measured by the relative strength of the functions of the respondents. By measuring the functions of the respondents one assumes that it is likely that the respondents will behave in a particular way when solving problems and making decisions (which is the research phenomenon). The assumed dependent variable (organizational effectiveness, e.g., degree of financial goal attainment) is measured by using secondary data from the departments and organizations for which the managers are responsible.

Research Method

Jung (1971) discussed the problem of measurement in psychology and claimed that there are facts that can be measured quantitatively. Relatively complicated aspects can be available by measuring methods. The MBTI and KTI instruments rest explicitly on Jung's theory. MBTI is no doubt one of the most applied psychological instruments in the world and its scientific qualities are well-documented. Samuels (1985) pointed out that MBTI has integrated Jung's hypotheses. The obstacle against using MBTI is partly that it is very extensive. The standard form of the MBTI in use in the early 1990s was form G with 126 items, of which 94 were scored for type. All versions of the MBTI measure the dimension judging and perceiving, which has no function other than (in relation to this study) isolating the dominant function.

The KTI instrument is less verified regarding reliability and validity and no written documentation on test results exists. The instrument can, however, be used in research. Measuring the attitudes (extroversion and introversion) is less relevant in leadership scholarship. Measuring the functions can be done by using the other part of the questionnaire. For measuring the functions the KTI instrument contains 32 items (compared with 94 items in the MBTI).

The following reasons were given for collecting data on managerial decision-making style by the KTI-instrument. The KTI is an instrument with fewer items and only collects variables relevant for the study. The instrument has acceptable face and content validity and is based explicitly on Jung's typology. This test was applied in connection with Keegan's work linking Jungian functions to managerial decision-making (Keegan, 1984). It is important to stress that the MBTI is a general test of the Jungian typology while KTI is a test for managers measuring decision-making styles based on Jungian type theory.

Sample

Data on decision-making styles in the study of Andersen (1994) came from 222 managers in eight Swedish industrial companies. The data were collected from managers working in various industrial trades, on different levels, in charge of different functions, who were geographically spread over the country. Data on decision-making behavior and effectiveness were obtained from one company in the service sector. The study contained 33 (79 percent) of the managers on the same level in the same industrial sector. All in all, 33 managers' decision-making styles and financial effectiveness were studied.

Conclusion: Decision Function and Effectiveness

The effectiveness of the managers in a service company was measured by the degree of financial goal attainment (Andersen, 1994). Those who managed departments which achieved the profit-margin goal (or surpassed it) were regarded as effective while those who did not were inefficient ones. Based on data from 33 managers in a service company and their decision-making style scores and the degree of effectiveness of their departments, the analysis aimed at assessing the degree (if any) of relationship between intuition in managers and their effectiveness.

Andersen (1994) reported that the covariance between effectiveness and less effectiveness was for the intuitive managers 1.5 (6:4). The covariance for the other managers was 0.5 (8:15). The implication of this is that intuitive factor in managers is three times more strongly related to effectiveness compared with other dominant functions that managers had. Intuitive managers with thinking function was 6.7 times stronger related to organizational effectiveness compared with managers with the other decision-making styles. As expected, value in one of the cells is less than 5; the chi-square test result is not presented. Fisher exact 2-tailed *p*-value is 0.26—the difference is *not* significant.

There are, however, some theoretical considerations for assuming a relationship between decision-making styles and organizational effectiveness. This empirical study indicated that there may well be such a relationship. The data were analyzed on the assumption of a direct relationship between intuition in managers and the effectiveness of their organizations. Several managers are intuitive and have an innovative and creative decision-making style. Whether they are more effective than others remains to be seen.

Intuition in Managers across Organizations

The study of Andersen (2010) aimed at finding out whether there were behavioral differences between public and private sector managers according to the public-private distinction tradition (Reiney et al., 1976). An analysis of data from 459 managers in four organizations in Sweden revealed significant differences in behavior between public and private managers. However, one similarity in behavior was reported: both public and private managers were mostly intuitive types.

Intuition in Managers and Gender

A number of empirical studies on male and female managers' decision-making styles were based on Jung's theory and Keegan's instrument (Andersen & Hansson, 2011). These studies contain data from 171 Swedish school headmasters (72 males and 99 females) and 61 managers in public social-insurance agencies (34 males and 27 females) and 117 vicars in the Church of Sweden (117 males and 36 females), and showed that there were no significant differences between these 385 managers in any of the decision-making functions.

As theories distinguishing between private and public organizations point out, previous research indicates that gender differences arise owing to the fact that managers are in charge of different organizations, which Hansson and Andersen (2008) and Andersen (2010) have suggested based on the same behavioral dimensions used in the study of Andersen and Hansson (2011).

Kanter (1977) has argued that leadership style of the few women in leadership positions (at that time) should be studied as a function of membership in a male-dominated group in which men shape work behavior. If the masculine model represents the universal and dominant model of leadership, women understand that they have to conform to it in order to escalate the ranks. Women repeatedly use the same strategies for gaining influence that have proven successful for men (Trinidad & Normore, 2005). Yet, we should note that women, who compose approximately 65 percent of all teachers, dominate the Swedish schools and, since the mid-1990s, have outnumbered male principals.

Consequently, it does not seem appropriate to argue that women have adapted to a male culture or leadership styles in Swedish schools. The analysis of the sample of principals yields no significant differences regarding the leadership variables. Findings of Franzén (2006) on Swedish principals are in line with the results reported by Andersen and Hansson (2011). We are justified in asserting that all teachers (principals are former teachers) have been influenced by the same school culture for several years. The school culture may explain the same pattern of leadership behavior among the principals.

Andersen and Hansson (2011) concluded—as have the majority of other studies—that no or only small and inconsistent differences in decision-making behavior exist. It was suggested that organizational differences and characteristics modify the phenomenon of leadership itself, which would explain the similarities of behavior regardless of gender. In this respect, a germane development is the rising trend that emphasizes the need to help women and men move away from gender stereotypes (Ferrario, 1991). The knowledge that there are few or no differences in leadership behavior between women and men may contribute to this movement.

Out of the 30 pair-wise comparisons of means for the samples consisting of 385 managers in three different organizations, only five comparisons (17 percent) yield significant differences in leadership behavior between women and men as managers ($p < 0.05$). In only one case is the significance at the level of 1 percent.

Regarding the first research question, we conclude that there are no or only small and inconsistent differences in leadership behavior between women and men. Trinidad and Normore (2005, p. 574) have claimed: "Women leadership styles are presented as alternative to traditional leadership models." But, when there are no differences between women's and men's leadership styles, this alternative does not exist.

As virtually no significant differences in behavior between female and male public managers were found, a second hypothesis was tested to find explanations for the similarities. The effect of organizational differences (private-public) has been eliminated here, as only public organizations are included in the study. Previous research indicates that managers' behaviors vary according to organizational types.

The importance of organizational influences on leadership behavior was also addressed. Few significant differences in leadership behavior between women and men in management surfaced in the comparison between predominantly male-led organizations. No differences emerged in leadership behavior in the predominantly female-led ones. Similarly, there were no differences in leadership behavior—including intuition and decision-making styles—in the comparisons between male-led organizations with a majority of female employees and female-led ones with a majority of women.

Conclusion

It is evident that the personality approach to leadership has been contested and more so over the years. What makes personality still a part of leadership and managerial research is the fact that the focus has changed from personality traits per se, to the behavioral consequences of specific traits. This is most evident when the psychological type theories like Jung's typology are used to describe the decision-making activities of formal leaders (managers). In that way the main focus is on the decision-making styles and the organizational outcomes of the decisions taken rather than the reasons for the decision-making behavior. Personality traits do exist.

This chapter concludes by referring to a study of 160 chief officers in the U.S. by Farkas and Wetlaufer (1996). They found that leadership styles were not a consequence of their personality traits. In effective companies the CEOs did not manage according to their personality, but according to organizational demands and the business situation at hand. The authors argued that leadership is not a question of personality. Successful managers suppress their specific personal inclinations and personality traits in order to manage their companies effectively. Importantly, Farkas and Wetlaufer (1996) claimed that until researchers can find a gene linked to leadership, which is most unlikely, the debate on leadership and personality will prevail. Leadership scholarship needs to be less focused on personality and more focused on leaders' behavior as behavior can be changed while personality cannot.

References

Andersen, J.A. (1994). *Leadership and Effectiveness*. (Ledelse og effektivitet), (in Norwegian—summary in English). Lund University Press, Lund.

Andersen, J.A. (2000). Intuition in managers: Are intuitive managers more effective? *Journal of Managerial Psychology*, Vol. 15 No. 1, pp. 46–67.

Andersen, J.A. (2010). Public vs. private managers: How public and private managers differ in leadership behavior. *Public Administration Review*, Vol. 17 No.1, pp. 131–141.

Andersen, J.A. & Hansson, P.H. (2011). At the end of the road? On differences between women and men in leadership behavior. *Leadership & Organizational Development Journal*, Vol. 32 No. 5, pp. 328–341.

Bass, B.M. (2008). *The Bass Handbook of Leadership: Theory, Research & Managerial Applications*. Free Press, New York.

Belbin, R.M. (1987). *Management Teams: Why They Succeed or Fail*. William Heinemann, London.

Benfari, R. (1991). *Understanding Your Management Style: Beyond the Myers-Briggs Type Indicators*. Lexington Books, Lexington, MA.

Blake, R.R. & Mouton, J.S. (1964). *The Managerial Grid*. Gulf Publishing, Houston, TX.

Blake, R.R. & Mouton, J.S. (1985). *The Managerial Grid III*. Gulf Publishing, Houston.

Briggs-Myers, I.B. (1962). *The Myers-Briggs Type Indicator*. Consulting Psychologists Press, Palo Alto, CA.

Briggs-Myers, I.B. & McCaulley, M.H. (1985). *Manual: A Guide to the Development and Use of the Myers-Briggs Type Indicator*. Consulting Psychologists Press, Palo Alto, CA.

Carlyn, M. (1977). An assessment of the Myers-Briggs Type indicator. *Journal of Personality Assessment*, Vol. 41 No. 5, pp. 461–472.

Driver, M.J., Brousseau, K.R. & Hunsaker P.L. (1990). *The Dynamic Decision-Maker: Five Decision Styles for Executive and Business Success*. Harper & Row, New York.

Eccles, R.G. & Nohria, N. (1992). *Beyond the Hype: Rediscovering the Essence of Mangement*. Harvard Business School Press, Boston, MA.

Farkas, C.M. & Wetlaufer, S. (1996). The ways chief officers lead. *Harvard Business Review*, Vol. 74, pp. 110–122.

Ferrario, M. (1991). Sex differences in leadership style: Myth or reality? *Women in Management Review & Abstracts*, Vol. 6 No. 3, pp. 16–21.

Fordham, F. (1964). *Introduction to Jung's Psychology*. Harmondsworth Penguin Books, London.

Franzén, K. (2006). Keeping a cool head and a warm heart: The construction of school leadership from a gender perspective. Umeå, Pedagogiska institutionen, Umeå University.

Gibb, C.A. (1969). *Leadership*. In L. Gardner & E. Aronson (Eds), *The Handbook of Social Psychology*, Vol. IV (pp. 205–281). Cambridge, MA: Addison-Wesley.

Hansson, P. & Andersen, J.A. (2008). Vicars as managers revisited: A comparative study. *Nordic Journal of Religion and Society*, Vol. 21 No. 1, pp. 91–111.

Hogan, R., Curphy, G.J. & Hogan, J. (1994). What we know about leadership: Effectiveness and personality. *American Psychologist*, Vol. 49 No. 6, pp. 439–504.

Jaques, E. (1990). In praise of hierarchy. *Harvard Business Review*, Vol. 68, pp. 127–133.

Jung, C.G. (1921/1971). *Psychological Types*. The Collected Works of C.G. Jung, Vol. 6. Bollingen Series XX. Princeton University Press, Princeton, NJ.

Jung, C.G. (1933/1992). *Modern Man in Search of a Soul*. Ark Paperbacks. Routledge, London.

Jung, C.G. (1964). *Man and His Symbols*. Aldus Books, London.

Jung, C.G. (1971). *Psychological Types*. In H.G. Haynes (trans.) and revised by R.F. Hall. The Collected Works of C.G. Jung (vol. 6). Princeton University Press, Princeton, NJ.

Kanter, R.M. (1977). *Men and Women of the Corporation*. Basic Books, New York.

Keegan, W.J. (1980). *How to Use the Keegan Type Indicator (KTI) and the Keegan Information Processing Indicator (KIPI)*. Warren Keegan Associates Press, New York.

Keegan, W.J. (1982). *Keegan Type Indicator Form B*. Warren Keegan Associates Press, New York.

Keegan, W.J. (1984). *Judgements, Choices and Decisions*. Wiley, New York.

Keirsey, D. & Bates, M. (1978). *Please Understand Me: Character and Temperament Types*. Prometheus Nemesis Books, Del Mar, CA.

McCaulley, M.H. (1990). The Myers-Briggs Type indicator and leadership. In K.E. Clark & M.B. Clark (Eds), *Measures of Leadership* (pp. 381–418). Leadership Library of America, West Orange, NJ.

McClelland, D.C. (1990). *Human Motivation*. Cambridge University Press, Cambridge

McClelland, D.C. & Burnham, D.H. (1976). Power is the great motivator. *Harvard Business Review*, Vol. 54 No.2, pp. 100–110.

Morgan, G. (1986). *Images of Organization*. Sage Publications, San Francisco, CA.

Quinn, R.E. & Hall, R.H. (1983). Environments, organizations, and policymakers: Toward an integrative framework. In R.E. Quinn & R.H Hall (Eds), *Organizational Theory and Public Policy*. Sage Publications, Newbury Park, CA.

Rainey, H.G., Backoff, R.W. & Levine, C.H. (1976). Comparing public and private organizations. *Public Administration Review*, Vol. 36 No. 2, pp. 233–44.

Robbins, S.P. & Judge, T.A. (2007). *Organizational Behaviour*. Person-Prentice Hall, Upper Saddle River, NJ.

Rowe, A.J., Mason, R.O. & Dickel, K.E. (1986). *Strategic Management & Business Policy. A Methodological Approach*. Addison-Wesley Publishing, Reading, MA.

Samuels, A. (1985). *Jung and the Post-Jungians*. Routledge, London.

Stevens, A. (1990). *On Jung*. Routledge, London.

Stogdill, R.M. (1948). Personal factors associated with leadership: A survey of the literature. *Journal of Psychology*, Vol. 25, pp. 35–71.

Stogdill, R.M. (1969). Validity of leader behaviour descriptions. *Personnel Psychology*, Vol. 22, pp. 153–158.

Stogdill, R.M. (1974). *Handbook of Leadership: A Survey of Theory and Research*. Free Press, New York.

Stoknes, P.E. (1992). What is the Myers-Briggs Type indicator? In D. Sharp (Ed.), *Personality Types: Jung's Model of Typology* (pp. 103–316). Moxnes Publishing, Oslo.

Trinidad, C. & Normore, A.H. (2005). Leadership and gender: A dangerous liaison? *Leadership & Organization Development Journal*, Vol. 26 No. 7, pp. 574–590.

Wallis, J. (2002). Drawing on revisionist economics to explain the inspirational dimensions of leadership. *The Journal of Socio-Economics*, Vol. 31 No. 1, pp. 59–74.

Yukl, G.A. (2010). *Leadership in Organizations*. Pearson, Upper Saddle River, NJ.

Chapter 5

Solving the Impossible: How to Harness Three Diverse Intuitions in Teams

Asta Raami

Contents

Introduction

This chapter elaborates upon three diverse types of intuitions integrated in our thinking. The use of these intuitions has been mentioned by distinguished inventors, successful business leaders, and domain-specific experts. The chapter outlines why it is important to understand and integrate these three types of intuitions when envisioning, innovating, or making complex decisions. Harnessing the full potential of intuition allows us to be more alert to respond to the challenges of our swiftly transforming environment.

The turbulent time around us calls for novel solutions. At the same time, in decision-making we have the tendency to emphasize reasoning over intuition. We try to squeeze all the juices out of System 2 while eliminating and amputating System 1 with a justification of the biasing effects it has. Furthermore, we are busy developing artificial intelligence to increase the amount of calculation for the benefit of our complex problems and decision-making—instead of looking at the research outcomes in studies of creative minds, which underline the role of intuition in high-cognition mental operations. It is true that from a historical perspective, the methods for reasoning have been indispensable especially when eliminating biases of thought, such as magical thinking and superstition. *But the point is not that intuition is prone to biases, instead that there is a lack of discernment skill while acquiring and evaluating intuitive information (Raami, 2015).* Every single type of information is prone to biases; intuition is not an exception. If our reasoning is not adequate, we end up with false information. To get accurate and reliable information while reasoning, we need to know that all the parameters involved are bulletproof and that the chain of reasoning is impeccable (Tart, 2009). This is seldom the case with the current problems.

For the past 10 years I have been researching intuition in creative practices. My continuous fascination has been why the concept of intuition remains too ambiguous to capture, and why the practical hands-on methods of intuition remain difficult to apply. Why does intuition slip out of our hands like soap? Why does it surprise us just when we thought that we finally understood how to utilize it?

This chapter brings together my 10 years of research in the fields of designers' creative processes, reinforced with recent interviews with Finnish artists, experts, inventors, and business leaders (Raami, 2016). These include discussions with seven successful artists, five domain-specific experts such as world-famous neurosurgeons, group discussions with 10 distinguished inventors, one of them holding 300 patents, as well as three deep interviews of exceptional business leaders, one of them constructing capital worth billions. Based on these perspectives, I have outlined the three most important types of intuitions, which form the basis of exceeding the known and of exceptional pioneering.

The Human Mind Is Equipped for Brilliance

The human brain has built-in ingenious abilities to invent novelties, to solve impossibilities, and to envision the future. Benefiting from this potential is essential, as we are surrounded by tremendously difficult problems. In short, we need more people who specialize in solving the impossible.* However, from the perspective of intuition, impossible problems do not exist. There is only inability to see the solution. Typically, we are unable to see the solution due to our restricted points of view. The reason why we do not see, as well as the methods how we could see, are both embedded in the human mind.

The way the human brain works can be compared to a snowy hill. When we slide down the slope for the first time, we can freely choose where to slide. While sliding, we leave a track behind. Then, when we slide down the second time, it is easiest to slide down in the already existing track. The human brain functions in a similar way. When we think or do something for the first time, we have an intact territory. As soon as we start thinking, a connection forms. Neurons that fire together, wire together.[†] Next time, the brain automatically chooses the most energy efficient and quickest route, which is the existing connection. (Pascual-Leone, n.d.) This process is the basis of our learning, as well as heuristics and automation. We practice something, and it becomes a well-wired connection in our brain. From the intuitive point of view there is a downside. When we have learned something extremely well, we are so deep in the track that the only thing we can see is the snowy wall. The hill disappears out of sight, or in fact even further, outside of our current understanding. Therefore, when the solutions for our impossible problems exist, they are unreachable to our understanding or even to our imagination.

The good news is that we can learn from the practices of the individuals who can make this leap and surpass the current understanding. Furthermore, we can benefit from the research outcomes of various fields of knowledge constructing understanding of the potential embedded in the human mind.

We Can Learn from Exceptional Inventors and Thinkers

Research made on Nobel Laureates and distinguished inventors reveals to us certain distinctive qualities and patterns of knowing which emerge when solving the impossible. People working with so-called "wicked problem solving" (Rittel & Webber, 1973) and with novel and radical innovation constantly report that their intuitive processes are profoundly based in a highly personal type of intuition (Keller, 1983; Larsson, 2002; Raami, 2015, 2018).

One of the most illuminating examples in history is the life and work of Nobel Laureate Barbara McClintock, who is the only woman in history awarded with an undivided Nobel Prize in Medicine. Her way of knowing and constructing scientific knowledge was so exceptional that she was heavily questioned by her peers, and

---

* Poet Theodore Roethke has said: "What we need is more people who specialize in the impossible."
† Neuropsychologist Donald Hebb first used this phrase in 1949 to describe how pathways in the brain are formed and reinforced through repetition.

hence quit all academic publishing for years. McClintock's crystallized observation on her personal working methods serves us a valuable insight related to surpassing the current level of knowledge. Typically, when we work with a complex problem or decision, we work *with* a problem: acquire information, classify, analyse, and acquire additional information. McClintock's way of working was the opposite. When faced with an unsolvable problem, she started to *work on herself*. Something in her was obstructing her from understanding the problem and from integrating the information and seeing the solution, rather than in the problem itself. She described being in the heart of her innovation and scientific work as being in a state of connectedness. Descriptions like these are present also with other Nobel Laureates and inventors (Keller, 1983; Holton, 1974; Larsson, 2001; Shavinina et al., 2004; Shavinina, 2009).

In other words, when we face a seemingly impossible problem, we are unable to see the solution. We obstruct the way ourselves due to the biological and psychological way in which our human mind works. Yet, we do not often understand *how* we obstruct the way. We often recognize the problems, but we are limiting our view by focusing *only* on the problem-solving. To solve the problem, we need to start working with ourselves. More precisely, the only thing we need to do is to remove ourselves from the way.

Further, when facing an impossible problem, we cannot find the solution with reason alone. The solution seems impossible since perhaps we cannot see the core question, or the solution is beyond our current logical understanding. We need to exceed the known. Therefore, we need intuitive information and integration of nonlinear ways of knowing when acquiring information, that is, various ways of intentional intuiting. In other words, often intuition appears as a ludicrous thought, the logic of which has been dared to be thought out thoroughly. Normally, instead of thinking these thoughts through, it is typical for us to turn away from a thought that otherwise overly challenges our preconceived notions. This is logical and natural since we have mental and emotional barriers restricting us (Mälkki, 2011; Mälkki & Raami, 2019). Therefore, in leadership, we need to learn how to tolerate seemingly unreasonable thoughts.

Instead of One Single Intuition, We All Have a Pool of Intuitions

The human brain is an elegant and ingenious organ with two joint system operations: System 1, intuition, and System 2, reasoning (Kahneman & Tversky, 1982). The nature of the human brain is inherently intuitive, and it occupies a majority of our thinking. System 1 processes several orders of magnitude more information than System 2 (Dijksterhuis et al., 2005; Zimmerman, 1989). In decision-making and creative work, it is always a question of integrating these two types of thinking. Often, intuition is considered as a monolithic phenomenon, yet System 1 is a pool of varying nonconscious processes founded on diverse knowledge bases (Glöckner & Witteman, 2010). Currently, cognitive science and psychology sees intuition as a continuum (Hogarth, 2001) consisting of varying instincts and evolution-based intuitions and domain-specific intuitions like heuristics and experience-based automated tasks.

The challenge is that intuitive experiences that are a part of inventing do not fit the current continuum of intuition, but rather represent an ambiguous territory of unmapped intuition. Therefore, the continuum of intuition is not a sufficient enough model to explain extraordinary intuitive experiences, which seem to have a remarkable role when inventing novelties. Therefore, when harnessing intuition for the use of personal and team decision-making and inventing, we need to be aware of the variety of intuitions and their role in intuiting. For example, not mixing the three "I" s—insight, intuition, and instinct (Shefy & Sadler-Smith, 2004). But in everyday life, while talking about intuition, it is more than obvious that we make constant confusions and end up referring to different types of intuitions without noticing it. (Raami, 2015, 2018).

An additional challenge is, due to our 300-year-long history of European culture and science, we think we can grasp intuitive experiences through natural language and verifiable observations. Therefore, the challenge of harnessing intuition cannot be solved "by rationalising the essential intuitive source of creative knowledge, but rather by *studying the way science proceeds when it is successful at being creative"* (Laughlin, 1997, p. 22).

We Can Acquire Specific Information through Intuition

Intuition is not just a way to receive information through moments of sudden flashes and revelations. Instead, it is a two-way channel (Bastick 2003). If we can receive intuitive information, we can acquire it through intentional intuiting. Intentional intuition allows us to access the untapped potential of the human mind. Some research states that through intuition we can acquire almost any information. Often we restrict the way ourselves. The most severe obstacle is our own mind in the form of restrictions and biases. (Kautz, 2005; Peirce, 2013; Raami, 2015).

When acquiring intuitive information, the demand for accuracy and reliability of information becomes integral. It is no use to acquire information if the reliability is unobtainable. According to Monsay (1997), the type of intuition is directly related to its reliability. She states that physical intuition is most likely reliable while sensible intuition rooted in sensing and common sense usually creates errors based on naïve experiences. In general, practice and trust appear to be crucial steps when interpreting intuitive signals and the reliability of intuition (Nadel, 2006). Davis-Floyd and Davis (1997) argue that the most essential components for testing reliability seem to be the personal and inner *feeling of connectedness as an embodied and spiritual aspect.* In other words, the reliability is related to the matrix of physical, emotional, and spiritual connectedness (Davis-Floyd & Davis, 1997). Further, intuition needs to be discerned from biases like imagination, magical thinking, storytelling, and such, otherwise we cannot build knowledge on it (Raami, 2015). Many individuals perceive signals like embodied sensations, absence of strong emotions, or experiences of serendipity and synchronicity, which work as confirmations of intuition (Raami, 2015; Mälkki & Raami, 2019). Of course, when creating, it is beneficial to integrate intuition and imagination since they feed each other. However, while making critical decisions, it may be a fatal error to rely on information based on biases and false associations.

The recent interviews in the autumn of 2018 with distinguished inventors started to outline the territory of intuition related to inventing. The coincidences and experiences inventors described while using intuition in their process of inventing were aligned with my previous interviews with business leaders. Elements like exceptional timing, unbelievable opportunities, strange synchronicity, and serendipity as well as unconventional recognition of meaningful weak signals and associations were repeatedly at the fore (Raami, 2016). Further, the inventors reported unconventional and remarkably similar stories of utilizing a special, highly personal way of intuiting. While inventing, they all described utilizing a similar kind of mental space as the basis of their thinking. For example, one inventor, an 80-year-old male who holds about 300 patents, describes:

> I have a white canvas. I turn my gaze upstairs. At the beginning, there is always an empty canvas, which afterwards starts to fill up. I can have a question in mind, to which the answer then appears early in the morning hours. I wake up at 2 a.m. and work until 6 a.m. The answer may be a text or a drawing, direct knowledge or a more emotional sensation. Sometimes the answer appears spontaneously, at other times I form questions and the canvas responds. The issue can be worded differently upon the canvas or otherwise moulded to another form. I can never erase the canvas, but every night I receive a new white canvas.

Similar experiences recur in the stories described by other interviewed distinguished inventors. However, this type of direct knowing experience is opposite from the perspective often seen in studies of expertise. Neither current psychology nor cognitive science recognize such a basis of knowledge, and it is perhaps excluded from the Western idea of a man. We have an illusion that problems are solved with hard work, analysis, and reasoning. It is true, that we need domain-specific expertise for integrating intuitive information to the existing practices. Many of these inventors report that when their domain-specific expertise has increased, they have been able to receive and apply more direct knowing information while making prototypes. Therefore, these two types of knowing are not exclusive but inclusive; they support each other. However, they are not equally credited. This is not made easier by the fact that our cultural comfort zone of handling intuition is limited due to personal, cultural, and historical reasons (Mälkki, 2011). Especially with this direct know-ing type of intuition, we are lacking the necessary vocabulary and the concepts are insufficient or nonexistent.

Another notable detail in the quotation is the difference between intuitive information and imagination: the inventor cannot erase or manipulate the infor-mation given. This is aligned with experiences reported by creative practitioners, since intuition and imagination are fundamentally different processes based on distinct knowledge bases (Davis-Floyd & Davis, 1997; Kautz, 2005; Raami, 2015). Imagination is adaptive; it has plasticity therefore you can easily manipulate the information in your mind. Often it comes jointly with emotions or wishes as guid-ing signals. Intuition instead resists manipulation and often comes jointly with the experience of emotional non-attachment (Kautz, 2005; Raami, 2015; Peirce, 2013). Further, intuitive information may take a form of multidimensional thought or clusters of information that seem to follow a logic of their own, while imagination is more prone to orchestrated association chains (Raami, 2015, 2016, 2018).

But this is not enough: we need to be alert to other biases too. We need to edu-cate ourselves about different types of intuitions and their specific biases. Since the model presenting intuition as a continuum is insufficient to capture many of the highly intuitive experiences, we need to widen our perspective.

Integrating the Three Types of Intuitions Creates Fertile Ground for Invention

The complexity of intuition results from its adhering to different knowledge bases in various fields. Further, the current understanding of intuition as a monolithic phenomenon or a continuum consisting of manifold variables explicates only intu-itions based on instincts, learning, and some types of expertise. However, these types of intuitions are not sufficient to capture intuitive processes related to excep-tional expertise and radical innovating that can surpass the known, as described by the inventors (Holton, 1973; Keller, 1987; Larsson, 2001; Raami, 2015, 2016). Therefore, I suggest including *a third dimension of intuition,* which supplements the field, since together with the two other types of intuition it helps us understand the difficulties of integrating intuitive knowledge in practice.

The continuum of intuition can be illustrated as a triangle, where in one corner is our most primitive type of intuition based on evolution and instincts (Figure 5.1). It is the primate and bestial in us, and we cannot ignore it even though we would like to see ourselves as developed, educated, and rational beings (Mälkki, 2011). The bestial lives inside us due to our strong animal-based genetics. From the instinct-based intuition rises our primitive urges and drives—which are extremely beneficial when, for example, they help us support our daily life, such as well-being, survival, and nurturing. It also helps us take care of our offspring, live in a social setting, and access and utilize physical qualities like embodied cognition

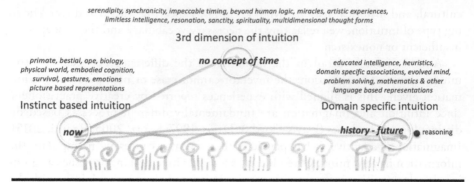

Figure 5.1 Three diverse types of intuitions and reasoning.

(Gigerenzer, 2007). At the same time this type of intuition is mainly unreachable to our reasoning due to herd-based functions such as primitive attachments, surviving, mating, pecking order, fears, and clinging.

In another corner is the domain-specific intuition, which is the one typically mentioned in expertise studies (Bastick, 2003; Glöckner & Witteman, 2010). This type of intuition is distinctive for the educated mind benefitting from intuitive processes such as heuristics, pattern matching and recognition, associations of accumulated evidence, automated tasks, and construction of mental representations. The information of domain-specific intuition is usually derived from subconscious memory traces and combined with new information, mental representations, or comparison with exemplars, prototypes, or images (Bastick, 2003; Glöckner & Witteman, 2010; Monsay, 1997). This type of intuition is an integral part of our expertise.

Further, it has an important role in discerning intuitive information, which can be illustrated as an ability to combine the right dots leading to understanding and outlining the correct pattern (Lloyd-Meyer, 2007). On the other hand, the same intuition produces severe biases such as mental loops and ingrained, rigid thought patterns (Kahneman & Tversky, 1987). Could it be that this stagnation is one of our most severe barriers in accessing and integrating the other two types of intuitions?

The problem is that domain-specific intuition does not explain the most radical and visionary types of insights, those which exceed the domain and our current understanding. Therefore, it is not sufficient to explain processes of intuitive revelations. The inventors interviewed used descriptions like connecting to "*the limitless intelligence,*" or working in "*the upper floor workroom,*" or "*the upstairs office*" and linked these experiences with components such as serendipity, synchronicity, resonation, sanctity, or beyond human logic. They see this dimension as different from their domain-specific thinking. The inventors describe that while working in this dimension of intuitive knowing, everything is possible since for them it is the source of free, limitless information. A male inventor, age 72, describes:

> There are two realities, an upper and a lower one. I call them the upstairs office and the office of the mind. In the upstairs office, nothing is impossible. Sometimes I reach it in the moments between being asleep and awake, or while driving. There, it is possible to examine the same things from multiple different angles at the same time.

This type of knowledge basis has been labeled with various names depending on the field of knowledge. For example, Kautz (2005) calls it superconscious, Tart (2009) as the transpersonal realm, László (2009) refers to it as Akashic Record or the Akashic Chronicle, and Wilber (1997) uses the term atomic consciousness. The reason why I call it the third dimension of intuition is due to its intrinsic intertwining with the two other types of intuition: instinct-based and domain-specific intuitions. Most likely, due to these other types of intuitions, we have difficulties in connecting and integrating the third dimension into our thinking capacity. These three intuitions are an inseparable part of our humanity; they intermingle endlessly, yet in fundamentally different ways since every one of them is embedded on entirely different knowledge bases.

Incoherence and Single-Lens Perspectives Are Indicators of Connection Flaws

An increase in incoherence and black-and-white thinking seems to be typical for our time. From the grassroot level to global affairs, an escalation of radical thoughts like populism can be observed. Could this be a result of our poor connection to intuitive faculties? Let's elaborate the idea a bit further. If our instinct-based intuition overrides rational thinking, we most likely end up over-reacting and making irrational emotion-based decisions. Could this lead to a power struggle and a situation where absurd and random arguments are considered more valid than the voice of experts? Moreover, if we deny the connection to the third dimension of intuition, could we end up explaining away genius ideas that simply do not fit into our current dogma?

Typically, we see and search for those perceptions which fit our worldview. When we educate our mind, we're able to examine and include other perspectives in our thinking too. However, if the perspective radically contradicts our own, accepting contradicting realities or points of view demands mental resilience and straining. However, when strong emotions are included, changing the perspective and maintaining contradicting views can become painful or impossible.

Per se, the perspectives of these three intuitions conflict radically with each other. This leads to blind spots and biased, hidebound thinking. Mental blocks are reactions to reject something that confronts our current understanding (Mälkki & Raami, 2019). When we ignore nonconscious processes they tend to have a stronger

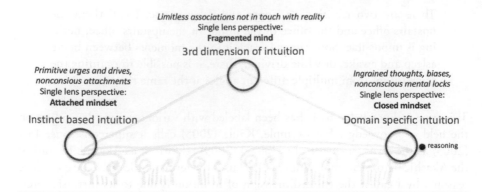

Limitless associations not in touch with reality
Single lens perspective:
Fragmented mind

3rd dimension of intuition

Primitive urges and drives,
nonconsious attachments
Single lens perspective:
Attached mindset

Instinct based intuition

Ingrained thoughts, biases,
nonconscious mental locks
Single lens perspective:
Closed mindset

Domain specific intuition

reasoning

Figure 5.2   The different logics in three diverse intuitions and examples of their typical biases.

influence underneath (Mälkki, 2011). All of us have inalienable primitive drives affecting us subconsciously even though we assume we are open-minded and think logically. For example, in a case of a trauma, pressure, conflict, or a strong emotional bond, we easily end up being in a black-and-white perspective, losing the connection to the other two types of intuitions (Figure 5.2). This may lead to a situation where our confrontation, stagnation, and primitive urges effectively override our other senses and we use our reasoning only for inventing acceptable-sounding explanations for our irrational decisions. All of us have most likely experienced a situation in which we have let ourselves be drawn in and stuck to a single perspective, for example being infatuated with something, so that we only see that one perspective—even if reality would be revealed later to be very different.

Let's elaborate how these three intuitions differ from each other in a case of single-lens perspective. It is essential to see the obstacles which are otherwise hidden, and which sever our connection to the other intuitions. When our instinct-based intuition controls our decisions and actions, we lose the connection to our logical reasoning, hence our actions are over-reactive, strongly emotion-based, and unpredictable. The single-lens perspective results in *an attached mindset* which is defensive and incoherent, dominated by primitive urges and drives. A typical reaction could be something like, "no matter if my arguments are logical or not, I just need to quickly exit the situation and return to my emotional comfort zone, preferably maintaining the power over others" (Mälkki, 2011, 2019; Mälkki & Raami, 2019). Actions brought about by instinct-based intuition are a consequence of herd activity and are dependent on the herd and the individual's place within it.

A person strongly bonded to an instinct-based, single-lens perspective lives in the very moment. Viewed from this attached mindset perspective the other two types of intuitions *are* intolerant and detached from reality—since they are not sharing the same intuitive reality. Therefore, the others look either weak, crazy, hypocritical, and lazy; or, powerless hairsplitters and lip service elitists. The circle of broken connection is fed by fears and separation (Figure 5.3).

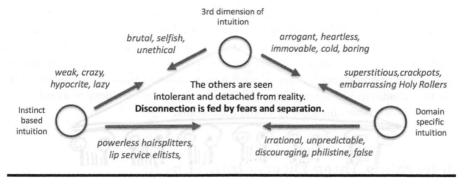

Figure 5.3   Disconnection between the three types of intuitions.

When we are stuck in the single-lens perspective of domain-specific intuition it causes intellectual rigidity, *a closed mindset* with mental barriers and limiting false beliefs. One inventor, holding 300 patents, described having a prototype of an invention that strongly challenges the current scientific knowledge as well as our traditional way of thinking. He had presented the invention to five professors, but all of them had rejected the invention without orienting themselves deeper into the theme, with comments "that is not possible." At the same time the inventor has two well-working prototypes of his invention. How is this possible? On the top of the closed mindset, the human mind is prone to more than a hundred different cognitive perception biases (Lieberman, 2009; Lieberman et al., 2015). One of them is called an investment bias. If an individual has invested enough of something valuable—it can be time, money, energy, thoughts, or whatever is considered valuable—they want to feel their investment is worth the value. Therefore, if a professor has invested several decades for a theoretical construction, it is easier to ignore or explain away the mismatching information than to let the collapsing belief destroy all the previous investments. Maintaining the coherence in our human mind is primary. Our consciousness can bend, shrink, or even split, but it cannot tolerate a break in coherence. The coherence is maintained even *at the cost of reality* (Hayles, 2014).

When looking at the other two intuitions from the perspective of domain-specific intuition, the other two look irrational, unpredictable, philistine, and false; or, superstitious crackpots and embarrassing Holy Rollers. Again, these other two *are* intolerant and detached from reality. When domain-specific intuition dominates, the perspective is well grounded in history and the future but typically has lost the connection to emotions and the body. The third dimension of intuition seems extremely hard to understand since it operates beyond human logic.

If we are driven to the single-lens perspective in the third dimension of intuition, the result is *a fragmented mind* where our thinking spalls with endless associations causing an inability to stay in touch with reality. Some of the interviewees report having periods when magical revelations of radical and unseen future inventions are reachable to their mind, due to the overkill speed of their mental, multidimensional associations. When looking at the other two intuitions from this perspective, they look either brutal, selfish, and unethical; or, arrogant, heartless, immovable, and boring. In this dimension, there is no concept of time. To sum up, we seldom live in just one perspective; instead we hover in between these all. However, if we do not recognize and acknowledge *all these three diverse intuitions in ourselves*, we are stuck with biases invisible to us and dichotomy.

Integrating Three Diverse Intuitions to Knowledge-Building Practices Is Possible

When we surpassed our current point of view from single-lens perspective and built a connection with another perspective of intuitive information, it did not guarantee us being able to maintain the connection and keep the access open. Contradictorily, we need to surpass our mental obstacles again and again. Therefore, including three diverse angles of intuitive knowledge simultaneously might require almost super-human skills. However, it is possible, and we can find ways to bind a working connection either by ourselves or in teams.

Let's return to McClintock's case. She had described, when the information was "not integrating," that it was an indicator of a problem. Correspondingly, when her internal system was working, she described it as "*integrating what you saw*," where she could simultaneously read the environment with her physical eyes as well as with her mind's eye. The physical spots she saw on maize kernels represented for her a hidden genetic meaning that she could read simultaneously. In this very moment, she saw directly into an ordered world of mental images. Her assistant has described what McClintock saw as "*completely unrelated to anything we knew, it was like looking into the twenty-first century,*" and "*just looking over her shoulder, looking at the spots, you could visualize what was going on—she made you see it* (Keller, 1983, p. 137).

Similar experiences of integration have been described by other Nobel Laureates too (Larsson, 2001). For example, Robert A. Millikan, a Nobel Laureate in Physics, was able to look with fresh, clear eyes at what was actually going on; he had intense powers of visualizing and an ability to connect what he saw with a preliminary theory of electricity; and on the top of these, he saw electrons with his eyes! (Holton, 1978, p. 38).

Studies of highly intuitive individuals' thinking suggest that when the information is not integrating, we barricade the way ourselves (Kautz, 2005). When we are unable to reach intuitive information, the problem is located in the connection (Davis-Floyd & Davis, 1997). Therefore, the only thing we need to do is to form a connection to intuitive information and connect ourselves to the solution. To enable this, we need to remove the obstacles blocking our connection to the other two intuitions. The connection flaw is not outside of us but inside of us. Therefore, in the end, all the problems might be connection flaws.

If we elaborate on this statement from the perspective of the three diverse intuitions, what does a well-working connection look like? In an optimal situation, combining these diverse intuitions takes place in the center of the triangle (Figure 5.4.). In this sweet spot, we are able to get the maximum bandwidth for the best qualities of all these intuitions. The main challenge seems to be how to *detach ourselves from attachments* and *surpass our ingrained thoughts,* which are the most severe biases of intuition (Raami, 2015).

In the optimal situation, our instinct-based intuition is free from attachments such as fears and clinging. To reach this situation, we need to educate our bestial mind to step out of the shadows and feel safe. When moving from single-lens perspective toward the educated mind, we are capable of getting rid of biases of magical thinking and superstitions as well as irrational, emotional reactions-based drives and urges. In the best situation, the instinct-based intuition offers us an ability to perceive with fresh eyes, a courageous drive to take forward visionary, brilliant ideas and integrate them into the practices of the physical world.

To enhance our connection to this type of intuition in practice, we may invoke our physical body. Hands-on work, going for a walk, or applying increasing kinematic playfulness in our work might be beneficial. Several researchers mention that these boost creative thinking (Keinänen, 2016); not to be forgotten are nourishment, sleep, and overall well-being. (Otherwise the primitive urge inside of us gets cranky!) But above all, the most important is to create an environment of physical and psychological safety. For example, mindfulness practices are often mentioned as being supportive, since they temporarily quiet down our fears, hence increasing our cognitive capacity (Williams et al., 2007).

When we have a working connection to the domain-specific intuition, seeing with fresh eyes integrates us with our expertise. We're able to apply skilled discernment in our process of constructing intuitive and domain-specific information.

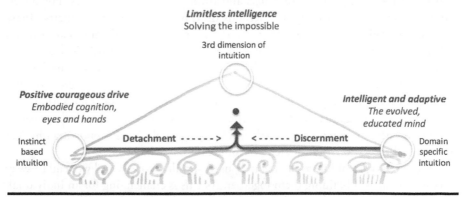

Figure 5.4　Integrating the potential of three different intuitions.

To fully harness the intuition of an educated mind, a resilient and tolerant approach is a prerequisite. This requires open-minded marveling and loosening of beliefs, since we as humans tend to rely on our minds, which may hold the answers but still find it difficult to question the learned dogmas. Therefore, we need to move toward the center of the triangle to get the maximum bandwidth in our thinking to fully access and integrate the third dimension of intuition.

To enhance this process, quieting the mind has been recognized to be highly beneficial. Studies in neuroscience state that any behavior quieting our thinking can support new insights (Bowden et al., 2005; Jung-Beeman, 2008). Creative practitioners often mention routine tasks like tinkering and crafting with deep concentration being helpful since this keeps the mind busy, which in turn creates porosity in thinking—thus easing access to intuitive faculties (Lee-Zlotoff, n.d.; Raami, 2015). Further, sensitiveness toward embodied signals is frequently mentioned as a beneficial tool. Numerous business leaders report utilizing gut feelings, goose bumps, or other embodied signals in decision-making (Gigerenzer 2007).

The most challenging source of intuition for an ordinary individual may be accepting and integrating the third dimension. This is no wonder since it has been excluded from our reason-based thinking—even so profoundly that it lacks decent scientific concepts and vocabulary. At best, when connecting to the third dimension of intuition we can access limitless intuition that flows freely (Kautz, 2005; Peirce, 2013; Targ, 2012). Yet we need to be alerted to the biases of the other two intuitions: the attachments of the primitive mind and expert-based ingrained thinking. But when reaching the state of detachment and discernment, we are capable of acquiring information from limitless intelligence and integrating what we see to our current expertise.

Typically, accessing this type of intuition is based on highly personal methods, which often are innate and originate from childhood. However, it is possible to develop the process of intuiting and enhance accessing and integrating intuitive information (Hogarth, 2001; Peirce, 2013; Raami, 2015). Typically, this requires constant unlearning from false beliefs and limiting mental structures. For boosting the process, we can study the methods used by highly intuitive experts. These include controlled remote viewing, radiesthesia, organizational constellations, and other direct knowing practices (Birkenkrahe, 2008; Targ, 2012; Kautz, 2005; Peirce, 2013; Roevens, 2008). For ordinary people these methods may sound weird, and instead we all benefit from dreams, exercises boosting intuition, creative arts, or meditation. For many people, the methods integrating physical relaxation with loosened mental rigidity work well. The classic external facilitators for creative insights are the three B's—bath, bed, and bus—typical places supporting physical and mental relaxation and the free flow of ideas (Bastick, 2003).

The three types of intuition are rarely used simultaneously, and we tend to sway between them as if braiding them together. As this is challenging for an individual, we can instead utilize the intuitions brought together by a team. This, of course, requires us to accept the existence of these three types of intuitions, be aware of their benefits, and acquire the power of discerning intuition. To achieve this, we can create a collective comfort zone supporting the culture of trust and acceptance, where both the limitations and the potentials of individuals can be harnessed for achieving these goals (Mälkki, 2011; Raami, 2015). In the solving of difficult problems or complex decisions it is important to integrate the entire potential of intuition, after all.

Summary

From the point of view of intuition, impossible problems do not exist. There is only the incapability of seeing the solutions. When acquiring information through intuition, the sole barrier we need to exceed is our human mind. This is not easy, since we do not understand how our mind restricts our view. Further, it is difficult to recognize our biases when perceiving intuitive information. While discerning what is accurate and reliable intuitive information, it is essential to remember we have different types of intuitions, which are based on diverse bases of knowledge. Based on interviews, it seems as if the continuum of intuition is not sufficient alone; in addition we need to include three separate dimensions of intuition. In decision-making and inventing, it is essential to recognize all three types of intuitions: instinct-based intuition, domain-specific intuition, and the third dimension of intuition. In a team, the information from diverse intuitions can be brought together. It is not necessary for every single person to have access to all the differing types of intuition, but it is imperative to be able to break down the barriers and mental blocks. Only then is it possible to harness the limitless potential of intuition to aid inventiveness and decision-making.

References

Bastick, T. (2003). *Intuition: Evaluating the Construct and Its Impact on Creative Thinking* Stoneman & Lang.

Birkenkrahe, M. (2008). System constellations as tool supporting organisational learning and change Processes. In *International Journal of Learning and Change*. doi:04/IJLC.2008.023179

Bowden, E., Jung-Beeman, M., Fleck, J., & Kounios, J. (2005). New approaches to demystifying insight. *Trends in Cognitive Sciences, 9*(7), 322–328. doi:10.1016/j.tics.2005.05.012

Davis-Floyd, R., & Davis, E. (1997). Intuition as authorative knowledge in midwifery and homebirth. In *Looking Intuit: A Phenomenological Exploration of Intuition and Attention* (pp. 145–176). New York: Routledge.

Dijksterhuis, A., Bos, M. W., Nordgren, L. F., & van Baaren, R. B. (2006). On making the right choice: The deliberation-without-attention effect. *Science, 311*(5763), 1005–1007. doi.org/10.1126/science.1121629

Gigerenzer, G. (2007). *Gut Feelings: The Intelligence of the Unconscious*. New York: Viking.

Glöckner, A., & Witteman, C. (2010). Foundations for tracing intuition: Models, findings, categorizations. In A. Glöckner & C. Witteman (Eds.), *Foundations for Tracing Intuition: Challenges and Methods* (pp. 1–23). Hove, East Sussex, New York: Psychology Press & Routledge.

Hayles, K. (2014). Cognition everywhere: The rise of the cognitive nonconscious and the costs of consciousness. *New Literary History*, *45*(2), 199–220. doi:10.1353/nlh.2014.0011

Hogarth, R. M. (2001). *Educating Intuition*. Chicago: University of Chicago Press.

Holton, G. J. (1973). *Thematic Origins of Scientific Thought: Kepler to Einstein*. Cambridge, MA: Harvard University Press.

Holton, G. J. (1978). *The Scientific Imagination: Case Studies*. Cambridge [England]; New York: Cambridge University Press.

Jung-Beeman, M. (2008). How insight happens: Learning from the brain. *NeuroLeadership Journal*, *1*, 20–25.

Kahneman, D., & Tversky, A. (1982). Judgment under uncertainty: Heuristics and biases. In D.Kahneman & A. Tversky (Eds.), *Judgment under Uncertainty: Heuristics and Biases* (pp. 3–22). Cambridge: Cambridge University Press.

Kautz, W. H. (2005). *Opening the Inner Eye: Explorations on the Practical Application of Intuition in Daily Life and Work*. New York: iUniverse.

Keller, E. F. (1983). *A Feeling for the Organism: The Life and Work of Barbara McClintock*. San Francisco: W.H. Freeman.

Keinänen, M. (2016) *Taking Your Mind for a Walk*. Springer.

Klein, G. (1998). *Sources of Power: How People Make Decisions*. Cambridge, MA: MIT Press.

Klein, G. (2004). *The Power of Intuition: How to Use Your Gut Feelings to Make Better Decisions at Work*. Crown Business.

Laughlin, C. (1997). The Nature of Intuition: A Neurophysiological Approach. In R. Davis-Floyd & P. S. Arvidson (Eds.), *Intuition: The Inside Story: Interdisciplinary Perspectives* (pp. 19–37). New York: Routledge.

Larsson, U. (2001). *Cultures of Creativity: The Centennial Exhibition of the Nobel Prize*. Canton, MA: Science History Publications.

Laszlo, E. (2009). In defense of intuition: Exploring the physical foundations of spontaneous apprehension. *Journal of Scientific Exploration*, *23*(1), 51.

Lee-Zlotoff, D. (n.d.) Podcast interview, *The Making of MacGyver With David Lee Zlotff*.

Lieberman, M.D. (2009). The brain's braking system and how to use your words to tap into it. *NeuroLeadership Journal* 2.

Lieberman, M.D., Rock, D., Grant Halvorson, H. & Cox, C. (2015). Breaking bias updated: The SeedsTM Model. *NeuroLeadership Journal* 2015 June.

Lloyd-Mayer, E. (2007). *Extraordinary Knowing: Science Skepticism, and The Inexplicable Powers of the Human Mind*. New York: Bantam Books.

Monsay, E. H. (1997). Intuition in the development of scientific theory and practice. In R. Davis-Floyd & P. S. Arvidson (Eds.), *Intuition: The Inside Story: Interdisciplinary Perspectives* (pp. 103–120). New York: Routledge.

Mälkki, K. (2011). Theorizing the nature of reflection (Doctoral dissertation). University of Helsinki, Institute of Behavioural Sciences.

Mälkki, K. (2019). Coming to grips with edge-emotions: The gateway to critical reflection and transformative learning. In A. Kokkos, F. Finnegan & T. Fleming (Eds.), *European Perspectives on Transformative Learning*. Palgrave Macmillan (forthcoming).

Mälkki, K: & Raami, A. (2019). Transformative learning to solve the impossible: Edge emotions and intuition in expanding the limitations of our rational abilities. In E. Kostara, A. Gavrielatos, and D. Loads (Eds.), *Transformative Learning Theory and Praxis: New Perspectives and Possibilities*. London: Routledge. (forthcoming)

Nadel, L. (2006). *Sixth Sense: Unlocking Your Ultimate Mind Power* (1st ed.). Lincoln, OR: ASJA Press.

Pascual-Leone, A. (n.d.) A researcher in Harvard mentioned the example in his lecture. Cited by Åhman, H. (2012) in *Mind Leadership in Organization*. 2014. Finland, Sanoma Pro.

Peirce, P. (2013). *Leap of Perception: The Transforming Power of Your Attention*. First Atria Books.

Raami, A. (2015). *Intuition Unleashed—On the Application and Development of Intuition in the Creative Process*. Helsinki, Finland: Aalto University, School of Art and Design.

Raami, A. (2016). Älykäs intuitio ja miten käytämme sitä. Helsinki: Schilds & Söderströms.

Raami, A. (2018). Toward solving the impossible problems. In J. W. Cook (Ed.), *Sustainability, Human Well-Being and the Future of Education* (pp. 201–233). London: Palgrave Macmillan.

Rittel, H. W. J., & Webber, M. M. (1973). Dilemmas in a general theory of planning. *Policy Sciences*, 4(2), 155–169.

Roevens, J. L. M. (2008). Systemic constellations work in organizations S.I.: ScienceGuide.

Shavinina, L. V. (2009). Innovation education for the gifted: A new direction in gifted education. In *International Handbook on Giftedness*. Dordrecht: Springer Netherlands. Retrieved from www.springerlink.com/content/x77186846177u1xh/

Shavinina, L. V., & Seeratan, K. L. (2004). Extracognitive phenomena in the intellectual functioning of gifted, creative, and talented individuals. In Larisa V. Shavinina & M. F. Ferrari (Eds.), *Beyond Knowledge: Extracognitive Aspects of Developing High Ability* (pp. 73–102). Mahwah, NJ: Lawrence Erlbaum Associates.

Shefy, E., & Sadler-Smith, E. (2004). The intuitive executive: Understanding and applying "gut feel" in decision-making. *Academy of Management Executive*, 18(4), 76–91.

Tart, C. T. (2009). *The End of Materialism: How Evidence of the Paranormal Is Bringing Science and Spirit Together*. Co-published with the Institute of Noetic Sciences. New Harbinger.

Targ, R. (2012). *The Reality of ESP: A Physicist's Proof of Psychic Phenomena*. Wheaton, IL: Quest Books.

Wilber, K. (1997). An integral theory of consciousness. *Journal of Consciousness Studies*, 4(1), 71–92.

Williams, M., Teasdale, J., Segal, Z. and Kabat-Zinn, J. (2007). *The Mindful Way through Depression: Freeing Yourself from Chronic Unhappiness*. New York: Guilford Press.

Zimmermann, M. (1989). The nervous system in the context of information theory. In R. F. Schmidt & P. D. D. G. Thews (Eds.), *Human Physiology* (pp. 166–173). Springer Berlin Heidelberg. Retrieved from http://link.springer.com/chapter/10.1007/978-3-642-73831-9_7

Chapter 6

Intuition and Deliberation in Morality and Cooperation: An Overview of the Literature

Ozan Isler and Onurcan Yilmaz

Contents

Behavioral sciences often rely on a dual-process model of the mind to describe human decision-making processes (Evans, 2008). Underlying this model is the evolutionary view of a "cognitive miser," of a mind constantly trying to save energy by reacting automatically to environmental cues (Fiske & Taylor, 2013). A long-standing debate revolves around the question of whether these intuitive reactions can be beneficial or whether we need effortful deliberation for achieving our goals (Kahneman & Klein, 2009). Here we first summarize this dual-process model of the mind and the arguments made on both sides of this debate. We then focus on a question that remains in relative neglect in the management literature—whether intuitions support ethical and cooperative behavior. As a provisional answer, we provide an overview of the literature and discuss the emerging picture on dual-process accounts of morality and cooperation.

The Dual-Process Model of the Mind

The model posits two distinct systems of cognitive processes. System 1 refers to the automatic, intuitive, and low-effort processes of the mind (Kahneman, 2011). Having emerged much earlier in our evolutionary history, we share this capacity for automatic thinking with many other animals. System 2 processes, on the other hand, are to a large extent what makes us distinctively human (Sapolsky, 2017). Directly related to the relatively recent evolution of the neocortex, System 2 corresponds to more deliberated, analytical, high-effort, and controlled processes (Kahneman, 2011; Tversky & Kahneman, 1974). While novel nontrivial decisions (e.g., multiplying two large numbers) often require System 2 thinking, we naturally rely on System 1 to conduct routinized behavior (e.g., driving our car, walking our dog, brushing our teeth). For example, try to answer as fast as you can, what is 2 times 2? And, what would be your ranking in a race, if you run past the person in the second position? Given that our intuitions often provide the correct answer to the first but not the second question (Thomson & Oppenheimer, 2016), research on the dual-process decision-making has sought to answer a third question.

Can We Rely on Our Intuitions?

System 1 processes, reflecting adaptations to our ancestral environment, have the evolutionary advantage of minimizing cognitive effort. Yet the environments we now inhabit and the problems we currently face are usually quite different than back in our days in the savannah. A prominent approach, the heuristics-and-biases (HB) view, emphasizes how this mismatch between our intuitions and our environments result in systematic cognitive biases (Kahneman, 2011). In contrast, the simple-heuristics (SH) and the naturalistic decision-making (NDM) views emphasize how intuitions can be reliable when they fit well with the environment (Gigerenzer, Hertwig, & Pachur, 2011; Klein, 2008).

According to HB, systematic errors in judgment are a natural by-product of our System 1 processes that have largely failed to catch up with our rapidly changing worlds. Take the conjunction fallacy, which demonstrates how our intuitions can systematically fail when making the probabilistic inferences that we regularly rely on in organizational settings. Linda, for example, is someone concerned with issues of social justice. Which do you think is more probable, that (A) Linda is a bank teller, or that (B) Linda is a bank teller and a feminist? While most people (over 80 percent) tend to answer B, deliberating on the correct answer makes it clear that B must be a subset of A and that it is hence less probable to occur (Tversky & Kahneman, 1983). A long list of other cognitive biases have been identified by research on the HB view (e.g., Tversky & Kahneman, 1974), which shows how human beings frequently and systematically fail the normative benchmarks of procedural rationality.

In contrast, the NDM and SH views emphasize the practical successes of automatic thought. The NDM view seeks to explain the efficiency of expert intuition in natural environments. For example, fireground commanders are often able to successfully make life-saving decisions (e.g., regarding how the flames will spread, whether a house will collapse) under acute time pressure (Klein, Calderwood, & Clinton-Cirocco, 1986). NDM explains such impressive intuitive judgments as the result of becoming skilled in the unconscious recognition of relevant cues in a complex environment (Klein, 1993). Rather than the instantaneous recognition of complex patterns, the SH view instead posits that "simple heuristics can make us smart" by providing practical and less error-prone results in a complex and uncertain world (Gigerenzer, Todd, & ABC Research Group, 1999). Accordingly, System 1 processes can become well-adapted to our current natural and social environments through the development of a repertoire of simple rules called heuristics. Take, for example, the equality heuristic, the simple rule of "allocating resources equally to each of N alternatives" (Gigerenzer, 2008). In the unpredictable world of financial investments, none of the sophisticated optimizing algorithms, including Markowitz's Nobel-winning mean-variance portfolio model, were found to outperform this simple rule (DeMiguel, Garlappi, & Uppal, 2007).

The contrasting views of HB on the one hand and NDM and SH on the other are mainly a matter of emphasis on the negative versus positive consequences of relying on intuitions. Despite the various differences in viewpoints (Gigerenzer, 2008), scholars tend to agree that intuitive performance can be improved by gaining experience through regular feedback, especially when the environment is conducive to such learning, and by relying on the right expertise in the right context (Kahneman & Klein, 2009).

These insights have gained increased attention in the management literature (Artinger, Petersen, Gigerenzer, & Weibler, 2015; Basel & Brühl, 2013). It is now widely reported that managers (Khatri & Ng, 2000; Parikh, Neubauer, & Lank, 1994) and entrepreneurs (Koudstaal, Sloof, & van Praag, 2018) routinely rely on intuitions and that reliance on intuition is positively associated with managerial seniority (Sadler-Smith & Shefy, 2004). In sum, the emerging picture indicates that although intuitive managerial decisions are often successful and although there is room for significant improvement (Loock & Hinnen, 2015), integration of individual deliberation as well as external analytical and empirical aids to managerial decision-making should be encouraged (Hodgkinson, Bown, Maule, Glaister, & Pearman, 1999), since reliance on intuitions in business settings have also been shown to result in systematic failures (Li & Tang, 2010; Rosenzweig, 2007; Simon, Houghton, & Aquino, 2000).

Despite the growing scholarship on the pros and cons of intuitive managerial decision-making, the literature understandably prioritizes the aspects of strategic business decisions and consequent corporate financial performance. However, dual-process theories in behavioral sciences have over the past 30 years been extended to decisions regarding morality and cooperation, which remain neglected in the management literature. As these findings may provide additional insights into managerial decisions (e.g., corruption, collusion, and social responsibility), we now review and summarize this relatively more recent literature.

Moral Intuitions

The origins and substance of moral judgments have been extensively examined for the last 50 years (Haidt, 2001, 2007; Kohlberg & Kohlberg, 1969; Piaget, 1965; Shweder, Much, Mahapatra, & Park, 1997). An early account, Kolhberg's *rationalistic theory*, which was for a long time the paradigmatic approach, posits that moral judgments are a result of advanced cognitive processes. According to this approach, even though emotional and intuitive processes may play a role, the necessary condition for arriving at moral judgments is to rely on reflective and analytic processes. Kohlberg defines moral judgments in hierarchical stages of universal applicability and consequently identifies three stages of moral development that proceed from pre-conventional to conventional and from conventional to post-conventional periods. Based on the justifications they provide when facing moral dilemmas, Kohlberg's method classifies those who refer to universal principles of justice (e.g., human rights) as having achieved the post-conventional stage of moral judgments. Kohlberg's implicit assumption here is that moral and cognitive development are intertwined, where reflective thought processes correspond to higher order moral judgments (i.e., post-conventional morality). Although Kohlberg's theory has been severely criticized as showing an essentialist bias toward Western liberalism (e.g., Haidt, 2007), more recent studies show that endorsement of the principles of universal justice (e.g., equality) indeed often requires more sophisticated, reflective processes (Napier & Luguri, 2013; Van Berkel, Crandall, Eidelman, & Blanchar, 2015; Yilmaz & Saribay, 2017a, 2017b).

A more recent approach that also assigns a pivotal role to cognitive processes in moral judgments is Greene's *dual-process model* (2007). The model predicts that moral judgments tend to be consistent with either utilitarian or deontological ethics depending on whether judgments are made deliberatively or intuitively. While utilitarianism prioritizes maximizing the aggregate social welfare (Mill, 1863), deontological judgments are guided by moral principles with simple rules of application ("you shall not kill"). Think of the classical trolley dilemma, for example: a runaway trolley is on the path to kill five people and you have the chance to save these lives by sacrificing the life of one other person. What would you do? Greene finds that people tend to approve of using a switch that diverts the trolley to a side track, where it will instead kill one person, while they tend to disapprove of making a similar sacrifice by pushing someone on the tracks to stop the trolley. Greene suggests that the idea of actively pushing someone to his or her death triggers a visceral reaction that results in an intuitive deontological response (i.e., it is wrong to kill), whereas lack of such emotions when using the switch engages utilitarian reasoning (i.e., it is right to save as many lives as possible).

Consistent with Greene's dual-process account, utilitarian judgments have been shown to correlate with activity in brain regions responsible for analytic thinking, whereas deontological judgments have been shown to coexist with emotional arousal (Greene, 2007; Koenigs et al., 2007). Greene's account finds further support in behavioral experiments. For example, it takes more time to make utilitarian judgments than to make deontological judgments about moral dilemmas (Greene, Sommerville, Nystrom, Darley, & Cohen, 2001). Similarly, activating analytic thinking increases (Paxton, Ungar, & Greene, 2012), whereas activating intuitive thinking decreases (Trémolière, De Neys, & Bonnefon, 2012), the endorsement of utilitarian moral judgments. More recently, Greene's account has been criticized by the fact that approval of sacrificial killing of one person (with the consequence of saving many others) does not necessarily require reliance on utilitarian ethics or analytical thinking (Kahane, Everett, Earp, Farias, & Savulescu, 2015). In particular, it has been shown that psychopathic tendencies may result in behavior similar to utilitarian moral judgments (Aktas, Yilmaz, & Bahçekapili, 2017).

In contrast to Kohlberg's and Greene's theories that assign a pivotal role to deliberation in the formation of normative judgments, Haidt's *social intuitionist model* (2001) predicts that moral judgments are exclusively made by System 1 processes, and that deliberation (i.e., System 2 processes) is merely used to rationalize these intuitively made moral judgments. For example, having read a hypothetical scenario involving an incestual relationship that does not result in any physical or psychological harm to the parties involved, people tend to immediately and strongly judge this relationship as morally wrong while often failing to provide deliberated justifications for their reactions. The natural process of making such moral judgment therefore seems essentially intuitive and not reflective (Haidt, 2001). In short, the social intuitionist model involves a foundational criticism of previous accounts of morality by prioritizing System 1 processes in moral judgments.

Whereas the social intuitionist model (Haidt, 2001) explains the role of cognitive processes in moral judgments, the more recent *moral foundations theory* (Graham et al., 2011; Haidt, 2012) seeks to explain the origin and substance of these moral judgments. The theory posits that moral judgments are evolutionary adaptions and that all societies rely on five distinct types or foundations of moral judgments in varying degrees. Care/harm relates to the protection of the off-spring or the weak. Fairness/cheating relates to the sustenance of group cohesion and detection of those who disrupt it. Loyalty/betrayal is about favoring one's own group. Authority/subversion corresponds to support for hierarchical social structures. Sanctity/degradation emphasizes sacredness as well as physical and spiritual cleansing. The theory has substantial empirical backing and practical relevance. For example, liberals have been shown to embrace the dimensions of care/harm and fairness/cheating, whereas conservatives are found to put equal emphasis on all five dimensions (Graham, Haidt, & Nosek, 2009). Most people are therefore inherently righteous, yet there is significant heterogeneity in their moral compass (Haidt, 2012).

Even though moral foundations theory does not explicitly rely on the dual-process model of the mind, when interpreted through the lens of the social intuitionist model, one might expect evidence for the five evolutionarily acquired moral foundations to be stronger for intuitively made judgments. However, recent evidence draws a more complicated picture. For example, directing conservatives to make intuitive moral judgments either via cognitive-load or ego depletion manipulations resulted in judgments to become more liberal (Wright & Baril, 2011). In addition, activating analytical thinking was found to strengthen some (e.g., care, fairness) but not all (e.g., loyalty, authority, sanctity) of the moral foundations (Yilmaz & Saribay, 2017b). Other studies have found, on the other hand, that priming intuition enhances the value given to the moral foundations of care and authority (Van Berkel et al., 2015).

In short, the emerging picture shows that people tend to rely on their moral intuitions but the specific effect of intuition and deliberation on moral judgments depends on which foundations are relevant in the context of the moral problem. There is consistent evidence that deliberation can strengthen endorsement of fairness and care foundations (Yilmaz & Saribay, 2017b). Nevertheless, a dual-process interpretation that encompasses the whole spectrum of moral judgments is not yet established. In particular, questions remain whether deliberated moral judgments reflect rationalizations of intuitive responses or whether they provide a more accurate account of their personally held moral views. It also remains to be established whether intuitive moral judgments reflect evolutionary visceral reactions or whether they exhibit culturally experienced social heuristics. A likely reason for these mixed results is that moral judgments have so far been mostly studied independently of the context of regular social interactions from which they likely have emerged. Most recently, the theory of *morality as cooperation* (Curry, Mullins, & Whitehouse, 2017) argues just that, predicting moral judgments to reflect cultural or evolutionary "solutions" to recurrent problems of cooperation. Indeed, behavioral research on the dual-process accounts of cooperation have provided significant insights into the role of intuition and deliberation in social life, which we now review.

Cooperative Intuitions

Cooperation is the act of working with others toward a common goal, such as expending effort to provide a public good (e.g., raising funds for a park in the local community) or curbing excess consumption for maintaining a common environmental resource (e.g., limiting one's CO_2 emissions). Although rightly seen as a defining feature of civilization, cooperation per se is not unique to humans: many other animals, in particular primates, cooperate with genetically unrelated others to gain future benefits and even positive reputation (Hauser, Chen, Chen, & Chuang, 2003). However, the scale of cooperation in human societies is second to none. More importantly, humans are characterized by a particular type of cooperation called *strong reciprocity*, which is not observed in other animals: cooperation with anonymous others at net personal cost even when reciprocal and reputational benefits are absent (Bowles & Gintis, 2011).

Evidence for this "strange" behavior is established using an experimental task called the public good game (PGG), which is regularly used to measure cooperation in social dilemma situations (Ledyard, 1995). In the PGG, each member of a group is asked to decide how much of an individual monetary endowment to contribute toward a group project and how much of it to keep for self (e.g., Fischbacher, Gächter, & Fehr, 2001). Importantly, contributing to the group project (i.e., the public good) in the PGG increases social welfare (i.e., the value of the project) while decreasing net personal earnings, thereby constituting a social dilemma (Dawes, 1980). Although standard theories of rational choice based on the assumption of pure self-regard predict absolutely no sharing of the endowment in the one-shot version of the PGG, participants in experimental studies across the globe have been found to routinely share large proportions of their endowment with anonymous others (Henrich et al., 2005).

This uniquely human trait of strong reciprocity can neither be explained by standard theories of evolution based on kinship, reciprocity, or reputation (Boyd & Richerson, 1989; Hamilton, 1964; Trivers, 1971). A widely accepted explanation of this phenomenon has been the idea that populations that culturally transmit a preference for strong reciprocity can gain benefits at the group level (Fehr & Fischbacher, 2003; Gintis, 2000). Given the likely evolutionary roots of strong reciprocity, alternative dual-process accounts of cooperation have also been proposed as explanations.

The predictions of these dual-process accounts of cooperation fall into one of two camps. A long line of research that we refer to here as *the self-control account* (SCA) argues that people are, mainly due to visceral reactions, intuitively selfish and that cognitive resources are needed to keep these urges under control in order to behave according to one's well-thought-out individual preferences or socially desirable ends (Hofmann, Friese, & Strack, 2009; Loewenstein, 1996; Metcalfe & Mischel, 1999; Myrseth & Fishbach, 2009). A more recent alternative, the self-labeled *social heuristics hypothesis* (SHH), instead posits that people often rely on prosocial heuristics and that they become more self-regarding with deliberation in social dilemmas (Bear & Rand, 2016; Rand, Greene, & Nowak, 2012; for an early formulation of SHH see Kiyonari, Tanida, & Yamagishi, 2000). While SCA is consistent with the explanation of strong reciprocity as a deliberated preference for achieving a socially desirable end, SHH assumes people to be strictly self-regarding and puts doubt on the evidence for strong reciprocity as a "misapplied" heuristic. So how does the current evidence weigh between the two accounts?

A long list of studies has sought to experimentally test SHH. As SHH predicts higher cooperation by System 1 as compared to System 2 processes, these studies primarily used cognitive process manipulation methods (e.g., time pressure, cognitive-load, or cognitive-resource depletion) to increase reliance on one or the other system and thus to compare intuitively made and deliberated PGG decisions. We focus here on the more prevalent method of comparing decisions under time pressure (for increasing heuristics use) and time delay (for inducing deliberation): while a large-scale multi-lab replication has recently failed to find a robust effect (Bouwmeester et al., 2017), the originating studies (Rand et al., 2012, 2014), other replication attempts (Everett, Ingbretsen, Cushman, & Cikara, 2017), and tests using improved methods (Isler, Maule, & Starmer, 2018) have found evidence for SHH. Indeed, a recent meta-analysis of time-pressure and other cognitive process manipulation studies have in the aggregate been shown to support SHH's prediction that intuition promotes cooperation in social dilemmas (Rand, 2016).

However, evidence against SHH remains non-negligible, and a broad range of experimental findings instead provide evidence for SCA. For example, extreme time pressure, which arguably is better equipped in inducing intuitive reactions compared to relatively long time limits that merely limit deliberation (Myrseth & Wollbrant, 2017), has been found to increase selfishness compared to a time-delay condition (Capraro & Cococcioni, 2016). In addition, a series of papers find positive correlation between cooperative behavior on the one hand and individual ability for self-control (Kocher, Martinsson, Myrseth, & Wollbrant, 2017; Martinsson, Myrseth, & Wollbrant, 2014), delayed gratification (Curry, Price, & Price, 2008; Fehr & Leibbrandt, 2011), and analytic thinking (Lohse, 2016) on the other. Similarly, supporting the idea that selfish impulses have free rein in the lack of cognitive resources for self-control, various other studies found that depletion of resources available for energy metabolism (DeWall, Baumeister, Gailliot, & Maner, 2008) and disruption of self-control related brain functions (Knoch, Pascual-Leone, Meyer, Treyer, & Fehr, 2006) weaken prosocial behavior. In a revealing study, younger children were found less likely to reject unfair offers, which is interpreted as a form of prosocial punishment of norm violators, not because they did not understand the norms in place but because the regions of their brains related to self-control were not yet fully developed (Steinbeis, Bernhardt, & Singer, 2012).

These conflicting findings for SHH and SCA imply that there may be missing moderators that are not taken into account in the aforementioned studies. A possible explanation is that past experiences forming social heuristics may be heterogeneous (Rand et al., 2014). Accordingly, people internalize prosocial heuristics if they are accustomed to environments that are conducive to cooperation but not when they are repeatedly exposed to situations where people act selfishly. Consistent with this explanation, people from relatively more cooperative environments (e.g., experimental participants from the U.S. who are not experienced with the one-shot PGGs) show intuitive cooperation, whereas those from relatively less cooperative backgrounds (e.g., participants from India with weaker institutions than the U.S. or participants who are experienced with one-shot PGGs where cooperation is a self-defeating strategy) do not have this prosocial tendency (Nishi, Christakis, & Rand, 2017; Rand et al., 2014; also see Peysakhovich & Rand, 2015; Santa, Exadaktylos, & Soto-Faraco, 2018).

Therefore, a more general perspective on the role of intuition and deliberation on cooperation suggests that the applicability of SHH and SCA may depend on whether people have internalized heuristics that are prosocial or selfish. Supporting this generalized account, a recent experimental study (Isler, Gächter, Maule, & Starmer, 2019) shows that deliberation increases cooperation when social dilemmas induce selfish heuristics (e.g., when cooperation involves maintaining an already existing common resource) but not when they induce prosocial heuristics (e.g., when it involves providing a previously nonexistent public good).

Discussion

So, can we rely on our intuitions? A comparison of the heuristics-and-biases, simple-heuristics, and naturalistic decision-making accounts indicated that expertise is built on regular feedback from a learning-friendly environment and that intuitions tend to be reliable when expertise matches the current decision environment. The question of whether intuitions can provide desirable judgments and behavior in moral and social dilemmas has a similar answer. Evidence on the dual-process accounts of cooperation indicates that both social heuristics and self-control may regulate intuitive cooperation to an extent dependent on the problem at hand (e.g., norms of strong reciprocity) and on the associations it may induce (e.g., selfish vs. prosocial heuristics). Likewise, the role of intuition and deliberation depends on which moral foundations are salient in the particular problem (e.g., hierarchy vs. fairness). Crucially, this overall result of context dependency does not imply a lack of systematic patterns of dependency. However, it implies the need for more research on the moderators and the boundary conditions regarding the consequences of intuitive and analytical thought processes. In conclusion, high returns should be expected from investigating the dual-process accounts of social and moral dilemmas, for example, in the managerial context.

References

Aktas, B., Yilmaz, O., & Bahçekapili, H. G. (2017). Moral pluralism on the trolley tracks: Different normative principles are used for different reasons in justifying moral judgments. *Judgment and Decision Making, 12,* 297–307.

Artinger, F., Petersen, M., Gigerenzer, G., & Weibler, J. (2015). Heuristics as adaptive decision strategies in management. *Journal of Organizational Behavior, 36*(S1), S33–S52.

Basel, J. S., & Brühl, R. (2013). Rationality and dual process models of reasoning in managerial cognition and decision making. *European Management Journal, 31*(6), 745–754.

Bear, A., & Rand, D. G. (2016). Intuition, deliberation, and the evolution of cooperation. *Proceedings of the National Academy of Sciences, 113*(4), 936–941.

Bouwmeester, S., Verkoeijen, P. P. J. L., Aczel, B., Barbosa, F., Bègue, L., Brañas-Garza, P., … Espín, A. M. (2017). Registered Replication Report: Rand, Greene, and Nowak (2012). *Perspectives on Psychological Science, 12*(3), 527–542.

Bowles, S., & Gintis, H. (2011). *A Cooperative Species: Human Reciprocity and Its Evolution.* Princeton, NJ: Princeton University Press.

Boyd, R., & Richerson, P. J. (1989). The evolution of indirect reciprocity. *Social Networks, 11*(3), 213–236.

Capraro, V., & Cococcioni, G. (2016). Rethinking spontaneous giving: Extreme time pressure and ego-depletion favor self-regarding reactions. *Scientific Reports, 6,* 27219.

Curry, O. S., Mullins, D. A., & Whitehouse, H. (2017). Is it good to cooperate? Testing the theory of morality-as-cooperation in 60 societies. *Current Anthropology 60*(1), 47–69.

Curry, O. S., Price, M. E., & Price, J. G. (2008). Patience is a virtue: Cooperative people have lower discount rates. *Personality and Individual Differences, 44*(3), 780–785.

Dawes, R. M. (1980). Social dilemmas. *Annual Review of Psychology, 31*(1), 169–193.

DeMiguel, V., Garlappi, L., & Uppal, R. (2007). Optimal versus naive diversification: How inefficient is the 1/N portfolio strategy? *The Review of Financial Studies, 22*(5), 1915–1953.

DeWall, C. N., Baumeister, R. F., Gailliot, M. T., & Maner, J. K. (2008). Depletion makes the heart grow less helpful: Helping as a function of self-regulatory energy and genetic relatedness. *Personality and Social Psychology Bulletin, 34*(12), 1653–1662.

Evans, J. S. B. T. (2008). Dual-processing accounts of reasoning, judgment, and social cognition. *Annual Review of Psychology, 59,* 255–278.

Everett, J. A. C., Ingbretsen, Z., Cushman, F., & Cikara, M. (2017). Deliberation erodes cooperative behavior—Even towards competitive out-groups, even when using a control condition, and even when eliminating selection bias. *Journal of Experimental Social Psychology, 73,* 76–81.

Fehr, E., & Fischbacher, U. (2003). The nature of human altruism. *Nature, 425*(6960), 785–791.

Fehr, E., & Leibbrandt, A. (2011). A field study on cooperativeness and impatience in the tragedy of the commons. *Journal of Public Economics, 95*(9–10), 1144–1155.

Fischbacher, U., Gächter, S., & Fehr, E. (2001). Are people conditionally cooperative? Evidence from a public goods experiment. *Economics Letters, 71*(3), 397–404.

Fiske, S. T., & Taylor, S. E. (2013). *Social Cognition: From Brains to Culture.* Los Angeles, CA: Sage Publications.

Gigerenzer, G. (2008). Why heuristics work. *Perspectives on Psychological Science, 3*(1), 20–29.

Gigerenzer, G., Hertwig, R., & Pachur, T. (2011). *Heuristics.* New York: Oxford University Press.

Gigerenzer, G., Todd, P. M., & ABC Research Group. (1999). *Simple Heuristics That Make Us Smart.* Oxford, UK: Oxford University Press.

Gintis, H. (2000). Strong reciprocity and human sociality. *Journal of Theoretical Biology*, *206*(2), 169–179.

Graham, J., Haidt, J., & Nosek, B. A. (2009). Liberals and conservatives rely on different sets of moral foundations. *Journal of Personality and Social Psychology*, *96*(5), 1029.

Graham, J., Nosek, B. A., Haidt, J., Iyer, R., Koleva, S., & Ditto, P. H. (2011). Mapping the moral domain. *Journal of Personality and Social Psychology*, *101*(2), 366.

Greene, J. D. (2007). The secret joke of Kant's soul, in Sinnott-Armstrong, W. (ed.), *Moral Psychology, Vol. 3: The Neuroscience of Morality: Emotion, Disease, and Development*. Cambridge, MA: MIT Press.

Greene, J. D. (2007). Why are VMPFC patients more utilitarian? A dual-process theory of moral judgment explains. *Trends in Cognitive Sciences*, *11*(8), 322–323.

Greene, J. D., Sommerville, R. B., Nystrom, L. E., Darley, J. M., & Cohen, J. D. (2001). An fMRI investigation of emotional engagement in moral judgment. *Science*, *293*(5537), 2105–2108.

Haidt, J. (2001). The emotional dog and its rational tail: A social intuitionist approach to moral judgment. *Psychological Review*, *108*(4), 814.

Haidt, J. (2007). The new synthesis in moral psychology. *Science*, *316*(5827), 998–1002.

Haidt, J. (2012). *The Righteous Mind: Why Good People Are Divided by Politics and Religion*. Vintage.

Hamilton, W. D. (1964). The genetical evolution of social behaviour. I. *Journal of Theoretical Biology*, *7*(1), 1–16.

Hauser, M. D., Chen, M. K., Chen, F., & Chuang, E. (2003). Give unto others: Genetically unrelated cotton-top tamarin monkeys preferentially give food to those who altruistically give food back. *Proceedings of the Royal Society of London. Series B: Biological Sciences*, *270*(1531), 2363–2370.

Henrich, J., Boyd, R., Bowles, S., Camerer, C., Fehr, E., Gintis, H., … Ensminger, J. (2005). "Economic man" in cross-cultural perspective: Behavioral experiments in 15 small-scale societies. *Behavioral and Brain Sciences*, *28*(6), 795–815.

Hodgkinson, G. P., Bown, N. J., Maule, A. J., Glaister, K. W., & Pearman, A. D. (1999). Breaking the frame: An analysis of strategic cognition and decision making under uncertainty. *Strategic Management Journal*, *20*(10), 977–985.

Hofmann, W., Friese, M., & Strack, F. (2009). Impulse and self-control from a dual-systems perspective. *Perspectives on Psychological Science*, *4*(2), 162–176.

Isler, O., Gächter, S., Maule, J., & Starmer, C. (2019). Intuitions and deliberated strong reciprocity explain cooperation in maintenance and provision dilemmas. Manuscript submitted for publication.

Isler, O., Maule, J., & Starmer, C. (2018). Is intuition really cooperative? Improved tests support the social heuristics hypothesis. *PloS One*, *13*(1), e0190560.

Kahane, G., Everett, J. A. C., Earp, B. D., Farias, M., & Savulescu, J. (2015). 'Utilitarian' judgments in sacrificial moral dilemmas do not reflect impartial concern for the greater good. *Cognition*, *134*, 193–209.

Kahneman, D. (2011). *Thinking, Fast and Slow*. London: Macmillan.

Kahneman, D., & Klein, G. (2009). Conditions for intuitive expertise: A failure to disagree. *American Psychologist*, *64*(6), 515.

Kahneman, D., & Tversky, A. (1979). Prospect theory: An analysis of decision under risk. *Econometrica*, *47*(2), 263–291.

Khatri, N., & Ng, H. A. (2000). The role of intuition in strategic decision making. *Human Relations*, *53*(1), 57–86.

Kiyonari, T., Tanida, S., & Yamagishi, T. (2000). Social exchange and reciprocity: Confusion or a heuristic? *Evolution and Human Behavior, 21*(6), 411–427.

Klein, G. (2008). Naturalistic decision making. *Human Factors, 50*(3), 456–460.

Klein, G. A. (1993). *A Recognition-Primed Decision (RPD) Model of Rapid Decision Making.* New York: Ablex Publishing Corporation.

Klein, G. A., Calderwood, R., & Clinton-Cirocco, A. (1986). Rapid decision making on the fire ground, in *Proceedings of the Human Factors Society Annual Meeting* (Vol. 30, pp. 576–580). Los Angeles, CA: Sage Publications.

Knoch, D., Pascual-Leone, A., Meyer, K., Treyer, V., & Fehr, E. (2006). Diminishing reciprocal fairness by disrupting the right prefrontal cortex. *Science, 314*(5800), 829–832.

Kocher, M. G., Martinsson, P., Myrseth, K. O. R., & Wollbrant, C. E. (2017). Strong, bold, and kind: Self-control and cooperation in social dilemmas. *Experimental Economics, 20*(1), 44–69.

Koenigs, M., Young, L., Adolphs, R., Tranel, D., Cushman, F., Hauser, M., & Damasio, A. (2007). Damage to the prefrontal cortex increases utilitarian moral judgements. *Nature, 446*(7138), 908.

Kohlberg, L., & Kohlberg, L. (1969). Stage and sequence: The cognitive-developmental approach to socialization, in Goslin, D. A. (ed.), *Handbook of Socialization: Theory and Research.* Chicago: McNally.

Koudstaal, M., Sloof, R., & van Praag, M. (2018). Entrepreneurs: İntuitive or contemplative decision-makers? *Small Business Economics,* 1–20.

Ledyard, J. (1995). Public goods: A survey of experimental research, in *Handbook of Experimental Economics.* doi:10.1016/0037-7856(73)90129-7.

Li, J., & Tang, Y. I. (2010). CEO hubris and firm risk taking in China: The moderating role of managerial discretion. *Academy of Management Journal, 53*(1), 45–68.

Loewenstein, G. (1996). Out of control: Visceral influences on behavior. *Organizational Behavior and Human Decision Processes, 65*(3), 272–292.

Lohse, J. (2016). Smart or selfish–When smart guys finish nice. *Journal of Behavioral and Experimental Economics, 64,* 28–40.

Loock, M., & Hinnen, G. (2015). Heuristics in organizations: A review and a research agenda. *Journal of Business Research, 68*(9), 2027–2036.

Martinsson, P., Myrseth, K. O. R., & Wollbrant, C. (2014). Social dilemmas: When self-control benefits cooperation. *Journal of Economic Psychology, 45,* 213–236.

Metcalfe, J., & Mischel, W. (1999). A hot/cool-system analysis of delay of gratification: Dynamics of willpower. *Psychological Review, 106*(1), 3.

Mill, J. S. (1863). *Utilitarianism.* London: Parker, Son and Bourn.

Myrseth, K. O. R., & Fishbach, A. (2009). Self-control: A function of knowing when and how to exercise restraint. *Current Directions in Psychological Science, 18*(4), 247–252.

Myrseth, K. O. R., & Wollbrant, C. E. (2017). Cognitive foundations of cooperation revisited: Commentary on Rand et al.(2012, 2014). *Journal of Behavioral and Experimental Economics, 69,* 133–138.

Napier, J. L., & Luguri, J. B. (2013). Moral mind-sets: Abstract thinking increases a preference for "individualizing" over "binding" moral foundations. *Social Psychological and Personality Science, 4*(6), 754–759.

Nishi, A., Christakis, N. A., & Rand, D. G. (2017). Cooperation, decision time, and culture: Online experiments with American and Indian participants. *PloS One, 12*(2), e0171252.

Parikh, J., Neubauer, F.-F., & Lank, A. G. (1994). *Intuition: The New Frontier of Management.* Blackwell.

Paxton, J. M., Ungar, L., & Greene, J. D. (2012). Reflection and reasoning in moral judgment. *Cognitive Science, 36*(1), 163–177.

Peysakhovich, A., & Rand, D. G. (2015). Habits of virtue: Creating norms of cooperation and defection in the laboratory. *Management Science, 62*(3), 631–647.

Piaget, J. (1965). *The Moral Judgment of the Child (1932).* New York: The Free Press.

Rand, D. G. (2016). Cooperation, fast and slow: Meta-analytic evidence for a theory of social heuristics and self-interested deliberation. *Psychological Science, 27*(9), 1192–1206.

Rand, D. G., Greene, J. D., & Nowak, M. A. (2012). Spontaneous giving and calculated greed. *Nature, 489*(7416), 427.

Rand, D. G., Peysakhovich, A., Kraft-Todd, G. T., Newman, G. E., Wurzbacher, O., Nowak, M. A., & Greene, J. D. (2014). Social heuristics shape intuitive cooperation. *Nature Communications, 5*, 3677.

Rosenzweig, P. M. (2007). *The Halo Effect—And the Eight Other Business Delusions That Deceive Managers.* New York: The Free Press.

Sadler-Smith, E., & Shefy, E. (2004). The intuitive executive: Understanding and applying 'gut feel'in decision-making. *Academy of Management Perspectives, 18*(4), 76–91.

Santa, J. C., Exadaktylos, F., & Soto-Faraco, S. (2018). Beliefs about others' intentions determine whether cooperation is the faster choice. *Scientific Reports, 8*(1), 7509.

Sapolsky, R. M. (2017). *Behave: The Biology of Humans at Our Best and Worst.* Penguin.

Shweder, R., Much, N., Mahapatra, M., & Park, L. (1997). Divinity and the "big three" explanations of suffering. *Morality and Health, 119*, 119–169.

Simon, M., Houghton, S. M., & Aquino, K. (2000). Cognitive biases, risk perception, and venture formation: How individuals decide to start companies. *Journal of Business Venturing, 15*(2), 113–134.

Steinbeis, N., Bernhardt, B. C., & Singer, T. (2012). Impulse control and underlying functions of the left DLPFC mediate age-related and age-independent individual differences in strategic social behavior. *Neuron, 73*(5), 1040–1051.

Thomson, K. S., & Oppenheimer, D. M. (2016). Investigating an alternate form of the cognitive reflection test. *Judgment and Decision Making, 11*(1), 99.

Trémolière, B., De Neys, W., & Bonnefon, J.-F. (2012). Mortality salience and morality: Thinking about death makes people less utilitarian. *Cognition, 124*(3), 379–384.

Trivers, R. L. (1971). The evolution of reciprocal altruism. *The Quarterly Review of Biology, 46*(1), 35–57.

Tversky, A., & Kahneman, D. (1974). Judgment under uncertainty: Heuristics and biases. *Science, 185*(4157).

Tversky, A., & Kahneman, D. (1983). Extensional versus intuitive reasoning: The conjunction fallacy in probability judgment. *Psychological Review, 90*(4), 293.

Van Berkel, L., Crandall, C. S., Eidelman, S., & Blanchar, J. C. (2015). Hierarchy, dominance, and deliberation: Egalitarian values require mental effort. *Personality and Social Psychology Bulletin, 41*(9), 1207–1222.

Wright, J. C., & Baril, G. (2011). The role of cognitive resources in determining our moral intuitions: Are we all liberals at heart? *Journal of Experimental Social Psychology, 47*(5), 1007–1012.

Yilmaz, O., & Saribay, S. A. (2017a). Activating analytic thinking enhances the value given to individualizing moral foundations. *Cognition, 165*, 88–96.

Yilmaz, O., & Saribay, S. A. (2017b). Analytic thought training promotes liberalism on contextualized (but not stable) political opinions. *Social Psychological and Personality Science, 8*(7), 789–795.

Chapter 7

Integrating Reason and Intuition: An Integrative Approach to Objectivizing Subtle Cues

Sharda S. Nandram, Gaëtan Mourmant,
Puneet K. Bindlish, and Danny Sandra

Contents

Introduction

Decision-making models suggest that decisions are only partly based on rational analyses. In fact, they are often a combination of rational and non-rational analyses, where the latter is still considered a black box and, therefore, rarely addressed in the business context. In a recent study, Nandram et al. (2018a) tried to explore this black box using an inductive approach to study the interplay between rational and intuitive decision-making.

Nandram et al. (2018a), who followed the classic grounded theory approach, studied entrepreneurs from the United States and Europe. They developed the theory of objectivizing subtle cues (OSC) as an explanation for how entrepreneurs make decisions when they do not have the data needed for rational analyses, when there is an overload of information, or when there is no data available at all.

Based on Nandram et al. (2018a), we define subtle cues as *conscious and unconscious emotions, thoughts, perceptions, and information.* Moreover, we define OSC as *the process of discovering, following, and making use of subtle cues.* This process has three important steps, starting with (1) becoming aware of the need to objectivize subtle cues and subsequently set up enablers for receiving those cues. This leads to (2) attuning to and being able to experience the cues. Finally, the decision maker (3) validates the cues, decides what to do with them, and observes the impact of any actions taken. The full model is explained in more detail based on research on decision-making in the clinical nursing setting.

OSC may be a relevant decision-making process for many professional fields. It does not create the split typically seen in the literature between decisions based on rational information and decisions based on intuitive information. It moves away from that discussion and creates the opportunity to think about how to enhance the use of subtle cues as a "neutral" input for information processing among professionals. Important questions that executives and managers have in this regard are the following: "How can we enable our subordinates to use subtle cues for decision-making?" and "What might be the consequences of using subtle cues?"

The emergence of subtle cues influenced by internal enablers can be trained by the organization, but these cues may need a long period of time to have an impact and they may be dependent on individual factors, such as personalities, attitudes, worldviews, and background. From a business perspective, it is important to facilitate the OSC process, as it may lead to better, more effective, and more efficient decisions.

Therefore, a CEO would encourage the use of subtle cues. However, he would probably choose to encourage subtle cues which are influenced externally, as that would be an area he could quickly influence compared to the cues that have an internal source. Therefore, the research questions that are addressed in this chapter are: "How are reason and intuition used together in the professional nursing setting?" and "How can organizations create a context that favors the process of objectivizing subtle cues?". The home-care nursing setting offers the potential place for significant interplay between rational and intuitive inputs for decision-making.

To address our research questions, we use data from a case study of Buurtzorg, a healthcare organization in the Netherlands. Buurtzorg works with around 14,000 nurses in a self-managed organizational structure. This case offers numerous examples of decision-making under various contexts. Buurtzorg's teams of 8 to 12 nurses make a range of decisions, from trivial to crucial, on their own. In a typical intrapreneurial fashion, they are responsible for the entire chain of care (e.g., setting up the team, finding clients, planning, coordinating) in the context of home care. To be able to work successfully, the organization has introduced certain enablers. The self-management structure is the main enabler, and it stimulates certain behaviors in which the nurses use many types of cues in order to deliver the best possible care in less time and at a lower cost than competitors. One such behavior is an integrating simplification approach, which uses the "needing," "re-thinking," and "common-sense" principles to arrange tasks and purposes (Nandram, 2015). The needs of the client serve as the starting point for the work, but there is a continuous process of re-thinking ways of improving the work while keeping the client at the center of care. Moreover, common sense is required in the overall decision-making process. These principles are a manifestation of a climate in which integrative intelligence is fostered with a minimum of conditioning (Nandram et al., 2017, 2018b). The implications of this enabler for the ways in which nurses arrange their tasks and strive to realize their goals are examined in this chapter.

Literature Review

The term *intuition* is derived from the Latin *intueri*, which means "to look upon." The Oxford dictionary defines intuition as "immediate apprehension by the mind without reasoning; immediate apprehension by a sense; immediate insight" (1990). Dane and Pratt (2007, p. 40) provide a universal definition for the management context: "affectively charged judgments that arise through rapid, non-conscious, and holistic associations." There are also more spiritually infused approaches to intuition. For example, Nandram (2017) discusses the Vedantic approach to intuition and concludes that it is a part of knowledge that comes from a spiritual level of consciousness, which is called the intuitive mind. Everyone has access to this intuition, but its applicability in the professional context depends on the intensity with which the mind is cleared using spiritual techniques (Nandram, 2017). Since the topic of spirituality has entered the business and management field, this broader perspective may provide new insights into the role of intuition in decision-making. However, the more important question is the following: What does the literature on intuition tell us about the conditions that influence an intuitive decision-making process?

Internal-conditions scholars have focused on several key areas as enhancing the use of intuitive decision-making (Table 7.1). These areas are mainly in the cognitive realm, as they are related to information processing. What are the internal enablers that entrepreneurs have mentioned in relation to the theory of OSC? In this regard, we again derive insights from Nandram et al. (2018a). Entrepreneurs used several types of internal enablers, such as trusting, letting go of fear, surrendering to what they sense within themselves about what is being asked, and accepting what is happening without judgments. These areas are all in the affective dimension, but there are also enablers in the cognitive dimension. In this respect, entrepreneurs mentioned such enablers as the belief that we need the mind, rational thinking, and the memory to help to trace subtle processes. Entrepreneurs also stated that certain behavioral conditions are required to let subtle cues emerge, including a courageous attitude, a willingness to leave the comfort zone, adoption of a third-person position to look at oneself and the business, and the ability to step back and be comfortable in silence.

Scholars have also addressed the implications of using intuition for decision-making. Such implications include development of capacities for rapid response, a capacity for direct immediate knowledge, insight skills, and foreknowledge (Table 7.2).

Table 7.1 Internal Enablers of Intuitive Decision-Making

Authors	Conditions That Influence Intuitive Decision-Making
Simon (1987), p. 63	Deliberate development of a vast repository of patterns in memory
Kahneman (2003), p. 697	Domain-sensitive expertise
Jung (1933), p. 567–568	Individual differences in thinking styles
Raidl and Lubart (2001)	Sensing information which brings cohesiveness in perception
Agor (1989)	Ability to interpret body language
Mitchel et al. (2005), p. 667	Closeness to consciousness of an opportunity
Allinson et al. (2000) and Shapiro and Spence (1997)	Understanding unstructured problems and the complexity of systems
Prietula and Simon (1989), p. 59	Implicit learning ability
Klein (2002)	Ability to make use of highly complex schema with domain relevance

Table 7.2   The Effects of Intuitive Decision-Making on Information Processing

Authors	Results of Using Intuition for Information Processing
Simon (1987), p. 63	Rapid-response capacity
Myers (2002), p. 128–129	Capacity for direct immediate knowledge
Waters (1980)	Insight skills
La Pira and Gillin (2006)	An understanding of the broader picture of events or opportunities
Agor (1989)	Logical skills
Rosenblatt and Thickstun (1994)	Intuitive cognition
Bradley (2006)	Foreknowledge
Rowan et al. (1986), p. 82; Holland and Baird (1968); Balthazard (1985); and Lewicki et al. (1992)	Knowledge without rational thought
Rotry (1967), p. 204	Apprehension
Policastro (1999), p. 89	Direction for decision-making
Bunge (1962)	Ability
Vaughan (1979)	Total comprehension
Shapiro and Spence (1997), p. 64	Judgment
Bowers et al. (1990), p. 74; Bastick (1982); and Epstein (1998)	Conclusions about the overall issue
Prietula and Simon (1989), p. 59	Expertise
Klein (2002)	Activities based on past experiences

In OSC theory, the implications are mentioned under the concepts of "attunement," "intuiting," and "sensing." This chapter's second research question, which relates to how to create a context that favors the OSC process, can be framed as: "What are the possible external enablers and what could be their consequences for the decision-making process?". One type of enabler that can be used to facilitate OSC is a learning structure. Hogarth (2001) mentions a learning structure as an external condition for facilitating intuition. In this regard, we propose the learning structure of integrative intelligence with deconditioning. To examine this structure, we use the Buurtzorg case.

Methodology

For this study, we conducted in-depth, face-to-face interviews with five nurses from the Dutch home-care organization Buurtzorg. The nurses were part of three different teams. We also observed two team meetings. Moreover, we used secondary data in order to understand the decision-making process among nurses in the home-care setting. In particular, we used the manual describing and explaining how the decision-making process was organized, and how the nurses in this organization worked in self-managed teams (Nandram, 2015). Additional texts in Dutch describing the client-centric approach at Buurtzorg were also utilized (Van Dalen, 2010, 2012; de Blok et al., 2010; Pool et al., 2011).

To code the data from the interviews and the manuals, we used the approach to coding found in the grounded theory methodology (Glaser & Strauss, 1967). The first two authors coded the available material separately and then discussed their coding with each other in order to build a coherent understanding. The third and fourth authors functioned as a sounding board to ensure that the understanding could be articulated well. Based on these inputs, the full model was developed. Our aim was to derive detailed insights into how external enablers influence decision-making and how nurses gain access to subtle cues for their decision-making processes.

Results: An Enhanced Model of Objectivizing Subtle Cues

In this section, we discuss the full model, which integrates both the initial research (Nandram et al., 2018a) and our new findings. Due to space limitations, the initial model has been simplified and summarized, but it can be found in Nandram et al. (2018a). We chose this form of presentation to ensure a coherent model for the reader.

The full model is described in Figure 7.1. In line with Nandram et al. (2018a), we define subtle cues as *conscious and unconscious emotions, thoughts, perceptions, and information*. OSC is defined as *the process of discovering, following, and making use of subtle cues*. The model encompasses three steps, each of which consists of several sub-processes.

The application of the OSC model to the nursing work at Buurtzorg was a fruitful process, which resulted in the emergence or new usage of the following constructs:

- A structure for deconditioning the mind, which is an external enabler
- A third strategy, which is described as a multilevel, dynamic, holistic perception
- Entrainment and holistic attunement

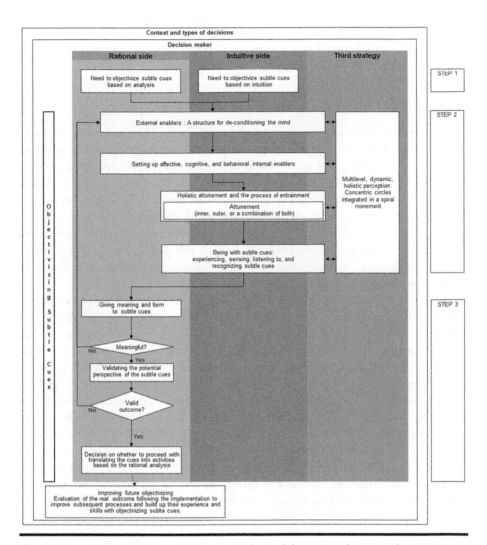

Figure 7.1 Objectivizing subtle cues. (Adapted from Nandram et al., 2018a.)

In the following, we provide more in-depth descriptions of the steps in the OSC process model.

Step 1: Awareness of the Need to Objectivize Subtle Cues

The model starts with the need to use subtle cues and, subsequently, the introduction of enablers for receiving those cues. This need could arise from the impossibility of conducting a purely rational analysis owing to an overload or lack of rational input in a certain situation. It could occur if one's intuition contradicts the results of a rational analysis. A statement made by an entrepreneur highlights this point: "My intuition says I should do something different, something that is in contrast to the rational path."

Step 2: A Multilevel, Dynamic, Holistic Perception

There are various strategies to cope with the subtle cues. A person may be triggered by earlier cues which may be stored somewhere in the memory and which may lead to new cues (rational realm mainly using expert intuition). Another strategy could be experiencing the subtle cues as instinctive reflexes (intuitive realm). We then consider a third strategy, which leads to a multilevel, dynamic, holistic perception. This strategy is pursued in parallel and in interaction with the sub-processes of establishing (1) external and (2) internal enablers, which lead to (3) a holistic attunement supported by the process of entrainment. The last sub-process in step 2 is (4) being with the subtle cues, i.e., experiencing, sensing, listening, and recognizing them. We first discuss this third strategy.

One important concept that emerged from the analysis of the interviews was "multilevel, dynamic, holistic perception," which occurs early on in the use of subtle cues in the context of a nurse working at a patient's residence. As mentioned earlier, decision-making is often a combination of rational and non-rational (or intuitive) analysis. However, in the nursing context, there may be conflicting cues. One nurse provided an example: "When I saw the client, I felt something, but the image I got when I checked the medical reports was something else. They did not match." This reflects a multilevel, dynamic, holistic perception, which leads to a dynamic process of scanning cues in opposite directions and, on that basis, arriving at an integrative, coherent interpretation. This strategy requires empathizing with the person that the decision-making concerns. In this study, these focal actors were the clients and their situations. The process is iterative and interactive, and it is characterized by a close relationship between the client's input and the input of the decision maker (i.e., the nurse).

This process has two possible directions. One is the sensing of a mismatch, followed by a scanning of the external and rational cues, and a slow move toward more internal cues. The decision maker interacts with the client, lets the client share, and then finds coherency among the various cues. The other possible result is the sensing of one's own feeling as a starting point, followed by the collection of more cues by interacting with the client. This can result in a mismatch with one's own feeling or a confirmation of that feeling, thereby leading to the collection of more cues from the external context in order to have a more comprehensive understanding of the situation. Ideally, both scanning processes are used, leading to several types of entrainment and, ideally, to coherence in the understanding of the situation.

We now describe this process in more detail.

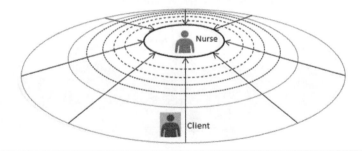

Figure 7.2   The outside-inside circle.

Two Concentric Circles

The concept of multilevel, dynamic, holistic perception can be described as two concentric circles in an iterative, dynamic interaction process. The first concentric circle moves from outside to inside (Figure 7.2). We call this the outside-inside circle. The nurse starts by scanning the given context and perceiving several cues. The nurse does so holistically while focusing on the client and incorporating the broader canvas around the client. In this process, the nurse works iteratively to try to understand the situation.

We call the second concentric circle, which moves from inside to outside (Figure 7.3), the inside-outside circle. The nurse has his or her own feelings and experiences from the past, which provide subtle cues. He or she brings those cues together to determine the best solution for the client in the given context. This process also works iteratively.

The concentric circles suit the dynamism and flexibility of the actors involved in the decision-making process. When the two circles reach an equilibrium, a holistic perception is achieved (Figure 7.4). This holistic perception is dynamic, as new elements are constantly incorporated.

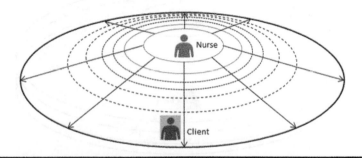

Figure 7.3   The inside-outside circle.

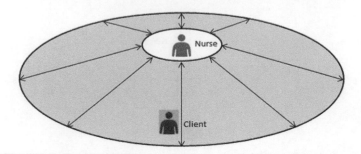

Figure 7.4 The integration of the two circles: Holistic perception.

Multilevel, Dynamic, Holistic Perception: Concentric Circles Integrated in a Spiral Movement

The circles function on different levels, including the emotional (e.g., empathy) and physical (e.g., smells, visual cues) levels. The nurses integrate the outcomes of the circles through an iterative process that spirals from the bottom up and from the top down over time (Figure 7.5). This process is a spiral movement because it involves continuous interactions between the circles at each level and at each point in time. We describe two examples of such movement in the following sections.

The Outside-Inside Circle

The professional psychological contract is already present as a given with the aim of helping the client in the best possible way. This connection starts with certain cues that result from visible facts and reasoning. Some nurses who enter a client's home to complete the intake process quickly perceive whether the client is one who will fit them well, and they quickly know that other clients would be best matched with

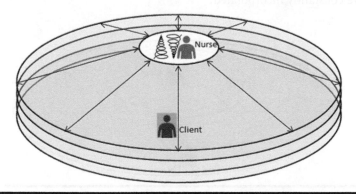

Figure 7.5 Multilevel, dynamic, holistic perception: concentric circles integrated in a spiral movement.

one of their colleagues. In the outside-inside concentric circle, the movement is from certain cues based on feelings. When those cues interact with facts, new cues arise, which leads to actions.

THE OUTSIDE-INSIDE CIRCLE

I can just look at someone: the posture, the tension, whether she is in pain, her preferences, her value system. How does she live? Who are the other family members?

My own emotions also tell me which cues I am receiving—how I can act and what I can ask.

I cannot just see or just listen. It is a whole. Only by considering all of the cues can I do something with them. I am there for the clients. I have time for them. They feel that I am there for them.

It is a combination of listening and seeing. I cannot give the same advice on the phone. I have to see the person. I have to be there to sense the whole.

The Inside-Outside Circle

In the inside-outside second concentric circle, the movement is from the feelings—relationships have to be built, and other family members and professionals have to be instructed, contacted, or heard. Things have to be arranged within the given canvas. New insights are slowly gained as to whether the decisions made are the best for that situation, client, and medical issue.

THE INSIDE-OUTSIDE CIRCLE

There are situations in which there is a mismatch between facts and feelings. For example, I had taken care of a client. Although I had a day off, I had to go to see the client to give her something. I felt it could not wait until the next day.

I went there in the evening and she was not doing well. I started to think about possible reasons. I studied the report and read what my colleagues had written. She had diarrhea. She had not eaten. She felt nauseous but did not vomit. All signals in the nurses' reports indicated the flu.

I had come to give her something but decided to stay for a chat. She was talking to me and I noticed that something else was going on—she was different than usual. Of course, I knew she was sick but there was no agreement between what was in the report and the image I had of her there.

Suddenly, I asked: Are you feeling tightness in your chest? She indicated that she was.

After I had asked the question, she started to pay more attention to her own signals. Ten minutes later I called the doctor's office. In the meantime, things progressed, as did the feeling that something was wrong. The doctor came and it ended in an emergency admission to the hospital.

My patient had experienced a heart attack. It had been festering all day. When I sat down and talked with her, it became apparent. Just by being there, I was able to understand that something completely different was going on than the records indicated. For the same reasons, I would have seen it as a flu at another time. There is something that happens to you emotionally. I cannot explain it. The signals differed from what I read. It is difficult to say exactly what it was—maybe it was her movements or her odor or her sweating or the fact that she was restless while talking to me. I do not know, but there are many things you look at and take into account. Something provides a signal, so that we see it differently at times. At other times, you immediately get to the right signal. That is why continuously identifying these things is important in our job.

The process of decision-making in both instances is about seeking out the boundaries and perceiving subtle cues, and iteratively matching those cues with previous knowledge, insights, and feelings. Does it feel right? Am I doing the best thing given the context and the client? If not, what should I adjust in the process or the context? Do I need to slow down or move faster? Do I need to focus on the short term (e.g., with terminally ill patients) or should I also consider the longer term?

Partial or Full Coherence as the Outcome

Both movements are part of the decision-making process and lead to coherence, at least to some extent. This coherence is not correct or incorrect. Instead, it is simply the coherence that can be achieved in that particular context. Everyone must trust that each nurse has followed the best possible decision-making steps. When a nurse informs other team members of how a decision was made and its consequences, everyone—including the nurse who made the decision—takes time for reflection. This leads to new learning and an analysis of whether it was the best decision. However, there is no point in judging the decision with regard to that particular case, which has already been solved. Instead, the discussion is helpful for learning purposes.

In parallel and in interaction with this multilevel, dynamic, holistic perception, other sub-processes are in action. We discuss those processes in the next section.

Step 3: Introducing Enablers, Holistic Attunement, and Being with Subtle Cues

A Structure for Deconditioning the Mindset: An External Enabler

We distinguish between two types of enablers: external enablers and internal enablers. We first discuss an important external enabler that emerged from the Buurtzorg case: the deconditioning process.

The theory of conditioning was developed by Nobel Prize winner Pavlov (1906). In conditioning, a natural stimulus is replaced to evoke certain behavior. Pavlov used an experimental setup focused on the quantity of saliva generated in a dog's mouth, which he measured under different conditions. As dogs depend on food for survival, the presence of food naturally causes salivation. The food is an unconditioned, or natural, stimulus. Pavlov used a bell to replace that natural stimulus in his experiments. The first time he used the bell, it did not cause salivation, as it was a neutral stimulus. However, when he repeatedly offered food while ringing the bell, the dog started to salivate. After a while, the food was no longer required to induce salivation—the sound of the bell sufficed. This process is called conditioning.

Conditioning can happen explicitly and implicitly through, for instance, processes, policies, guidelines, organizational workflows, and IT systems. Conditioning is not good or bad on its own. Instead, the quantity and quality of these processes, policies, guidelines, organizational workflows, and IT systems are dynamically assessed by the organization. Nandram et al. (2018b) studied conditioning in the context of Buurtzorg. They suggest that this dynamic assessment requires a certain form of intelligence, which they term "integrative intelligence." They define integrative intelligence as the ability to pursue a holistic understanding for decision-making and action-taking (Nandram et al., 2017). It implies an ability to discern how much individual intelligence and systems intelligence can be built into the organizational design while maintaining the natural, instinctive responses of employees and others involved in the organization's context.

In their study of Buurtzorg, Nandram et al. (2018b) conclude that the more an organization embodies integrative intelligence, the greater is its tendency to exhibit an organizational design characterized by self-managed organizational structures and decision-making authority decentralized to its employees. In such situations, extensive conditioning is usually not necessary (See Figure 7.6). They stress that as integrative intelligence is an innate human ability, many forms of conditioning can have a negative impact on that intelligence and, subsequently, one's ability to be part of a self-managed organization.

The study of decision-making at Buurtzorg led to the emergence of the concept of deconditioning the mindset through the structure of self-management. Nandram (2015) explained this in detail and addressed the various dimensions: an entrepreneurial context, consideration of work as a craft, attunement to the needs of clients by putting them at the center, simplified IT systems, and leadership focused on a higher collective purpose. This context can be described as encompassing mindful tasks, holistic perceptions, intra- or entrepreneurial freedom, autonomy, independence, "waking up people," "jack-of-all-trades," self-control teams, promotion of willingness to try or to participate, "replacement of bureaucracy with humanity," and fostering. How much individual intelligence and systems intelligence is required for the effective and efficient functioning of the organization depends on the amount of conditioning present in the organization's worldview.

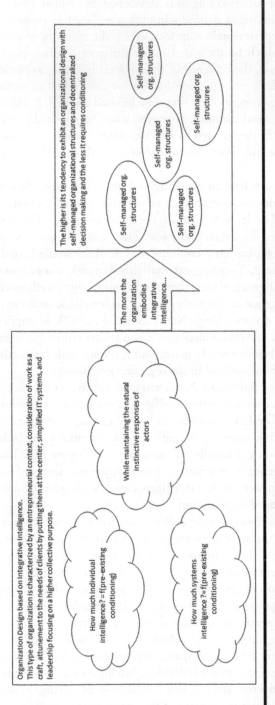

Figure 7.6 Deconditioning an organization.

The implication of deconditioning through a self-managed structure is that nurses rely on more kinds of input for their work. It also results in an increase in OSC compared to a more traditional and hierarchical organizational structure. The following quotes from the interviews illustrate how the nurses work in the self-management context.

CLIENT, RATHER THAN CARE, AT THE CENTER

There is no rulebook for hiring decisions. This is a very important decision for the whole team. It is a holistic process. The person should fit into the team and make the team more complete. There are criteria related to the professional expertise that is required to work as a nurse. However, that is not enough. A fit with the Buurtzorg philosophy is important, but there is also such a thing as the team philosophy. We need to see the total picture and all of the capacities, experiences, and personalities of all of our colleagues before deciding what we would expect from a new colleague. The person should see the client, and not care, as the main focus.

TRUSTING OTHERS

We need people who can fit into our atmosphere of trust. We all trust that the others have made well-considered decisions. If a decision turns out to be wrong, then we still have to support that individual. We then rely on the analysis of what went wrong and why.

We are all educated to deal with all types of care-related issues. However, you need more when you are in the field. We have our expertise and our experience. If you do not know how to deal with a certain situation, there are team members to ask and even a general practitioner whom you can call.

FREEDOM AND RESPONSIBILITY GO HAND IN HAND

At Buurtzorg, a nurse should be able to cope with the freedom that comes with the self-managed structure. It does not tell you how to do things or how to organize your work. However, you are responsible for your activities as a team. You have the responsibility to make it all happen together. There is no one else to go to. You have to solve things as a team.

We have a lot of decision-making power within the safeguards set by Buurtzorg. Freedom to carry out the care as we think is best. Responsibility for the whole. We make joint decisions here.

On a more individual level, we suggest that the process of conditioning and the impact on OSC can be described as follows. Conditioning decreases the integrative intelligence of the individual. This leads to an increase in apathy and a decrease in the ability to ask questions. Consequently, there is a decrease in awareness, as the nurse will simply apply purely technical procedures. This leads to a decrease in the perception of subtle cues and, thereby, an overall decrease in OSC.

On the contrary, Buurtzorg is promoting a space that encourages de-conditioning and "replacing bureaucracy with humanity." As expressed by one nurse, employees are asked to be "less robots, more human beings." Therefore, nurses are encouraged to ask questions in order to develop a holistic perception of the situation, thereby increasing their awareness and further enhancing their perception of subtle cues, leading to the objectivization of subtle cues.

Interestingly, in the initial study of objectivizing subtle cues (Nandram et al., 2018a), the focal population was composed of entrepreneurs. Hence, they already had many of the deconditioning attributes. For example, autonomy and independence are strong entrepreneurial attributes, while development of a holistic perception allows for the perception of entrepreneurial opportunities. The ability to constantly ask questions is also an important characteristic of entrepreneurs for whom adapting to new technology and change is paramount. Therefore, the deconditioning context was implicit in the first study of objectivizing subtle cues for entrepreneurs, but it had to be made explicit for nurses, which led to the success of Buurtzorg.

Internal Enablers

There are three types of internal enablers. They can be affective (e.g., trust, lack of fear), cognitive (e.g., openness to new signals, quieting the mind), and behavioral (e.g., a courageous attitude, adoption of a third-person perspective). Through such enablers, the decision maker is able to perceive more subtle cues.

When both types of enablers are established, the decision maker proceeds to holistic attunement.

Entrainment and Holistic Attunement

This sub-process of step 2 can involve different approaches to attunement: inner attunement (e.g., an inner voice about what is right or wrong), outer attunement (e.g., attunement to a greater wholeness, attunement to people), or a mixture of the two. In the first study with entrepreneurs (see Nandram et al., 2018a), some entrepreneurs used mixtures of attunement. One entrepreneur explained the interplay between the two: "I think there are outer and inner features and knowledge and insights to be used for everything."

Our new study with nurses offers more insights. We introduce the term *holistic attunement*, which covers all three types of attunement found in the first study. Holistic attunement means attuning to cues by taking the decision maker, the decision-making process, and the stakeholder with whom the decision is concerned

	inner entrainment (within system)	outer entrainment (between systems)
symmetrical entrainment	I self-entrainment intraentrainment	II interpersonal and collective entrainment
asymmetrical entrainment	III environmental (cultural) entrainment extraentrainment	IV environmental (social) entrainment

Figure 7.7   Integral entrainment matrix (Sandra and Nandram, 2013).

into account. In the home-care context, the stakeholders are the client and his or her family members.

Holistic attunement can be explained in terms of the process of entrainment.

The client's context is a given, as the residence cannot be changed to solve problems. However, in decision-making, the nurses following the dynamic, holistic perception process also pay attention to things that can be changed, such as the arrangements with the client, his or her family members, and other actors in the "care chain." Sandra and Nandram (2013) conceptualize four quadrants of entrainment (Figure 7.7), which may improve our understanding of the holistic attunement process. Bluedorn (2002, p. 149) defines entrainment as *"a process over time whereby two or more autonomous rhythmic processes interact with each other in such a way that they adjust towards and eventually lock-in to a common phase and/or periodicity, most often to the rhythm being more powerful or dominant. Afterwards, the processes maintain a consistent relationship."*

Entrainment involves two basic components: two or more autonomous rhythmic processes, and interactions between them. As such, each human being can be considered as an autonomous process. In that case, the nurse and the client interact. Other autonomous processes can also be involved, such as the client's family members and other medical-care providers. The integral entrainment matrix is based on two major aspects of entrainment: whether rhythms mutually entrain each other (symmetric) or not (asymmetric), and whether the entrainment occurs within the system (inner) or between systems (outer).

We can consider this situation from the nurse's point of view. First, the nurse's state of being plays an important role in the way he or she perceives the environment. This reflects his or her level of self-entrainment (Figure 7.1, quadrant 1) (e.g., Childre & Martin, 1999). The higher this level, the more the nurse will be able to perceive. The nurse might ask himself or herself: What is happening with the client? What are his or her needs? How does the family help? What is the role of others in the care chain? In this state, the nurse is interacting with an environment that he or she can influence and change (i.e., the nurse, the client, and others; quadrant 2: interpersonal), and with an environment he or she cannot change and is subjected to (i.e., the housing; quadrant 4). The nurse moves from seeing cues in the close environment to seeing, perceiving, and recognizing subtle cues related to the client, while also experiencing internal cues (quadrant 1). From this inner and outer entrainment, the nurse sees a solution to the problem emerge. After that solution is introduced, the client needs to adapt to it (i.e., the client is entrained by the solution; quadrants 3 and 4) and gradually feel alignment with all of the rhythms around him or her, thereby achieving the goal of the treatment. The nurse will evaluate and fine-tune where required based on the holistic attunement process. In the following quote, a nurse explains part of this process.

> *I always tell colleagues, "you come to the client's house expecting action," but that is where it all starts. There is a person behind the action—it is more than putting on a support stocking or helping the client take a shower. There is a person behind your actions and it is important that you understand him or her. You see, listen, smell, and hear. You try to develop a whole picture before you act. You continuously perceive and fine-tune and share with colleagues. You talk with the family. You talk with the general practitioner. You look at the client's history. You apply your clinical reasoning. You use all of these as inputs and make your own decisions. So much is possible. Sometimes you may have another judgment than your colleagues regarding a particular client. Some clients will complain to your colleagues, while they are totally relaxed and happy when you are there. There is a special bond that you feel with that client. With other clients, you feel they would rather see you leaving than coming. It is not predictable. There is always more to see—that makes the work fun.*

Being with the Subtle Cues

With regard to being with the subtle cues, we distinguish among intuitive experiences (e.g., hunches, instincts), sensing the environment and people (e.g., perceptions of energy in people, warning signs), sensing subtle mental activity (e.g., gaining insight, knowingness), sensing the future, sensing a trend toward wholeness, and sensing connection and direction (e.g., inspiration, the inner voice). These subtle cues can be experienced, sensed, listened to, and recognized.

We now turn to the last step in the model.

Step 4: Validating and Observing the Impact of Using Subtle Cues

To further enhance our understanding of decision-making in the nursing context, let us examine a typical visit to a client. The nurse enters the client's residence and (1) holistically contextualizes the situation, (2) consciously or unconsciously collects subtle cues from the context, (3) builds a relationship with the client, and (4) decides on the best care for that client. In order to make this decision, she or he combines all of the subtle cues that she or he has consciously or unconsciously collected from the context and the patient. The nurse also integrates those subtle cues with her or his professional and clinical reasoning. On that basis, the nurse determines the type of care that best fits that context for that specific patient/client and that medical need.

From the data, the following decision-making logic emerged:

■ Give meaning and form to subtle cues, and then determine whether those subtle cues are meaningful. In this step, we found another validating path. Nurses check by sharing with colleagues and others (e.g., general practitioners, other medical service providers, and family members) before acting.
■ Determine whether the subtle cues lead to a valid outcome.
■ The nurse proceeds with translating the cues into activities based on a rational analysis.

Finally, the nurses mentioned that they measured the results of the application of subtle cues in order to improve the process.

Discussion and Conclusion

In this chapter, we have shown that decision-making involves interactions between reason and intuition. Based on two populations (entrepreneurs and nurses), we have enhanced the OSC model for decision-making. This study contributes to the insights provided by our previous study (Nandram et al., 2018a). If we abstract from the findings, we can state that the context of decision-making is important for letting subtle cues emerge to enable comprehensive decision-making. We have explained how several subtle cues, when integrated, lead to a holistic, coherent understanding of what happens when decision makers act in a context that is not conditioned but creates room for natural stimuli. We have enriched the previous OSC model with several constructs: a learning structure for deconditioning the mind as an external enabler; a strategy of multiple, dynamic, holistic perception; and holistic attunement as explained by entrainment.

Two concepts can be considered in future research. Researchers may wish to study the nature of the relationship between the decision maker and the person whom the decision-making concerns. In the nursing context, there is an *empathic dependency* between the client and the nurse. The relationship is not equal, as the client needs the nurse to solve an issue. In the entrepreneurial context, dependency exists in relation to suppliers, customers, and employees, but the element of empathy may be different. In the nursing context, the nurses' dynamic, holistic perceptions seem to be able to remove the barrier between them and the client and his or her family members. The empathic base should be studied further as an important influencer of integrative decisions in other populations and contexts. Typically, a barrier is present in interactions between two persons who do not know each other but who have to work together. The more the two people become acquainted, the better they can cope with expectations, preferences, and subtle aspects of communication.

The concentric circles also need further research. What is the starting point for how people make decisions? Do they start with themselves or do they start with another actor? In a management context, does the entrepreneur start with what he can give, what he finds important, or the needs of the others? In economic terminology: Does he adopt a *supply-demand approach* or a *demand-supply approach*. An awareness of the starting point is important for defining the subsequent steps. In one case, one could try to push one's own views, while in another case, one is open to the voices (needs and demands) of the others. As we have seen in the case of nursing, there is a third *integrative decision strategy*. An important aspect may be to strive for a coherent view from an integrative intelligence perspective. This can lead to a coherent outcome by incorporating everyone's perspectives (e.g., from different levels, medical disciplines, levels and types of experiences, various ways of dealing with policies) and purposes (including the decision-making timeframe). It does not matter how they start as long as they reach a coherent outcome in which the client is served in the best possible way in the given context.

Future research focused on other areas of decision-making (e.g., expats in a new culture context) and the intentions behind decision-making (e.g., to solve a problem, to understand how something works, or the need for a short- or long-term response) would probably be useful for extending and modifying this theory, while gradually making it more universal.

Acknowledgment

We would like to thank the nurses from Buurtzorg Nederland for their input during in-depth interviews and team meetings.

References

Agor, W. H. 1989. *Intuition in organizations: Leading and managing productively.* Thousand Oaks, CA: Sage Publications.

Allinson, C. W., Chell, E., and Hayes, J. 2000. Intuition and entrepreneurial behaviour. *European Journal of Work and Organizational Psychology, 9*(1): 31–43.

Balthazard, C. G. 1985. *Intuition.* Unpublished doctoral dissertation, University of Waterloo, Ontario, Canada.

Bastick, T. 1982. *Intuition: How we think and act.* John Wiley and Sons.

Bowers, K. S., Regehr, G., Balthazard, C., and Parker, K. 1990. Intuition in the context of discovery. *Cognitive Psychology, 22*(1): 72–110.

Bluedorn, A. C. 2002. *The human organization of time: Temporal realities and experience.* Stanford, CA: Stanford University Press.

Bradley, R. T. 2006. *The psychophysiology of entrepreneurial intuition: A quantum-holographic theory.* Paper presented at the 3rd International Entrepreneurship Research Exchange conference held at UNITEC, Auckland, New Zealand (7–10 February 2006).

Bunge, M. A. 1962. *Intuition and science.* Prentice-Hall.

Childre, D., and Martin, H. 1999. *The heartmath solution.* San Francisco, CA: HarperCollins.

Dane, E., and Pratt, M. G. 2007. Exploring intuition and its role in managerial decision making. *Academy of Management Review, 32*(1): 33–54.

De Blok, J., Pool, A., and Keesom, J. G. M. 2010. *Buurtzorg: menselijkheid boven bureaucratie.* Amsterdam, the Netherlands: Boom Lemma Uitgevers.

Epstein, S. 1998. Cognitive-experiential self-theory. In D. F. Barone, M. Hersen, & V. B. Van Hasselt (Eds.), *Advanced personality* (pp. 211–238). Springer.

Glaser, B. G., and Strauss, A. L. 1967. *The discovery of grounded theory: Strategies for qualitative research.* Piscataway, NJ: Aldine Transaction.

Hogarth, R. M. 2001. *Educating intuition.* Chicago, IL: University of Chicago Press.

Holland, J. L., and Baird, L. L. 1968. The preconscious activity scale: The development and validation of an originality measure. *The Journal of Creative Behavior, 2*(3): 217–226.

Jung, C.-G. 1933. *Psychological types.* Geneva, Switzerland: Georg Editeur.

Kahneman, D. 2003. A perspective on judgment and choice: Mapping bounded rationality. *American Psychologist, 58*(9): 697.

Klein, G. A. 2002. *Intuition at work: Why developing your gut instincts will make you better at what you do.* Doubleday.

La Pira, F., and Gillin, M. 2006. Non-local intuition and the performance of serial entrepreneurs. *International Journal of Entrepreneurship and Small Business, 3*(1): 17–35.

Lewicki, P., Hill, T., and Czyzewska, M. 1992. Nonconscious acquisition of information. *American Psychologist, 47*(6): 796.

Mitchell, J. R., Friga, P. N., and Mitchell, R. K. 2005. Untangling the intuition mess: Intuition as a construct in entrepreneurship research. *Entrepreneurship Theory and Practice, 29*(6): 653–679.

Myers, D. 2002. *Intuition: Its powers and perils.* New Haven, CT: Yale University Press.

Myers, D. G. 2004. *Intuition: Its powers and perils:* New Haven, CT: Yale University Press.

Nandram, S. S. 2015. *Organizational innovation by integrating simplification.* Springer.

Nandram, S. S. 2016a. *Organizational innovation by integrating simplification: Lessons from Buurtzorg Nederland.* Springer.

Nandram, S. S. 2016b. How do spirituality, intuition and entrepreneurship go together? *Philosophy of Management, 15*(1): 65–82.

Nandram, S. S. 2017. Spirituality in the field of entrepreneurship: The relationship between spiritual-based intuition and entrepreneurship. In Hense E., Hubental, C., Speelman, W.M. (Eds.), *The quest for quality of life: Approaches, concepts and images with a special focus on the Netherlands.* Germany: Aschendorff Verlag.

Nandram, S. S., Mourmant, G., Norlyk Smith, E., Heaton, D. P., and Bindlish, P. K. (2018a). Understanding entrepreneurial decision-making by objectivizing subtle cues. *Journal of Management, Spirituality and Religion, 15*(5): 398–423.

Nandram, S. S., Bindlish, P. K., and de Blok, J. 2018b. What if business revisits Pavlov's kennel: The case of Buurtzorg. *The European Financial Review*, June–July.

Nandram S. S., Bindlish, P. K., Keizer, W. A. J. 2017. *Understanding integrative intelligence*. Netherlands: Praan Uitgeverij.

Oxford Dictionaries. 1990. *The concise Oxford dictionary* (R. E. Allen, Ed.). New York: Clarendon Press–Oxford University Press.

Pavlov, I. P. 1906. The scientific investigation of the psychical faculties or processes in the higher animals. *Science, 24*(620).

Policastro, E. 1999. Intuition. In P. S. Runco (Ed.), *Encyclopedia of creativity* (Vol. 2, pp. 89–93). San Diego, CA: Academic Press.

Pool, A., Mast, J., and Keesom, J. G. M. 2011. *Eerst buurten, dan zorgen: Professioneel verplegen en verzorgen bij Buurtzorg*. Amsterdam, the Netherlands: Boom Lemma Uitgevers.

Prietula, M. J., and Simon, H. A. 1989. The experts in your midst. *Harvard Business Review, 1*.

Raidl, M.-H., and Lubart, T. I. 2001. An empirical study of intuition and creativity. *Imagination, Cognition and Personality, 20*(3): 217–230.

Rosenblatt, A. D., and Thickstun, J. T. 1994. Intuition and consciousness. *The Psychoanalytic Quarterly, 63*(4): 696–714.

Rotry, R. 1967. *The linguistic turn: Recent essay in philosophical method*. Chicago, IL: University of Chicago Press.

Rowan, R., Track, F., and Delran, N. J. 1986. *The intuitive manager*. Farnham, UK: Gower.

Sandra, D., and Nandram, S. S. 2013. The role of entrainment in the context of integral leadership: Synchronizing consciousness. *Advances in Management, 6*(12): 17–24.

Shapiro, S., and Spence, M. T. 1997. Managerial intuition: A conceptual and operational framework. *Business Horizons, 40*(1): 63–68.

Simon, H. A. 1987. Making management decisions: The role of intuition and emotion. *The Academy of Management Executive (1987–1989), 1*: 57–64.

Van Dalen, A. 2010. *Uit de schaduw van het zorgsysteem: Hoe buurtzorg nederland zorg organiseert*. Amsterdam, the Netherlands: Boom Lemma Uitgevers.

Van Dalen, A. 2012. *Zorgvernieuwing: Over anders besturen en organiseren*. Amsterdam, the Netherlands: Boom Lemma Uitgevers.

Vaughan, F. E. 1979. *Awakening intuition*. Anchor Press.

Waters, J. A. 1980. Managerial skill development. *Academy of Management Review, 5*(3): 449–453.

Chapter 8

How to Filter Cognitive Bias from Intuition: Evolved Decision-Making: A Hunch?

Francesca McCartney; Interviewed by Kirk Hurford

Contents

Introduction

The idea of intuition is increasingly used in discussions about business management and decision-making, sometimes as if it were a new concept. But it is hardly so. A manager in the days before the Internet had little choice but to use intuition—the raw data simply was not accessible. Often, "a hunch" was all there was. Today, so much data is available that the inverse is true—in mere seconds, we can summon enough data to support any decision we want to make—good or bad. Sorting through this flood of data makes the use of intuition more crucial than ever. Are we back to the idea of a hunch?

What is a hunch? Where does it come from, and how can we tell if a hunch is coming from intuition or false beliefs? Let's ask an expert.

For the past 40 years, Francesca McCartney, Ph.D., has been researching and teaching the use of intuition in daily life and as a modality for medical healing. She has published several books, is a featured lecturer on the topic of intuition, and is the founder of three schools: the Academy of Intuition Medicine®, founded in 1984; Energy Medicine University, founded 2006; and the Academy of Intuition Medicine Online, founded in 2017.

[Kirk Hurford]

Dr. McCartney, I know this sounds simple, but to begin with, what is intuition?

[Francesca McCartney]

That was exactly the question I asked in 1976, and I am continuing to explore and expand upon that topic. Recent research shows that humans have more than 21 senses. Most people assume that we operate with only the five common senses. That belief was given to us by Aristotle and is long overdue for a revision. Those over the five senses are accessed via intuition.

The Oxford Dictionary defines intuition as *"the faculty of knowing as if by instinct, without conscious reasoning."* But what does that mean? It is the sense of knowing or perceiving something without knowing exactly *how* you know. How does this work? Can we develop this ability in ourselves for decision-making and more? Yes!

Humans are wired from birth to receive inner- and outer-world information signals, but too often we ignore or don't trust our subtle intuitive perceptions. The world is constantly communicating with us and the secret is learning to pay attention.

We are so much more than our five common senses, and learning to listen to, trust, and act upon your intuition develops super-consciousness, and with practice, becomes the normal way you live in your body and operate in the world.

We experience intuition in many perfectly ordinary, everyday ways. Intuition is the sudden "Aha!" that seemingly comes from nowhere after wracking your brain for an analytical solution that refuses to come—the light bulb over your head. Intuition is the flash of insight that reveals where your lost keys are. Intuition is the picture of someone in your head just before they call on the phone or walk into your office. Intuition is that feeling in your gut when something is not right, or someone is lying. Intuition is that *inner knowing,* so often drowned out by other, more insistent noises, that warns or advises us, and to which we often say (after the fact), "If only I had listened …"

[KH]

Listened to what?

[FM]

Intuition has location signal points within your body. Intuition is a learned language of interpreting those signals—just as a child learns how to decipher the signal language from sight, smell, sound, touch, and taste. Each of the five common senses has a receptor location that delivers signals to the nervous system and the brain for decoding and informing. The language of intuition operates in the same way.

In business, and in life, operating with a wide perspective of information yields the best outcome in the decision-making process. Five points of perception is a limited range of information and often is filtered through bias from conditioned data entry. An excellent starting place to stimulate stronger intuitive language signals is to listen to your first hit, go with your hunch, trust your gut feeling. The more you listen, trust, and follow through with your hits and hunches the stronger the signal wiring in the nervous system becomes, whereupon your decisions are memory imprinted in your brain, which develops a cognitive intuitive language.

[KH]

When we say cognitive bias, we're referring to a personal perspective, right? How is this different from intuition?

[FM]

Cognitive bias is a language of personal perspective that for the five-sense person is developed from a limited perspective of the five senses. Western-minded people lean toward using analysis and rote educational sources for deductive decision-making. This system of analytical decision-making does not recognize the larger menu of possible choices available with the expanded human sense of intuition, and therein is a limited decision-making process. Decisions made in a box rather than inspirational choices streaming from outside of the box—where intuition, inspiration, and invention operate.

Limited perception developed as a survival mechanism as our body is bombarded by two million bits of information every minute. The common senses and analytical mind act as a filter. If we were unable to filter out most of these bits, we would go mad in one second. We use our filters—the purpose of which was to weed out information irrelevant to our species—for the task: to lock into those objectifications alone which are in tune with cultural, informational, and survival purposes.

To survive with a semblance of sanity, we need some sort of filters to pick out those events, interactions, or relationships that we want or need to focus on. This doesn't mean that we should always keep filters in place or use them for purposes other than they were originally intended. Filters require intentional management. If properly handled, filters can both isolate the objects that we need to focus on and reveal their relationship with other objects and the whole. They can be both—like two sides of a coin.

Intuitively sourced information does not pass through the same perceptual filters that process analytical information. The sense of sight, for example, gathers five points of data through the rods and cones in the eyes, travels through a decoding filter in the optic nerve that chooses three of the five data points based on the most common memory—that is the memory pattern that has the most charge stored in the brain and delivers a composite image to the brain built on that three of five choice of repeated experience. This creates visual image perception based on repeated data and most likely probabilities and excludes new data/new perception as a primary choice for decision-making. These filters become so internalized and automated that alternative perspectives, such as intuitive sensing, are not even recognized. This mostly unconscious control mechanism obstructs the ability to think outside of the box, thus limiting new knowledge, inspiration, and the "quick hit."

Historical and cultural contexts also influence perception and create bias. A Coke bottle dropped from an airplane into a society of bushmen in South Africa's Kalahari Desert in the movie *The Gods Must Be Crazy* is seen as many things, but never as a container for carbonated beverages. It has been reported that some pre-Columbian Native Americans could not see the large sailing vessels of the first European explorers to approach their shores because they had no cultural precedent for such an event or object, and no appropriate words in their vocabulary to describe it. Thus, in their reality, such things simply did not exist. Even the "objective" cognitive act of seeing in the material world requires a synergy of senses.

Genius is often described as highly creative, clever, and brilliant—characteristics of a person who has access to knowledge and data beyond the norm—which is a definition that also applies to intuition.

[KH]

So, you're saying intuitive information is from outside the box, and cognitive bias is an attempt to restrict information from inside the box?

[FM]

In the broadest sense, yes. Information is more than just facts. Facts also have context. Context is a powerful influence on how we perceive facts. Context is what gives facts meaning. For example, you might be reading a story about animals on a farm and, at some point in events, you realize that there is a bigger story being told (Orwell, 1945). As the context changes, so does your perception of the facts. The pig is no longer a pig. Intuition allows for a richer context. Cognitive bias comes from a failure to perceive and appreciate the contextual information that comes from our extra-normal senses.

[KH]

Can we apply these ideas in a real-world circumstance? Let's say I'm interviewing three people for a critical position. How would I include intuition in the decision-making process?

[FM]

Once you have all the information, interviews, etc., clear your mind and go into meditation and visualize all three of the candidates sitting around a table with you.

Which one appears most prominently? This should be a first, quick hit, such as they look bright, active, more animated and the others look dull, lethargic, quiet. The one that responds best to this intuitive inquiry is the best person for the position.

[KH]

I can see where some people might have a problem with what you are proposing. You're suggesting that I not think about the facts? What about the person's resume? Experience? Shouldn't I compare those things?

[FM]

You're touching on the reason why some people choose to take courses on this topic. There is a lot of unlearning required to make full use of intuitive information. You can use all those pieces of information to vet the person's suitability to be considered, but that is what qualifies them to be considered a candidate. The intuitive method of picking a qualified candidate is to place them in the context of your company and their job, and let your imagination coupled with intuition show you who will be the best fit.

[KH]

Now something less organic—how about a new logo design for my company?

[FM]

Again—clear your mind and go into meditation and pose the inquiry question: "What colors, symbols, words represent my company?" This inquiry posture is dependent on you not mentally responding and letting go of preconceived ideas. Simply hold quiet mind and observe—you are sitting in a movie theater watching the film, not controlling the film. This means that you are allowing your imagination the freedom to respond with anything. Imagination is a powerful tool for intuitive language-building. It is the bridge between your subtle abstract knowing and fully formed intuition as a practical decision-making sense. Imagination/intuition allows the combination of diverse types of knowledge and ways of thinking to create new ideas and allow existing ideas to be built on and improved—all through the creation of novel thoughts and ideas including metaphors and symbols.

[KH]

So, you're saying imagination is an intuition tool—a sense?

[FM]

Not exactly. Imagination is a bridge language that uses metaphor and symbol that the mind is familiar with as interpretative process for creating connection into the intuitive senses and thereby either removing a bias filter and/or creating a new filter that receives subtle signals from outside the learned, conditioned, rote information stored in the brain and emotional body.

Albert Einstein once said "Imagination is more important than knowledge. For while knowledge defines all we currently know and understand, imagination points to all we might yet discover and create."

[KH]

It seems like the idea is to "trust" my intuition, but is there any hard science supporting the use of intuition?

[FM]

There is about 50 years of research on the human sense of intuition—hard science, as you call it. Several renowned and respected organizations are conducting research on intuition. The Rhine Research Center began research in 1965; the Princeton Engineering Anomaly Research lab (PEAR) began research in 1979; and the Institute of Noetic Sciences (IONS), which has a large online research results library, started their research in 1971. In 2000, I received a seed grant from IONS to do intuition research and conducted that research project in the IONS lab. We had 100 test subjects participate in four weekly sessions, in a randomized, controlled study, testing how the subjects use intuition as a decipherable sense-language. The results were significant with a statistical outcome above chance.

I'd like to include an excerpt from a PEAR paper about the "filter tuning process":

> More subtle mechanisms for acquisition of information, such as intuition, instinct, inspiration, and various other psychical modalities, also can enhance the flux of incoming information. Although commonly experienced, these channels involve less readily identifiable sensors and therefore are less susceptible to orderly reasoning, and they are correspondingly less respected and utilized in modern scientific practice, traditional education, and contemporary social activity. In the extreme materialistic view, this imbalance extends to total dismissal of these subtler capacities, thus restricting experience to the five primary sensory capabilities and their technological extensions alone. Consequently, the inferred models of reality are limited to those substances, processes, and sources of information that constitute conventional contemporary science.

[KH]

So, intuition is a well-researched tool that we can use to make better decisions. In other words, intuition is a critical decision-making tool. If I want to improve my intuitive decision-making ability—you said there are courses—what do people study?

[FM]

Yes, intuition is a discipline with a wide range of study. I have focused on teaching intuition as a natural human sense that should be used in all endeavors of life along with the five common senses, as well as methodology for assessing spiritual maladies that largely get ignored by modern medicine. This method includes a broad study of the nature and use of intuition and what I call a reinvention of ancient and indigenous medicines into a Western healing system that includes the Spirit as well as body and mind. At the Academy of Intuition Medicine, classes first teach meditation, grounding, and basic energy system concepts.

[KH]

I understand what you mean by meditation, but what do you mean by "grounding"?

[FM]

Have you heard the expression "that person is well grounded"? What did you think when you heard that? Being grounded is a state of being completely and totally present while having full control of all your perceptive abilities—active and balanced. Meditation helps you get there, but there is no reason why you can't be grounded all the time. In class, students learn about how to sense the state of being grounded, and especially, being not grounded.

[KH]

You're saying that intuition is a valuable decision-making tool and that being grounded is necessary to make use of intuitive information. Do you have any other advice?

[FM]

We spoke earlier about meditation—and that deserves consideration as a foundation for this process. There are many techniques for meditating, but they all seek one main goal—a quiet mind.

[KH]

Isn't thinking like breathing? How does one stop thinking?

[FM]

Your question reveals a potential misunderstanding—do you believe thinking is the principal activity taking place inside you? Learning to meditate will teach that the thing that is "you" is perfectly capable of being present and aware without thinking. You will learn to notice the presence of ideas and notice the analytical engine that processes those ideas and puts them in conveniently labeled boxes: good, bad, happy, sad, exciting, depressing, important, not important—often sizing and coloring the ideas in the process. Meditation will return to you the ability to experience raw ideas—you could call them organic ideas. From that larger, richer perspective will come fresh ideas along with new ways to see old ideas.

It's not uncommon for meditation students to experience powerful emotions in the beginning. These come from the process of rediscovering oneself—not unlike greeting a long-lost friend—with a combination of joy and grieving for the lost time. Ultimately, once reunited with your full, complete, true self—you will be happy, peaceful, and well grounded.

[KH]

You make meditation sound like a cure for everything.

[FM]

Not meditation, but the intuitive awareness that comes from meditation—which ultimately results in a reconfiguration of a person's entire energy system, and the way one lives in the body. Modern research is increasingly supporting the model of the constant interaction between body and mind. Not only that, there is increasing evidence that the body *is* the mind—mind traditionally considered located in the brain. The evolving field of mind-body medicine known as psycho-neuroimmunology (PNI) has added a new layer to the mind-body dynamic by introducing the vital role played by the immune system within this network. It has provided many new insights into the various hormonal and chemical connections between emotional stress and illness. A key characteristic of the cells of the immune system is that they travel through the body to wherever they are needed to mount a defense or repair damage. PNI refers to the multidirectional network of commu-nication between the psyche—the intangible aspect of being human—the mind, emotions, and soul; the human biologic processes of neurology and physiology; and the function of our body's immune system.

[KH]

When you say modern research, can you give an example?

[FM]

One of the pioneers in this recent field of mind-body research is Dr. Candice Pert. She started her career in neuroscience with measuring receptors, molecules made up of chains of amino acids that respond to energy and chemical cues by vibrat-ing. These receptors basically work as scanners. They are attached to a cell's mem-brane, waiting for the right chemical to come along to bind to—called receptor specificity. This chemical is called a ligand, and it is a molecule itself. As soon as the message, the chemical cue, is received, the receptor transmits it deep into the cell's interior, where a reaction of biochemical changes is started. The actual change depends on the message, but the changes in this single cell influence on a much larger scale.

The largest category of ligands is called peptides. They are the chemicals that play a wide role in the regulation of almost all life processes. A peptide that is brain involved is called a neuropeptide. It turns out that almost every peptide that has ever been found anywhere is a neuropeptide. These neuropeptides also have recep-tors in the brain. The research found that neuropeptides exist in all parts of the brain. What amazed me was the discovery that neuropeptides and their receptors are to be found in the body as well. In the study, it is noted that neuropeptides are "abundantly distributed in subtly different intricate patterns all the way down both sides of your spine."

As mentioned earlier, it is the connection with the immune system that provides the vital link between body and brain. Monocytes and other white blood cells travel along in the blood and at some point, come within "scent" distance of a given neuropeptide, and because these white blood cells have receptors for that given neuropeptide on their surface, they begin to move toward it. Candice Pert discovered that every neuropeptide receptor they could find in the brain was also on the surface of the human monocyte. It has been known for over a century that the pituitary gland—located near the middle of the brain—spews out peptides throughout the body. But a few years ago, it was found that these peptide-producing cells also inhabit the bone marrow—the place where immune cells are generated. Human immune system cells have receptors for opiates and other emotion-affecting peptides which appear to control the routing and migration of the monocytes, which are very pivotal to overall health. However, they don't just have receptors on their surface for the various neuropeptides. Immune cells also make, store, and secrete the neuropeptides themselves.

In other words, the immune cells are making the same chemicals that control our moods. Immune cells clearly do not only take care of the physical health of the body, they also create information chemicals that can regulate mood and emotion.

What this illustrates is two-way communication—brain communicating with immune cells in the body, and immune cells in the body communicating with the brain. It seems fair to conclude that intelligence is located in these cells distributed throughout the body.

According to Dr. Pert, it is the emotion-affecting peptides and their receptors that make the dialogue between the conscious and the unconscious processes possible. Since neuropeptides and their receptors are in the brain as well as in the body, and since there is a multidimensional exchange of information between the various systems of the body, we can reasonably take the step that the mind is in the body, with all that that implies. The thing we call mind is immaterial. However, the mind has a physical basis, which is the whole body, including but not limited to the brain. The mind is what holds this psychoneuroimmunology information network together.

The traditional separation of mental processes, including the emotions, from the body need to be reconsidered in this context. If the mind is defined by brain-cell communication, as in contemporary science, then this model can now be naturally extended to the entire body. Hence, the ideas of Intuition Medicine® and Energy Medicine from which the respective academies are founded.

[KH]

The research on psychoneuroimmunology is fascinating. Is there a real-world example you can provide?

[FM]

Certainly. Let's look at the idea of "conscious breathing," a technique taught and practiced in prenatal classes all around the Western world, and deeply practiced in the Eastern world. A wealth of data shows that changes in the rate and depth of breathing produce changes in the quantity and kind of peptides that are released from the brain stem. And vice versa! One can do this by bringing the process of breathing into consciousness and doing something to alter it. By either holding your breath or breathing extra fast, you can cause the peptides to diffuse rapidly throughout the cerebrospinal fluid. This is an attempt by the body to restore balance. Since many of these peptides are endorphins—the body's natural opiates—you soon achieve a lessening of your pain.

[KH]

So, if I understand you correctly, meditation can influence more than just my decision-making?

[FM]

Much, much more. And this is because meditation has a beneficial effect on the total organism that is you. You are healthy, vibrant, and this results in your ability to make quality decisions. The thing is, there is a bigger organism that responds the same way to your positive state of health—your company. Professor Richard Pascal believes that businesses must recognize that they are living organisms, subject to the same dynamics of life as all other organisms: adapt or die. "Rapid rates of change, an explosion of new insights from the life sciences, and the insufficiency of the old-machine model to explain how business today really works have created a critical mass for a revolution in management thinking."

Intuition is what will give you the ability to be in synchronicity with the organism that is your company. People and companies who recognize this are the ones that will adapt and thrive.

[KH]

In other words, using intuition in business is revolutionary?

[FM]

Darwin's theories are true for all organisms. Let's call it evolutionary.

[KH]

We've covered a lot of ground in this conversation. Is there anything you'd like to say in closing?

[FM]

We need to overcome the bias built into the current Western idea that the mind is totally in our head. We need to start thinking about how the mind manifests itself in various parts of the body, and beyond that, how we can bring that process into consciousness. Using consciousness techniques, such as visualization, we can consciously influence reality at a micro level. By selectively influencing certain micro-events, it is possible to create a much larger effect. If we genuinely believe that we have a greater ability to influence ourselves and the world around us, and if we learn to focus our consciousness in very specific ways, our consciousness will produce an energetic effect and will shape our reality accordingly. All people have the ability to be intuitive. We all have the ability to develop a heightened sensitivity to the world around us.

Ultimately, this will lead to an expanded ability to become the intuitive decision makers and business leaders we need to direct the course of human history toward happiness and prosperity.

Bibliography

Jahn R. & Dunne B. (2004). Sensors, filters, and the source of reality. *Journal of Scientific Exploration*, Vol 18, No 4, 547–570.

McCartney, F. (2007). An empirical study of the transmission of healing energy via the Internet. *Subtle Energies & Energy Medicine Journal*, Vol 18, No 2, 21–33.

McCartney, F. (2005). *Body of Health: The New Science of Intuition Medicine®*. Nataraj Publishing: Novato, CA.

Orwell, G. (1945). *Animal Farm*.

Pascale, R. T. (2000). *Surfing the Edge of Chaos*. Retrieved Dec. 5, 2018, from http://str andtheory.org/images/spirituality_in_the_workplace-mitroff_denton.pdf

Chapter 9

The Role of Intuition in Risk/Benefit Decision-Making with Research Human Subjects

David B. Resnik

Contents

Introduction

Weighing risks and benefits is an essential part of the ethical evaluation of research involving human subjects. Regulations, international guidelines, scholarly articles, and books affirm the principle that risks to human subjects are ethically acceptable in relation to the expected benefits of the research to subjects or society (Resnik, 2018). For example, the Common Rule requires that risks to human subjects "are reasonable in relation to anticipated benefits, if any, to subjects, and the importance of the knowledge that may reasonably be expected to result" (Department of Homeland Security et al., 2017 at 45 CFR 46.111a2).* The World Medical Association's Declaration of Helsinki states that, "medical research involving human subjects may only be conducted if the importance of the objective outweighs the risks and burdens to the research subjects" (World Medical Association, 2013). In a highly cited review article, Emanuel et al. (2000) summarize this principle as "risks to the subject are proportionate to the benefits to the subject and society" (p. 2703).

Decisions pertaining to the weighing of risks and anticipated benefits[†] in research with human subjects can be extraordinarily complex and difficult, because they are affected by many different factors, including the study's design, procedures, tests, and interventions; prior human and animals research; the target population; the local research infrastructure and environment; and privacy/confidentiality protections (Resnik, 2018). Compounding the problem of risk/benefit decision-making is the fact that regulations and guidelines do not clearly define risks and benefits or explain how to apply these concepts to real cases (Resnik, 2017).

Given the complexity and difficulty of these decisions and the lack of clear regulatory guidance, it is not surprising that some studies have shown that there is significant variation in how oversight committees (known in the U.S. as Institutional Review Boards or IRBs) evaluate risks and anticipated benefits. For example, one study found significant variation in how IRBs at 43 different research sites evaluated the same protocol for observing health services provided at Veteran's Administration centers. Ten IRBs determined that the protocol qualified for expedited review because it was no more than minimal risk; 31 determined that the protocol needed to be reviewed by the full board because it was more than minimal risk; one determined that the study was exempt from review; and one decided not to approve the study because they judged it to be too risky (Green et al., 2006).[‡] A survey conducted by Shah et al. (2004) found significant variation in how IRB chairs evaluate risks. For example, 48 percent of IRB chairs responding to the survey judged a single magnetic resonance imaging scan with no sedation to be minimal risk, 35 percent judged it to be a minor increase over minimal risk, 9 percent judged it to be more than a minor increase over minimal risk, and 8 percent said they couldn't evaluate its risk (Shah et al., 2004).

One of the main reasons why risk/benefit decision-making in research with human subjects exhibits such variation—and inconsistency—is that IRBs often

---

* The Common Rule is a regulation for research with human subjects adopted by 16 U.S. federal agencies.
† Though most commentators simply use the term *benefit* I will use the term *anticipated benefit* to emphasize the important point that this concept, like the concept of risk, includes a probabilistic component. See further discussion later in this chapter.
‡ The Common Rule defines minimal risk as "probability and magnitude of harm or discomfort anticipated in the research are not greater in and of themselves than those ordinarily encountered in daily life or during the performance of routine physical or psychological examinations or tests" (Department of Homeland Security et al., 2017 at 45 CFR 46.102j).

rely on intuition to make judgments concerning risks and benefits (Resnik, 2017). Van Luijn et al. (2002) found that only 12 percent of the 53 IRB members they surveyed assessed benefits and risks systematically while 20 percent made assessments based on an overall impression or feeling of the balance of risks and expected benefits. Other studies have found that IRB members often make risk/benefit decisions based on personal experiences and gut feelings (Stark, 2012; Klitzman, 2015).

Variation and inconsistency in risk/benefit decision-making arising from the use of intuition in the oversight of research with human subjects raises significant ethical and practical concerns. When IRBs disagree about risk/benefit assessments, they may overestimate risks and underestimate anticipated benefits, or vice versa. In the first case, variation and inconsistency may impede valuable research needlessly and waste resources by delaying or impeding approval of studies; in the second, variation and inconsistency may lead to inadequate protection of the rights and welfare of human subjects by exposing people to unjustifiable risks (Resnik, 2017).

Given these practical and ethical concerns, numerous commentators have argued that IRBs should minimize their use of intuition in risk/benefit decision-making and take an approach that relies on empirical data and systematic reasoning (Levine, 1988; Meslin, 1990; Weijer, 2000; National Bioethics Advisory Commission, 2001; Wendler et al., 2005; Rid et al., 2010; Rid and Wendler, 2011; Bernabe et al., 2012; Kimmelman and Henderson, 2016). In this chapter, I will discuss how intuition impacts risk/benefit decision-making in research with human subjects and examine strategies for reducing its use. I will argue that while it is desirable to reduce the use of intuition in risk/benefit decision-making involving the oversight research with human subjects, there are practical and conceptual limits to achieving this goal.

What Is Intuition?

Before considering how intuition impacts risk/benefit decisions in research with human subjects, we need to address a prior question: what is intuition? For the purposes of this chapter we can understand intuition as "*a mental process in which one forms a belief or judgment immediately, without any conscious awareness of an inference process at work*" (Resnik, 2017, p. 3). More informally, we might call an intuition a gut feeling or hunch (Liebowitz, 2014). Intuition contrasts with reasoning, which involves forming beliefs or judgments as a result of conscious awareness of one's inference or deliberation (Kahneman, 2011; Resnik, 2017; Pust, 2017). For example, suppose that two people are buying cars. JJ develops a list of desirable qualities for a car (such as cost, fuel economy, reliability, etc.), rates prospective vehicles according to these criteria, and buys the car with the highest overall rating. When asked the question, "why did you buy car X?," JJ can give a coherent account of inferential steps she took in making the decision. KK takes a different approach to buying a car. KK examines different vehicles, considers some qualities he finds desirable in cars, and buys the one that he likes best. When asked the question, "Why did you buy car X?," KK cannot give a coherent account of the inferential steps he took in making the decision and can only say, "I chose the one I thought was best." The difference, then, between intuition and reasoning, boils down to conscious awareness of an inference process at work. JJ had such awareness; KK did not.

Thinking of intuition as a thought process we are not aware of would seem to shroud it in mystery. However, psychologists and neuroscientists have understood for over a hundred years that subconscious activities of the brain play a key role in sensory perception, cognition, emotion, and feeling. For example, we are not aware of the brain activity that transforms electrical signals from our optic nerves into visual images that we perceive as three-dimensional. Nor are we aware of how our physical stimulation of our skin can produce feelings of pleasure or pain (Kahneman, 2011).

One potential source of intuition is emotion or feeling (Kahneman, 2011). Emotions or feelings, such as empathy, anger, disgust, jealousy, or fear, can impact our beliefs, judgments, or decisions (Haidt, 2001). For example, one may decide that aborting a 20-week-old fetus is immoral based on emotional response (e.g., empathy) to viewing an ultrasound image of a fetus or seeing the discarded remains of a fetus following an abortion. Or one might decide to have a romantic relationship with someone based on a strong feeling of attraction to that person or desire for him or her (Resnik, 2017).

Another source of intuition occurs when we form judgments that stem from subconscious inference. A subconscious inference is one we are not aware of when it occurs, but which can we can reconstruct after the fact. For example, suppose that two police officers, a rookie cop and a veteran, are interrogating a suspect. After the questioning is finished, the veteran declares that the suspect was lying. The rookie says to the veteran, "how do you know?" The veteran replies, "trust me, I just know." While the veteran may not be aware of the source of his belief that the suspect is lying, one could argue that it could be explained by a series of inferences he was not aware of. For example, he might have observed, during his time on the police force, that most suspects who are lying exhibit certain mannerisms, and he could have noticed that his suspect also exhibited those mannerisms. We could explain his belief as resulting from a form of inductive inference that he was not aware of. Much of what counts of common sense or professional judgment may involve such subconscious inferences (Kahneman, 2011).

Cognitive psychologists have studied some types of subconscious inference processes, called heuristics, which are rules for forming empirical judgments (Kahneman et al., 1983; Kahneman, 2011). One of these is known as the availability heuristic, which leads one to estimate probabilities based on one's ability to recollect or imagine similar events. For example, one might estimate the probability of being bitten by a shark while swimming at the beach based on recollecting media coverage of a shark attack. Another is the anchoring heuristic, which leads one to fail to revise probability estimates based on new evidence. For example, a person who estimates the probability of being attacked by a shark while swimming at the beach as 1/100, despite learning of evidence that the probability is much lower than this, would be following the anchoring heuristic. Heuristics are inductive rules for operating in the world that serve us most of the time but can lead to biases and errors. For example, the anchoring heuristic could lead one to overestimate or underestimate probabilities (Kahneman et al., 1983).

Intuition also plays an important role in moral judgment. For years, psychologists and philosophers have debated about the issue of whether moral judgments are based on reasoning or intuition. In psychology, Lawrence Kohlberg proposed a highly influential theory of moral development based on his observations of how children make moral decisions. According to Kohlberg (1981), children go through different stages of moral development. Young children make moral choices to avoid punishment, older children make choices to conform to social conventions, and adolescents make choices based on their grasp of general moral rules or principles. Others have challenged the rationalist approach. Experiments have shown that test subjects often cannot clearly articulate their reasoning after they have made moral choices, and that sometimes moral principles they claim to accept have no impact on their choices (Haidt, 2001, 2007). Haidt (2007) argues that we make moral judgments based on intuition and that reasoning enters the picture only later, when we try to rationalize our judgments. Other psychologists have conducted experiments that show that rational and intuitive processes work together to influence moral judgment (Feinberg et al., 2012).

In philosophy, there is a long tradition, dating back to Plato, which holds that morality is based on human reasoning. Aristotle (2003) argued that human goodness (or virtue) is a form of rational activity of the soul. A virtue is a habit (or behavioral disposition) we acquire by following the examples of virtuous people and using practical wisdom to make choices. Eighteenth-century British philosopher David Hume (2000) challenged this viewpoint by arguing we can use reasoning to form descriptive judgments or beliefs relating to natural science or mathematics/logic, but that reasoning cannot provide us with normative judgments concerning what is good, right, or just. Moral judgments and beliefs are based on emotion, not reason. Immanuel Kant (1964) countered Hume's skepticism concerning the role of reason in morality by arguing that moral judgments are derived from a general rule, known as the categorical imperative, which is a principle that would be adopted by rational beings who are trying to decide how to live together in society. We can use the categorical imperative, according to Kant, to infer what we should do when faced with moral dilemmas.

While Kant has had a tremendous influence on philosophy, he was not able to prove that intuition plays no role in moral thinking. Many philosophers argue that all moral theories rest on some basic axioms, such as the categorical imperative or the principle of utility,* that are accepted without further argument or justification, which is another way of saying that such axioms are based on intuitive beliefs or judgments (Audi, 2004). Others argue that intuition comes into play when we lack sufficient time or information to use reasoning to make moral choices (Resnik, 2017).

In the 20th century, John Rawls developed a highly influential approach to justifying moral principles and decisions that combines intuition and reasoning. Rawls (1971) argued that we can use a method, known as reflective equilibrium, to justify moral principles that guide our decisions and actions. To use the method, we imagine a hypothetical situation, known as the original position, in which rational agents (or contractors) are attempting to form a social contract that includes principles for living together in society.† The contractors are behind a veil of ignorance that prevents them from knowing who they are in society: they know nothing about their race, gender, age, socioeconomic status, and so on. The purpose of the veil is to ensure that their judgments are unbiased or impartial. To arrive at principles, the contractors start with their considered judgments (or intuitions‡) of what is right/wrong, good/bad, just/unjust in different situations. They then develop principles (or theories) to systematize these intuitions and then test those principles against their intuitions, modifying or rejecting them if they conflict with their intuitions. They may also expand their set of intuitions as time goes on to provide additional testing for their principles. Eventually, the contractors reach a point, known as reflective equilibrium, in which their principles agree with their intuitions. Under Rawls's approach, reasoning plays a key role in developing, testing, and applying principles, which are ultimately grounded on intuitive judgments.

What Are Risks and Anticipated Benefits?

Two other prior questions must be addressed before we can consider how intuition impacts risk/benefit decision-making in research with human subjects: what are risks? and what are anticipated benefits? A risk is the possibility of an adverse outcome (or harm). Risk includes two components: (1) a quantitative one, i.e., the probability of the harm occurring and (2) a qualitative one, i.e., the severity or magnitude of the harm. We would consider an event with a high probability but a low severity to be less risky than one with high severity but low probability. For

---

* The principle of utility is based on 19th-century philosopher John Stuart Mill's approach to morality, known as utilitarianism. According to Mill's version of the principle: "actions are right in proportion as they tend to promote happiness; wrong as they tend to promote the reverse of happiness" (Mill, 1979, p. 7).

† Rawls's theory fits within the social contract approach to moral and political philosophy, which appears in the works of Hobbes, Locke, Kant, and Rousseau (Rawls, 1971).

‡ A considered judgment is an intuition that has been purged of various biases because it is made behind the veil of ignorance.

example, we would say that a study involving a 1 percent chance of death is much riskier than a study involving a 50 percent chance of headache. There are several different types of risks in research involving human subjects, including: medical risks (e.g., bleeding, bruising, nausea, toxicity, disability, death); psychosocial risks (e.g., pain, inconvenience, stress, stigma, discrimination), and economic risks (e.g., loss of income, owing money for medical treatment due to research injuries) (Resnik, 2018).

Anticipated benefits also include quantitative and qualitative components, i.e., the probability of the beneficial (or good) outcome occurring and the value of that outcome. Anticipated benefits in research with human subjects include those that accrue to research participants, such as: receiving treatment for a disease or information about one's health, obtaining a sense of satisfaction by contributing to research, or earning money for participating in a study; as well as those that accrue to communities or society, such as: advancement of human knowledge, and practical applications of knowledge, including treatments, diagnostic tools, preventative measures, and social policies (Resnik, 2018).

Intuition in Risk/Benefit Decision-Making

Intuition can impact risk/benefit decision-making in research with human subjects in two different ways. First, when IRBs lack data concerning probabilities related to risks and anticipated benefits, they cannot use reasoning to make these judgments, but they must make them nevertheless. Their only recourse, it would seem, is to rely on intuition (Resnik, 2017). In some cases, data may be available. For example, the risk of a serious adverse event (SAE) occurring in allergy skin testing is 1/100,000, but 8/100 for general anesthesia (Resnik, 2018).* We could therefore say that a study involving only allergy skin testing is less risky than one involving general anesthesia. In other cases, perhaps the vast majority, data may be nonexistent or scarce. For example, suppose we know that it is possible that a person could fall into a deep depression after recalling a traumatic event during a research interview, but we do not know the probability that this will occur. To estimate this probability, we would need to rely on intuition. Or suppose that we know that producing knowledge that leads to the development of a new drug to treat a disease is an anticipated benefit of a Phase I drug safety test on healthy volunteers, but we do not know the probability that a given treatment will pass Phase I, II, and III testing and receive marketing approval, nor do we know whether a given treatment will produce more good than harm once it reaches the market. To estimate the probability of this anticipated benefit, we would again need to rely on intuition (Resnik, 2017). In general, data concerning anticipated societal and community benefits are likely

---

* A serious adverse event is an event that is life-threatening or results in death, hospitalization, permanent damage or disability, or congenital/birth defect (Resnik, 2018).

to be less available than data concerning risks and benefits to individuals, because most studies related to the impacts of research focus on individual risks and anticipated benefits (Resnik, 2018).

It might be argued that we can use reasoning to make probability judgments even when we lack data related to the outcomes in question, since we can use our background knowledge to estimate probabilities. For example, an investigator might estimate the probability of an SAE occurring in a Phase I study based on the results of prior animal studies and knowledge of the drug's chemical structure and its interaction with the body's metabolic pathways and waste elimination systems. However, judgments that are not grounded in data are likely to be biased or erroneous, because they often depend on assumptions we make about how our knowledge applies to the situation in question (Resnik, 2017). For example, in 2006, six healthy volunteers participating in a Phase 1 study at St. Mark's Hospital in London needed to be hospitalized due to severe immune reactions they had to a monoclonal antibody that had been tested in animals but not in humans. The investigators had considerable knowledge about the antibody but did not anticipate how it would interact with the human immune system (Resnik, 2018).

Second, even when IRBs have sufficient data to estimate probabilities related to risks and anticipated benefits, they may need to rely on intuition concerning the qualitative components of risks and benefits, because assessments of the severity of harms and the value of benefits are moral judgments, which are at least partly intuitive. For example, suppose that investigators plan to study the effectiveness of a malaria vaccine by administering it to healthy volunteers from an African country where malaria is prevalent but who have not contracted the disease. They will expose the participants to malaria-carrying mosquitos to determine whether the vaccine is effective at preventing the disease. Participants who test positive for malaria will receive free treatment (Sauerwein et al., 2011). To evaluate the risks and anticipated benefits of the study, an IRB must be able not only to answer empirical questions concerning the probability of contracting malaria in the African country and the effectiveness of treatment but also qualitative questions like: What is the value of developing a malaria vaccine? For the country? For the world? Does the value of the knowledge gained from this study justify the risk of exposing healthy volunteers to malaria? Answering questions like these requires IRB members to place the risks and anticipated benefits of the study in a larger moral framework, because these questions deal with human values, not probability estimates. If moral judgments are at least partly intuitive (see earlier discussion), then the answers to these questions must also be based on intuition.

Some commentators have argued that we can rely on reasoning to make qualitative judgments related to risk by using a rating scale that classifies different adverse outcomes for human subjects. Rid et al. (2010) have developed a scale for classifying harms to human subjects based on their duration and magnitude (or quality). The categories of adverse outcomes include: negligible (e.g., mild nausea), small (e.g., headache), moderate (e.g., insomnia lasting one month), significant (e.g., ligament tear with no permanent disability), major (e.g., permanent, disabling arthritis), severe (e.g., loss of a limb or paraplegia), catastrophic (e.g., permanent, severe dementia or death). Although using something like the scale proposed by Rid et al. (2010) may allow IRBs to use reasoning in making judgments concerning the qualitative components of risks, it does not completely eliminate the use of intuition, because the scale itself is based on moral judgments we make concerning the ranking of adverse outcomes and one may need to rely on intuition when deciding where an adverse outcome lies on the scale (Resnik, 2017). For example, suppose that a study requires subjects to undergo a magnetic resonance imaging (MRI) test that involves spending 30 minutes sitting still inside a small imaging chamber. While some people might rate the adverse outcome of MRI testing as negligible or small, those with claustrophobia might rate it as significant or major. Or suppose a study involves a venipuncture to collect 100 ml of blood. There is a 20 percent chance of minimal bleeding or bruising due to the venipuncture. Although many people might rate the adverse outcome of the venipuncture as negligible or small, those who are afraid of being stuck with a needle might rate it as moderate or significant. Because people are likely to disagree about how to classify adverse outcomes on the scale, it is plausible to suppose that judgments that apply the scale to actual cases result, at least in part, from intuition. If these judgments were based entirely on reason, then we could achieve agreement on how to classify adverse outcomes by appealing to rational arguments (Resnik, 2017).

In theory, one could also develop a rating scale for classifying the anticipated benefits of research, but no one, to my knowledge, has done this. However, it is likely that such a scale would not eliminate reliance on intuition from qualitative judgments concerning anticipated benefits, because the scale itself would be based on moral judgments concerning the ranking of desired (or good) outcomes and one would still need to rely on intuition when deciding where an outcome lies on the scale (Resnik, 2017).

Bernabe et al. (2012) argue that we can eliminate intuition from qualitative judgments related to risks and anticipated benefits by basing our judgments on the values and beliefs of the "reasonable person," an idea first suggested by Levine (1988). For example, to evaluate the harm associated with an MRI, one could form a judgment based on how a reasonable person would view the harm. Likewise, one could appeal to the values and beliefs of the reasonable person to evaluate benefits related to knowledge produced by a study. While relying on the values and beliefs of the reasonable person may bring reasoning to bear on qualitative judgments concerning risks and benefits, it does not eliminate reliance on intuition, because the "reasonable person" is a normative concept based on a larger moral framework. For example, most people would say that a "reasonable person" would regard death as a catastrophic outcome that should be avoided in research, but this claim assumes a moral view about the value of life and the importance of avoiding death (Resnik, 2017).

Conclusion: Prospects for Reducing Reliance on Intuition

As we have seen, intuition impacts quantitative and qualitative components of judgments concerning risks and anticipated benefits in research involving human subjects. However, there are good reasons for reducing the use of intuition to avoid variation and inconsistency in risk/benefit decision-making when human beings participate in research. To protect human subjects and promote the advancement of science, it is important to reduce reliance on intuition in risk/benefit decision-making involving research with human subjects. What are the prospects for reducing reliance on intuition in this context?

The barriers to reducing the use of intuition regarding the quantitative components of judgments concerning risks and anticipated benefits are largely practical, because they are due to a lack of empirical data pertaining to probabilities concerning possible research outcomes. To address this problem, more research is needed on the risks of procedures, tests, interventions, and study designs. Moreover, IRB members need to become aware of this data and use it in decision-making. Investigators can provide IRBs with data concerning risks and anticipated benefits when they submit their research proposals to the board. To do this, they need to familiarize themselves with the published literature and summarize and interpret it for the IRB. Investigators should inform the IRB about gaps in knowledge concerning risks and benefits, as well as assumptions used to estimate probabilities. In some situations, data are not likely to be available because the protocol is testing a drug, biologic, or medical device that has not been used in human beings (Kimmelman, 2004). When this happens, investigators can make probability estimates based on prior animal studies and background knowledge, while implementing precautionary measures to protect human subjects from harm.* Funding agencies can support data collection efforts by sponsoring research on risks and anticipated benefits related to research involving human subjects. Research on anticipated benefits should include not only benefits to human subjects but also benefits to society related to knowledge advancement, drug development, health policy, etc.

Some barriers to using intuition in risk/benefit decision-making in research involving human subjects are not likely to be overcome, however, because they are conceptual, rather than practical, in nature. As we have seen, moral judgments, depend, in part, on our intuitions concerning matters of right/wrong, good/bad, and so on. We can use reasoning to develop principles for moral decision-making and scales for classifying risks and anticipated benefits, but reasoning can only go so far. Some reliance on intuition is inevitable when we make moral judgments.

---

* Some precautionary measures might include starting subjects on low doses of drugs or biologics and proceeding slowly with dose escalation; frequent monitoring of subjects for signs of toxicity, pain, and discomfort; and careful screening of subjects to ensure that they are healthy enough to participate in research without undue risk.

None of the preceding discussion implies that IRBs should forgo the attempt to reduce the use of intuition in making risk/benefit decisions, since over-reliance on intuition can have negative impacts on the protection of human subjects and the advancement of science. However, IRBs should understand that intuition often impacts their decision-making and should take steps to reduce their use of it, wherever possible.

Acknowledgments

This research was supported by the Intramural Program of the National Institute for Environmental Health Sciences (NIEHS), National Institutes of Health (NIH). It does not represent the views of the NIEHS, NIH, or U.S. government.

References

Aristotle. 2003 [350 BCE]. *Nichomachean Ethics*. Tredennick, H (ed.), Thompson, JA (transl.). New York: Penguin Books.

Audi, R. 2004. *The Good in the Right*. Princeton, NJ: Princeton University Press.

Bernabe, RD, van Thiel, GJ, Raaijmakers, JA, and van Delden, JJ. 2012. The risk-benefit task of research ethics committees: an evaluation of current approaches and the need to incorporate decision studies methods. *BMC Medical Ethics* 13:6.

Department of Homeland Security, Department of Agriculture, Department of Energy, National Aeronautics and Space Administration, Department of Commerce, Social Security Administration, Agency for International Development et al. 2017. Federal policy for the protection of human subjects. *Federal Register* 82(12):7149–7274.

Emanuel, EJ, Wendler, D, and Grady, C. 2000. What makes clinical research ethical? *Journal of the American Medical Association* 283(20):2701–2711.

Feinberg, M, Willer, R, Antonenko, and O, John OP. 2012. Liberating reason from the passions: overriding intuitionist moral judgments through emotion reappraisal. *Psychological Science* 23(7):788–795.

Green, LA, Lowery, JC, Kowalski, CP, and Wyszewianski, L. 2006. Impact of institutional review board practice variation on observational health services research. *Health Services Research* 41(1):214–230.

Haidt, J. 2001. The emotional dog and its rational tail: a social intuitionist approach to moral judgment. *Psychology Review* 108(4):814–834.

Haidt, J. 2007. The new synthesis in moral psychology. *Science* 316(5827):998–1002.

Hume, D. 2000 [1739]. *A Treatise of Human Nature*. Norton, DF, and Norton, MJ (eds.). New York: Oxford University Press.

Kahneman, D. 2011. *Thinking, Fast, and Slow*. New York: Farrar, Straus, and Giroux.

Kahneman, D, Slovic, P, and Tversky, A. (eds.). (1983). *Judgment under Uncertainty: Heuristics and Biases*. Cambridge: Cambridge University Press.

Kant, I. 1964 [1785]. *Groundwork for the Metaphysics of Morals*. H.D. Paton (transl). New York: Harper and Rowe.

Kimmelman, J. 2004. Valuing risk: the ethical review of clinical trial safety. *Kennedy Institute of Ethics Journal* 14(3):369–393.

Kimmelman, J, and Henderson, V. 2016. Assessing risk/benefits trials for using preclinical evidence: a proposal. *Journal of Medical Ethics* 42(1):50–53.

Klitzman, RL. 2015. *The Ethics Police? The Struggle to Make Human Research Safe.* New York: Oxford University Press.

Kohlberg, L. 1981. *The Philosophy of Moral Development, Volume One.* New York: Harper and Rowe.

Levine, RJ. 1988. *Ethics and the Regulation of Clinical Research,* 2nd ed. New Haven, CT: Yale University Press.

Liebowitz, J. (ed.). 2014. *Bursting the Big Data Bubble: The Case for Intuition-Based Decision Making.* Boca Raton, FL: Taylor & Francis Group.

Meslin, EM. 1990. Protecting human subjects from harm through improved risk judgments. *IRB* 12(1):7–10.

Mill, JS. 1979 [1861]. *Utilitarianism.* Sher, G (ed.). Indianapolis, IN: Hackett.

National Bioethics Advisory Commission. 2001. *Ethical and Policy Issues in Research Involving Human Participants. Volume I: Report and Recommendations of the National Bioethics Advisory Commission.* Bethesda, MD: National Bioethics Advisory Commission.

Pust, J. 2017. Intuition. *Stanford Encyclopedia of Philosophy.* Available at: http://plato.st anford.edu/entries/intuition/. Accessed November 5, 2018.

Rawls, J. 1971. *A Theory of Justice.* Cambridge, MA: Harvard University Press.

Resnik, DB. 2017. The role of intuition in risk/benefit decision-making in human subjects research. *Accountability in Research* 24(1):1–29.

Resnik, DB. 2018. *The Ethics of Research with Human Subjects: Protecting People, Advancing Science, Promoting Trust.* Cham, Switzerland: Springer.

Rid, A, and Wendler, D. 2011. A framework for risk-benefit evaluations in biomedical research. *Kennedy Institute of Ethics Journal* 21(2):141–179.

Rid, A, Emanuel, EJ, and Wendler D. 2010. Evaluating the risks of clinical research. *Journal of the American Medical Association* 304(13):1472–1479.

Shah, S, Whittle, A, Wilfond, B, Gensler, G, and Wendler, D. 2004. How do institutional review boards apply the federal risk and benefit standards for pediatric research? *Journal of the American Medical Association* 291(4):476–482.

Stark, L. 2012. *Behind Closed Doors: IRBs and the Making of Ethical Research.* Chicago, IL: University of Chicago Press.

Sauerwein, RW, Roestenberg, M, and Moorthy, VS. 2011. Experimental human challenge infections can accelerate clinical malaria vaccine development. *Nature Reviews Immunology* 11:57–64.

Van Luijn, HE, Musschenga, AW, Keus, RB, Robinson, WM, and Aaronson NK. 2002. Assessment of the risk/benefit ratio of phase II cancer clinical trials by institutional review board (IRB) members. *Annals of Oncology* 13(8):1307–1313.

Weijer, C. 2000. The ethical analysis of risk. *Journal of Law, Medicine & Ethics* 28(4):344–361.

Wendler, D, Belsky, L, Thompson, KM, and Emanuel EJ. 2005. Quantifying the federal minimal risk standard: implications for pediatric research without a prospect of direct benefit. *Journal of the American Medical Association* 294(7):826–832.

World Medical Association. 2013. Declaration of Helsinki: ethical principles for medical research involving human subjects. Available at www.wma.net/policies-post/wma-declaration-of-helsinki-ethical-principles-for-medical-research-involving-human-subjects/. Accessed November 1, 2018.

Chapter 10

On Leading and Making Data-Driven Decisions, or Not

Kenneth Carling

Contents

To Err Is Human

I have worked during the past two decades at Dalarna University in Sweden. In both formal and informal meetings outside the university, I frequently hear the question: What is the stand of Dalarna University on issue *x*? This is a question which I find bewildering. Working within a university, the idea of a unified stand on any one issue across its faculty members is beyond understanding, since the faculty consists of too many diverse, strong-minded individuals and decision makers with idiosyncratic objective functions. Formed in such an environment, I will limit what follows to individual decision-making after the following ingenuous remark. Humans are most certainly faced with collective decision-making. Unfortunately, Kenneth Arrow's Impossibility Theorem defines collective decisions achievable only as a dictatorial imposed decision (Arrow, 1963), which undeniably implies individual decision-making. Sen (1999) in his Nobel Laureate address puts forward an optimistic view on overcoming the impossibility by informational broadening that, inter alia, could be achieved by the members in the collective internalization of the other members' preferences (in their idiosyncratic decision-making). In what follows, I disregard the issue of collective decision-making by assuming that individual decision-making can be made collectively satisfactory by the internalization of other members' preferences, values, and beliefs, retrieved by the individual in the collective decision-making process (for instance, via decision engineering; March, 1978).

By this disclaimer, we focus in what follows on an individual decision maker, which, for the sake of concreteness, is a business leader with a high degree of dictatorship in his decision-making. He faces a (very simple) business decision where he has to evaluate the return-on-investment (ROI) of only one possible investment. The cost of investment is uncertain to him, and the long-term, future return is even more uncertain. In fact, at the outset he only has a hunch about the cost and the return. Let us assume that the statistical distribution characterizing the cost uncertainty is $g(c)$, and the corresponding statistical distribution for the discounted return is $f(r)$. Arguably, the business leader should decide for the investment if

$$E[R-C] - \lambda \text{Var}(R-C) > 0, \tag{10.1}$$

where the uppercase letters indicate the random variables return and cost, and λ indicates the decision maker's penalty coefficient, representing his risk willingness. A risk-neutral decision maker would set $\lambda = 0$, or else positive (negative) for a risk-avert (risk-loving) decision-maker.

The decision rule in Equation (10.1) implies some technical issues (and some assumptions that I do not elaborate on for the sake of simplicity). The business leader needs, in addition to knowing his risk willingness, to submit an estimate for f and g, and, even more difficult, the joint distribution $h(r,c)$, and on top of that be able to derive the expectation and variance, which requires a decent command of probability calculus. For the time being, assume that the business leader already knows or possesses data that is helpful for estimating the joint distribution $h(r,c)$ (from which the marginal distributions can be derived). What are the odds that his *instinct* is sufficient for applying the decision rule in Equation (10.1) in a rational way?

Here is a little eye-opening test, inspired by the works of Tversky and Kahneman (1974), that I have used with several cohorts of students. These students are somewhat proficient in probability calculus. "You are walking on a street in Washington, D.C., in the United States. In the unlikely event that you meet Barack Obama, is he more likely to … (a) be wearing a suit *or* (b) be surrounded by six hefty bodyguards while he is dressed in a suit?" The students are asked to pick their choice promptly, relying on their instinct. The vast majority choose the (b) alternative, in spite of having been trained to know that the probability for an outcome of a single event is at least as high as the corresponding probability for a joint event. In a slightly less trivial test, they are also asked to evaluate the following:

> A cab was involved in a hit-and-run accident at night. Two cab companies, the green and the blue, operate in the city. Here are some facts:
>
> (A) 85 percent of the cabs in the city are green and 15 percent are blue.
> (B) A witness identified the cab as blue. The reliability of the witness was tested and he correctly identified each one of the colors 80 percent of the time, and failed 20 percent of the time.
>
> Are odds in favor of the cab belonging to the blue company?

Again, the students get it wrong by instinct. However, if the facts are presented to them in a sequential order, so they are first given (A), and thereafter (B), the students protest and say that they need some time to process the new information provided by the (B) alternative. In the latter situation, they first realize that the best shot for the probability of the cab being blue is 0.15, and upon receiving the (B) information, they realize that they need Bayes' rule to update the probability, which can be worked out with some effort to be 0.41.

In yet another test, the students are introduced to a scary, wild, Swedish landscape at nighttime, in a text about an unidentified, large, and furry animal watching a girl, where the students are asked to choose between the possibility of the animal being a wolf or an elk. Invariably, the students promptly suggest that the animal is a wolf, in spite of there being only 200 wolves in Sweden, but some 138,000 elk. Apart from data science students obviously having limited experience of game hunting, it is remarkable that no student has ever posed the question of whether predators are more common than their prey, or the other way around.

Kahneman's (2011) elegant summary of research on cognitive biases in humans suggests a pessimistic view on humans' ability to manage rational decisions whenever uncertainty, probability calculus, and data are involved. Hence, the odds for the decision maker instinctively and rationally managing the investment decision above are gloomy.

Machines Don't Err...

It is a trivial task to write a script for the cab example above that generates the odds for the involved cab to be blue, where the odds are updated via the Bayes' rule on new facts being added to the case. In fact, it is also a fairly simple task to write a script for the business leader's investment decision. The script could be set up as follows. It would ask for historical data on returns and costs for comparable investment projects (not forgetting the non-realized projects), as well as the business leader's hunches on the return and cost for the investment. The data is thereafter used for Kernel-estimating $h(r,c)$ and obtaining the expectation and variance quantities by numerical approximation, via Monte Carlo simulations. To obtain λ, as the remaining quantity to feed into the decision rule, the classical approach to extracting individuals' risk preferences could be applied. The machine places, for instance, $1000 on the table, and offers the business leader a game with a 50-50 outcome, where the business leader gets the $1000 from the machine if he wins. To enter the game, he must risk losing an input that could range from $500, to be stepwise increased by $100 per call. Suppose the business leader is willing to play at all inputs of $1000 and less, then it can be deduced that he is risk-neutral, and $\lambda = 0$, and so forth. By this setup, the machine can assist the business leader in order to ensure that he complies with the decision rule, in spite of his potential cognitive biases.

Actually, the machine can be of even greater assistance. Add to the script a visualization tool and a user interface, where the business leader can modify the quantities involved to examine various outcome scenarios for the not-yet-decided-for investment project. The visualization tool serves to depict the uncertainty of the outcome. It is divided in a part that relates to the incompleteness in the input data that leads to uncertainty in estimating $h(r,c)$ with a recommendation on what data acquisition action to take to reduce this uncertainty, and another part that relates to the outcome uncertainty of the investment. For instance, the probability that the cost exceeds the returns could be depicted with a complementary histogram of the distribution of losses of the investment, to allow for the identification of the worst-case scenario.

... but Leaders Don't Embrace Machines

Upon receiving the machine, I guess the business leader would initially be happy and go play with it. But I also guess that he would return shortly with a series of complaints after realizing that the machine is of little assistance for fundamental concerns in his decision-making. One concern would be when a good-enough analysis has been attained. Creativity can infinitely be allocated to feeding the machine with new data to improve the estimate of $h(r,c)$, but does it pay off? Along the same lines, the business leader may well appreciate the machine's usefulness for operational decisions, where, most likely, data is less costly to acquire, but he may claim "I have subordinates to run the operation; I worry about the strategical decisions where 'comparable' data is very hard to come by." And most disappointedly remarks, "when the machine encounters an outlier it does not know what to do with it and asks for my expert opinion." And at the end of the day, is it the machine or the business leader that will convince the financial people and the staff to embark on the investment if deemed worthwhile?

No wonder that leaders, on a strategic level, are skeptical of over-riding their intuition for data-driven, formal decision-making. Loechner (2014) relates a report on executives that suggests a strong prevalence and preference, among the executives, to invoke intuition in the decision-making (as a complement to data-driven decision-making).

Intuition and Analytics (the Machine) as a Trade-Off

Consider the following quote of Syd Finkelstein: "Many senior executives believe the key to improving decision making is to move fast and learn from your mistakes. Learning from your mistakes is difficult and people often overestimate their ability to do it." From computer design, operations management, as well as from practical life, we know that being readily available helps in moving fast—putting the car keys and the smartphone in the pocket of your clothes, for instance, is wise. Intuition has the good attribute of being readily available when a decision is called for, while the decision maker may not know where to find the machine (if even aware of its existence), or the data, and might (rightly) assume that the machine needs to be customized for being useful for the particular decision to be taken.

Here a paradox arises. The decision maker would possibly make a better decision if he calls upon the machine. But who should assess "possibly" if not the decision maker? And by what means should that assessment be made, if not by the decision maker's intuition with regard to the value added to the decision by calling upon the machine? Let us return to the investment decision at the beginning of the chapter, and the machine constructed in the second section. The business leader should pose several questions: How good a decision can I make promptly, without the machine?; How good would it be with the help of the machine?; How will the ROI be affected if I delay the decision?; and How long would it take to have the machine up and running? In short, the business leader arrives at a situation of having to trade between the benefits of a prompt decision and the benefits of a more analytically based decision.

It goes without saying that the business leader must be aware of the machine-aid as an option for addressing (actually posing) these questions, and it would be quite helpful to have some informed intuition about the machine's benefits, and what machine parts could be bought directly off the shelf. And it would be even better if some of the best machine parts were already built-in, in the mind of the decision maker. Figuratively speaking, it would be good if Equation (10.1) was readily available in the business leader's cache memory, with his value on λ, whereby the added benefits from the machine would be reduced, and an intuitive and prompt decision without engaging the machine would be good enough. This strategy to improve decision-making has recently been explored in the literature, and I now turn to reiterate some key findings in this strand of the literature.

Statistical Numeracy and the Feasibility of Developing It

Cokely et al. (2018) state "effective decision making in our complex and uncertain world often requires the same kinds of reasoning and metacognitive skills (e.g., evaluating thinking, feelings, and risk) that are used when solving various practical probabilistic math problems." Other researchers have highlighted the need for *debiasing* the decision makers' cognitive biases associated with our, as humans, effort-saving heuristics, which are either insensitive to factors that normative (decision) theories suggest we should take into account, or sensitive to factors we should ignore (Chang et al., 2016).

It seems that the concern over poor decision-making, where poor here means deviation from what normative decision theory suggests, arose with the findings of Tversky and Kahneman (1974), who indicated numerous flaws in people's intuitive understanding of probability. These findings were followed by many others that have helped us to understand the magnitude of the problem and provided us with a collection of terms to denote various forms of cognitive biases, when faced with uncertainty and probabilistic reasoning. Chang et al. (2016) point, however, to the fact that little attention has been dedicated to addressing the problem, an activity that has been referred to as debiasing with the scope of improving statistical numeracy (Cokely et al., 2018).

However, a first question is whether debiasing is possible. Starting in the 1990s, educational systems around the world recognized that it would be desirable for future generations to develop a basic statistical numeracy (at first it was [mathematical] numeracy that was of concern) (see also Dow, 1990 and Watson & Callingham, 2003). In an early paper on the issue, Fischbein and Gazit (1984) examined pupils, from 10 to 13 years, who received basic statistical training, on their ability to transfer this training to practical reasoning and decisions in their environment. They concluded that "implementation of a systematic program on probability may be carried out without particular difficulties, possibly starting from grade six" and "a course on probability (including practical activities) might have a positive beneficial effect on children's prejudices and misconceptions."

Another observation that speaks in favor of the realism of debiasing is that humans generally have good intuition about things that are similar to everyday encounters, and that we are able to make instinctive decisions that are generally good, based on comparisons with our experience in such situations. This has been pointed out by Kahneman (2011) and also Parkinson (2014), but as the latter phrased it, "we have poor intuition about things that are outside of everyday experience and very poor intuition about things that are totally alien."

To study if training debiases, and thereby improves, decision-making in very complex problems (things that are totally alien), Chang et al. (2016) report on putting trainees to the tough test of making geopolitical forecasting, by employing a training program titled CHAMPS KNOW. They found quite large, positive effects, in spite of the trainees having received a modest amount of (arguably, well-targeted) training. So I conclude this section by claiming that debiasing is possible by training and thereby allowing for statistical numeracy to be incorporated into the readily available cache memory of the intuitive decision maker (see also Fong et al., 1986). So how should we develop these skills?

How and What Numeracy to Develop?

Confronted with a decision problem, looking out for the so-called base rate is a good start. In the cab example above, it is wise to note that 85 percent of the cabs are green, and to revise the belief that the involved cab was green, much context-specific auxiliary information pointing toward the blue company would be required. Likewise, it would have been wise to find out the size of elk and wolf populations in Sweden before forming the beliefs in that example. In my review of research related to the topic of this chapter, I found (at least) four relevant strands of literature that are weakly connected, namely, studies in behavioral science, educational science, management science, as well as the intelligence community disciplines. In spite of the apparent lack of cross-fertilization between these four strands, they share the recommendation of being alert to the base rate. In what follows, I will rely on guidelines for developing intuitive awareness proposed in the management discipline (Sadler-Smith & Shefy, 2004), and, when justified, invoke best practice that has emerged in other disciplines, as well as adding my own reflections.

Sadler-Smith and Shefy (2004) offer seven recommendations, which will serve as the starting point. They are:

1. *Open up the closet.* That is, to reflect on one's openness to intuition, feelings, hunches, and so forth in judgments and decisions.
2. *Don't mix up your I's.* The I's refers to instinct, insight, and intuition, which should not be confused; that, in turn, asks for practicing in distinguishing between them.
3. *Elicit good feedback.*
4. *Get a feel for your batting averages.* That is, to benchmark one's intuition.
5. *Use imagery.* That is, to make use of images instead of formal languages such as words and mathematical symbols.
6. *Play devil's advocate.*
7. *Capture and validate your intuitions.*

Parallel with the above, Liebowitz (2017) and Liebowitz et al. (2017) have argued for the informed, intuitive decision maker who ought to possess analytic skills, such as problem-solving, intellectual curiosity, issue diagnosis, insight generation, synthesis of internal and external data, problem framing, and synthesis of financial and qualitative data. To this list, Liebowitz adds other skills. These are: (a) *Collaboration abilities*, such as team building, project management, and interpersonal communications (oral and written), (b) *creativity-enhancing* skills to think outside the box, (c) *business-speak, summarization, and data visualization* techniques for the analyst to explain their results to C-level executives, as well as (d) *learning by doing*, or testing by learning methods to sharpen the analytical and decision-making skill sets.

Chang and Tetlock (2016) stress that high-quality feedback is key to developing intuition in judgment and decision-making (cf. Sadler-Smith & Shefy [2004], and recommendations 3 and 4, and Liebowitz [2017] and Liebowitz et al. [2017], d), and they also elaborate on how to structure training problems in a way that elicits such feedback. Nonetheless, the question of how to achieve "learning by doing" in an environment of reduced cognitive bias begs an answer. Cokely et al. (2018) claim, on compelling grounds, that statistical numeracy is the strongest predictor of general decision-making skill.

In my view, the most appealing approach to developing intuitive decision-making skill is laid out in the CHAMPS KNOW training program, providing numerical feedback on historical judgment as an operational solution to the feedback issue (Chang et al., 2016). The acronym is built from probabilistic reasoning principles. CHAMPS stands for: Comparison classes (C); Hunt for the right information (H); Adjust and update forecasts when appropriate (A); Mathematical and statistical models (M); Post-mortem analysis (P); Select the right question to answer (S). And, in their context of judgment and decision in geopolitics, political reasoning principles; KNOW stands for: Know the power players and their preferences (K); Norms and protocols of institutions (N); Other perspectives should inform forecasts (O); Wildcards, accidents, and black swans (W).

Across the four literature strands, there is a consensus that feedback is crucial and that (repeatedly) practicing good judgment and decision-making are imperative for developing a better, intuitive decision-making skill (see also Paas, 1992). These aspects have carefully been included in the CHAMPS KNOW training approach: And while it is not made explicit by the acronym, the training draws on data visualization to enhance graphical literacy, as an important technique in fostering good decision-making (cf. Chang et al., 2016, and training in the second and third years).

I note that three crucial prerequisites need to be in place with the trainee for developing intuitive decision-making skills. The first is an awareness of the existence of the cognitive biases, and the second is a self-motivation for debiasing. This is perhaps not surprising. A more surprising finding was provided by Chang et al. (2017). They examined the quality in decision-making under decision process accountability as well as outcome accountability. It has been argued elsewhere that feedback based on uncertain outcomes related to the decision might be detrimental in developing decision-making skills, as such feedback would confound a good decision-making process with a random outcome beyond the trainee's management. In spite of this objection, Chang et al. (2017) report that judgment performance is enhanced in a setting where both process and outcome accountability are put on the trainee. It is nevertheless important to recognize that developing good intuition for decision-making requires an environment that is tolerable to decisions with unfortunate outcomes, as long as the decision-making process is well executed.

Having said this about training principles, I now return to the question of what constitutes important training topics. I will divide these topics into (i) probabilistic reasoning (i.e., statistical numeracy), (ii) decision context reasoning, and (iii) intrapersonal reasoning, where (ii) and (iii) connect to the KNOW part of CHAMPS KNOW. Scholarly literature and traditional academic education in course modules offer an exhaustive range of topics, including also the topics needed here. The core problem is the lack of integration of the topics for effective developing of general decision-making skills, because the goal of training should be to debias the cache memory for a readily available library of decision rules.

I claim that for probabilistic reasoning (i) it is imperative to develop skills in counterfactual analysis, a topic that seldom constitutes a course module in its own right, but appears as a mindset in a vast range of courses offered by heterogeneous academic disciplines. Counterfactual analysis can be both backward- and forward-looking and serves to assess the potential outcomes of competing actions (and, if backward-looking, the action undertaken, i.e., the outcome of the factual). Counterfactual analysis develops skill in identifying potential, competing actions, and finding the means of assessing actions, either for deciding on the action to take, or for future learning, or both.

It is important to stress counterfactual analytical skills, since any ensuing data analysis will inevitably be used for judgment (or, in statistical jargon, estimation) within the counterfactual framework of the decision maker. Relating to CHAMPS KNOW, I claim that counterfactual analysis covers C, H, P, and S in the training program, but, to the best of my knowledge, there is no university that offers a counterfactual analysis course applying best practice across academic disciplines. However, it seems obvious that practicing scenario analysis and simulations would be a part of an apt curriculum.

Furthermore, the decision-making process involves joining disparate, uncertain judgments, most likely, attaching unequal weights to these judgments, where the judgments might arrive at different instances. A fundamental, statistical skill is the ability to effortlessly make use of Bayes' rule, which is the workhorse for updating probabilities upon receiving new information. Effortlessness is key here, as the rule is a challenge for the human brain. I dare say that no more probability calculus skills are required for attaining general decision-making skills than what are required for automating Bayes' rule in one's mind.

In statistics, the term estimation normally replaces judgment. It is true that statistical estimation is concerned with extracting the essence of numerical data;

however, the theory of estimation as developed within the statistical discipline offers strategies for best practice in judgment beyond numerical data. For instance, an old and celebrated principle in estimation theory is to minimize the mean squared errors (MSE). Technically, it implies selecting a model that fits the data in such a way that the summed, squared errors (the misfits) are the smallest possible. As a principle, this concept provides ground for weighting the more well-known concepts of validity and reliability into a single quantity. The many insights that have emerged in the last centuries in estimation theory are (and should be) transferable to judgment in general. Thus, estimation theory is a good source for anyone wishing to enhance his/her decision-making skills.

Tangent to estimation theory is extreme-value theory. For computer scientists the worst case is an important benchmark quantity, and rightly so (cf. W, in CHAMPS KNOW). Extreme-value theory, unfortunately, being generally inaccessible due to a sophisticated, mathematical machinery, provides a great source of principles and tools for assessing the unknown, unexperienced, and the extreme— that is, everything that provides wonderful business opportunities.

It is unfortunate that the many useful results from humankind's study of probability and uncertainty, that one wishes the decision maker to have built into his/her cache memory, are so hard to access, due to the mathematical and logical rigor and formalism by which they are presented. Deconinck (2015) published a paper upon completing his Ph.D. to advise fellow Ph.D.s on tricks to overcome the difficulty of succeeding with the doctoral degree. Here is a passage from his paper (his first name is Koen):

> I almost did not notice, but I just applied a trick here: if you want to know more about a subject, try to read a popular science book or article instead of diving straight into the academic literature. "But, Koen," you might be saying, "I don't have time to read those popular science books!" Ah, but if you can find a good popular science book about a topic you are working on, it will actually save you a lot of time down the road. You will be more knowledgeable, it will be easier to understand arguments in the literature, and it will be easier to see to which other studies your own work can be linked. Of course, not every field or topic has good popular science books, but you would be surprised at how many good popular science books are out there, even about topics such as statistics or game theory.

I very much agree, and hasten to recommend Christian and Griffiths (2016) as an example that in a popular and humorous way explains Bayes' rule, and "overfitting," which is a central theme in estimation theory, as well as randomness in itself.

I recognize that statistical numeracy is key to good decision-making skills, but good probabilistic reasoning is insufficient. The KNOW part contains additional skills needed. I claim that game theory, and strategies to address undesirable outcomes in a game referred to as "Mechanism Design," offer a great many insights valuable to an intuitive decision maker, and I advocate that the key findings in this discipline are loaded into one's cache memory (cf. K, in the CHAMPS KNOW). To this topic, I would want to add stopping theory as a great tool to manage the trade-off dilemma in decision-making, as well as scheduling theory to intuitively assess the implementability of a decision. Obviously, the scholarly literature on these three topics is immense, but the fundamental lessons are possible to find from a handful of papers per topic.

To underscore the point that an exhaustive search of the literature on a topic is overly ambitious, I point the reader to the paper by Gächter and Renner (2018) that can be read in an hour. It outlines that the fundamental role of a (business) leader is to manage the social dilemmas in an organization (i.e., to take care of situations where the employees' self-interests are in conflict with the organization's common interests). It demonstrates that the leader needs to be thick-skinned and act as an altruistic role model with regard to the dilemma, in order to foster an organizational culture that effectively overcomes social dilemmas. And the leader needs to be steadfast from day one. While speaking of collectivism, which is another collection of findings to load into the cache memory, it is helpful for the decision maker to be aware of some cultural variation in the degree of collectivism. Van Hoorn (2014) relates geographical variation in cultural individualism that affects how the members cooperate within an organization around a decision, and how they respond to individualized incentive schemes to attain the organization's goals (cf. Liebowitz, point [a] in the list earlier in this chapter).

I conclude this commentary by supporting Liebowitz's point (c) that recognizes communication skills as highly desirable for the decision maker. Graphical literacy and the use of imagery are helpful to the intuitive decision maker both in shaping the decision and in conveying it to bodies concerned. Regrettably, my working knowledge of communication theory is insufficient for a further elaboration on how to develop such skills.

Concluding Discussion

Up to this point I have tried to integrate my intuition about developing informed intuition for decision-making with analytics in the form of retrieving theories and best practice from the research literature, and to process these data with analytical methods. This strategy brought me to a preliminary position subject to devil's advocate testing. I circulated the thoughts to a large set of heterogeneous decision makers and academics asking for their holistic feedbacks. This feedback led to my desire to add three things.

I am skeptical of the possibility of successfully reconciling intuition with a mechanistic view. I have deliberately refrained from trying to define intuition in my writing, leaving it to the reader to load the concept with a meaning while reading.

For anyone finding this unsatisfactory, I point to Gobet (2017) and confess that I concur with the view labeled G&C in his paper.

Fernand Gobet, like many others, including Daniel Kahneman, has studied or reflected on the "clinical eye" supposedly developed by experts in healthcare such as physicians and nurses. My wife, who is a senior physician, made the following prosaic remark on "clinical eye": "You see the patient, have a hunch, initiate the investigation, take the lab tests, and have the hunch confirmed or rejected in a few days by the outcome of the lab tests and the patient's response to the treatment." That is, in her view the "clinical eye" is developed by good feedback and a good estimate of the batting averages (cf. Sadler-Smith & Shefy [2004], and recommendations 3 and 4). However, I do not believe that this context-specific intuition transfers to general decision-making skills.

I do not believe I have given the appropriate weight to spatial reasoning skills for a training curriculum, for individual decision-making as well as for collaborative reasoning and decision-making. So I conclude with the following assertions. I do believe that spatial intelligence enhances creative and good decisions (Cooper, 2000). I do believe that spatial reasoning can be effectively trained (Deshpande & Huang, 2011). And I do believe that tools for visualization are helpful for decision-making individually as well as collaboratively (Clarke & Mackaness, 2001).

Acknowledgments

Several persons have affected this work, but I foremost want to mention Moudud Alam, Maria Carling, Irene Gilsenan Nordin, Johan Håkansson, Bin Jiang, Luis Oliveira, Lena Nerhagen, and Torbjörn Swenberg who had a direct impact on the final outcome. And there would not have been an outcome if it had not been for Jay Liebowitz stimulating my thinking on the topic. However, any errors in the chapter are mine alone.

References

Arrow, K. (1963). 1951. *Social Choice and Individual Values*. London, UK: Yale University Press.

Chang, W., & Tetlock, P. E. (2016). Rethinking the training of intelligence analysts. *Intelligence and National Security*, 31(6), 903–920.

Chang, W., Atanasov, P., Patil, S., Mellers, B. A., & Tetlock, P. E. (2017). Accountability and adaptive performance under uncertainty: A long-term view. *Judgment and Decision Making*, 12(6), 610.

Chang, W., Chen, E., Mellers, B., & Tetlock, P. (2016). Developing expert political judgment: The impact of training and practice on judgmental accuracy in geopolitical forecasting tournaments. *Judgment and Decision Making*, 11(5), 509–526.

Christian, B., & Griffiths, T. (2016). *Algorithms to Live By: The Computer Science of Human Decisions*. Macmillan.

Clarke, I., & Mackaness, W. (2001). Management 'intuition': An interpretative account of structure and content of decision schemas using cognitive maps. *Journal of Management Studies*, 38(2), 147–172.

Cokely, E. T., Feltz, A., Ghazal, S., Allan, J. N., Petrova, D., & Garcia-Retamero, R. (2018). Decision making skill: From intelligence to numeracy and expertise. In K.A. Ericsson, N. Charness, P.J. Feltovich, R.R. Hoffman, eds, *Cambridge Handbook of Expertise and Expert Performance*. Cambridge University Press.

Cooper, E. E. (2000). Spatial-temporal intelligence: Original thinking processes of gifted inventors. *Journal for the Education of the Gifted*, 24(2), 170–193.

Deconinck, K. (2015). Trust me, I'm a doctor: A PhD survival guide. *The Journal of Economic Education*, 46(4), 360–375.

Deshpande, A. A., & Huang, S. H. (2011). Simulation games in engineering education: A state-of-the-art review. *Computer Applications in Engineering Education*, 19(3), 399–410.

Dow, M. A. (1990). A unified approach to developing intuition in mathematics. In R. K. Wallace, D. W. Orme-Johnson, & M. C. Dillbeck, eds, *Scientific Research on the Transcendental Meditation and TM-Sidhi Program: Collected Papers*, Vol. 5. Fairfield, IA: Maharishi International University, pp. 3386–3398.

Fischbein, E., & Gazir, A. (1984). Does the teaching of probability improve probabilistic intuitions?. *Educational Studies in Mathematics*, 15(1), 1–24.

Fong, G. T., Krantz, D. H., & Nisbett, R. E. (1986). The effects of statistical training on thinking about everyday problems. *Cognitive Psychology*, 18(3), 253–292.

Gächter, S., & Renner, E. (2018). Leaders as role models and 'belief managers' in social dilemmas. *Journal of Economic Behavior & Organization*, 154, 321–334.

Gobet, F. (2017). Three views on expertise: Philosophical implications for rationality, knowledge, intuition and education. *Journal of Philosophy of Education*, 51(3), 605–619.

Kahneman, D. (2011). *Thinking, Fast and Slow*. New York: Farrar, Straus and Giroux.

Liebowitz, J. (2017). Educating informed 'intuitants'. *SAS Exchange*. Retrieved from www.sas.com/en_us/insights/articles/analytics/educating-informed-intuitants.html.

Liebowitz, J., Paliszkiewicz, J., & Gołuchowski, J. (eds.) (2017). *Intuition, Trust, and Analytics*. Boca Raton, FL: CRC Press.

Loechner, J. (2014), Executive decisions: Gut feel, big data or collaborative? Center for Media Research, June 18. Retrieved from www.mediapost.com/publications/article/228031/executive-decisions-gut-feel-big-data-or-collabo.html.

March, J. (1978). Bounded rationality, ambiguity, and the engineering of choice. *The Bell Journal of Economics*, 9(2), 587–608.

Paas, F. G. (1992). Training strategies for attaining transfer of problem-solving skill in statistics: A cognitive-load approach. *Journal of Educational Psychology*, 84(4), 429.

Parkinson, J. (2014), The role of intuition in a world of Big Data. *CFO*, Jan. 29. Retrieved from www.cfo.com.

Sadler-Smith, E., & Shefy, E. (2004). The intuitive executive: Understanding and applying 'gut feel' in decision-making. *Academy of Management Executive*, 18(4), 76–91.

Sen, A. (1999). The possibility of social choice. *American Economic Review*, 89(3), 349–378.

Tversky, A., & Kahneman, D. (1974). Judgment under uncertainty: Heuristics and biases. *Science*, 185(4157), 1124–1131.

Van Hoorn, A. (2014). Individualism and the cultural roots of management practices. *Journal of Economic Behavior & Organization*, 99, 53–68.

Watson, J., & Callingham, R. (2003). Statistical literacy: A complex hierarchical construct. *Statistics Education Research Journal*, 2(2), 3–46.

Chapter 11

Studying Intuition and Creativity: Identifying Intuition-Rich Contexts and Candidates for Research

Eric W. Stein

Contents

Introduction

This chapter addresses links between creativity and intuition, although it is easy to argue that the task is much too large for a single chapter (or even a few). Creativity itself is a huge topic and encompasses many disparate experiences. Similarly, intuition is a rich and multivariate construct. Therefore, to make headway, I chose to contextualize creativity in terms of four behavioral and cognitive outcomes, and to identify the types of people who express them.

This approach is consistent with a line of inquiry I have been pursuing for the past decade. I have been engaged in explorations in creativity in the following four areas: real-time decision-making using improvisation (I), creative problem-solving using design (D), knowledge creation using scientific methods and experimentation (E), and perception and flow as part of the aesthetic (A). Conveniently, these attributes spell out the word, IDEAS (where S stands for strengths). I have used IDEAS as a vehicle to explore creativity in a variety of works (Stein, 2011, 2014a, 2014b). Interestingly, the study of creativity (and intuition) is in alignment with my earlier works on organizational memory (e.g., Stein and Zwass, 1995; Stein, 1995), knowledge management (e.g., Stein, Pauster, and May, 2003; Stein, Manco, and Manco, 2001; Stein and Miscikowski, 1999), organizational learning (e.g., Stein and Vandenbosch, 1996), human expertise (e.g., Stein, 1995), and communities of practice (e.g., Stein, 2005, 2007; Hornett and Stein, 2007).

Why have I chosen these four expressions of creativity? There are several reasons. First, creativity is a bit of a garbage can in which there are many streams of research ranging from psychology to education to strategy. I wanted to focus on specific and concrete behaviors and cognitions that are aligned with modern organizations. Second, they each represent key areas of strength that it can be demonstrated all organizations, and individuals, should possess to be effective. Indeed, one could argue that IDEAS is a key to competitive advantage. For instance, Apple has been rated to have the highest market cap in the world more than once at over a trillion dollars (*Forbes*, 2018). Why? Apple's remarkable growth is the result of its extraordinary design capabilities as evidenced by the iPhone and other products. Design requires an appreciation of both function and form. Apple nails both, which allows it to sell its products at premium prices. Aesthetic awareness is a key competitive advantage that Apple has had since its inception. Furthermore, its ability to improvise and to experiment in order to get the right value-proposition to the consumer is written into its DNA. Apple, Amazon, Microsoft and a host of other industry leaders leverage IDEAS to great advantage. I think it is important to understand how they do it and how to cultivate these skills.

In this chapter, I will begin by reviewing some of the research on intuition while borrowing key insights and distinctions from the literature for this analysis. I introduce a scorecard that indicates the degree to which a person's problem-solving context is considered "intuition rich." Next, I examine each of the four areas for

Figure 11.1 Creative types in four key areas.

creative expression and indicate the potential role intuition plays in each area. The four key creative types are illustrated in Figure 11.1.

In my opinion, each creative type is a fruitful target for continued research on intuition. In each section, I discuss the strengths that these individuals exhibit and the degree to which they exercise those skills in intuition-rich environments. I close each section with a scorecard as to the degree to which each area of creative expression aligns with intuition-rich contexts. In the penultimate section, I discuss a means to help identify potential candidates for intuition study. I briefly describe an instrument that I have developed that assesses the degree to which an individual scores as an improviser, designer, scientist, or artist. I close the chapter with my conclusions and ideas for future research.

What Is Intuition?

The study of intuition has a long and rich history. Einstein famously remarked that, "The intuitive mind is a sacred gift and the rational mind is a faithful servant" (Culham, 2015, p. 294). Multiple disciplines including psychology, philosophy, and management have made contributions, although not in consistent ways, prompting one researcher to quip, "it makes one wonder whether the term has any meaning at all" (Epstein, 2008, p. 23). Fortunately, recent reviews of the topic have restored some order to the concept and provided a much needed roadmap for continued work.

Akinci and Sadler-Smith (2012) provide a thorough review of the various streams of thought on the topic and the reader is referred to their work for a complete understanding of the progression. They break intuition research into two major streams: (i) research from base disciplines such as psychology and (ii) research from the management literature. The former stream includes the early work of Jung's personality types in the 1930s. It also includes Herbert Simon's seminal work on bounded rationality, the implication being that intuition falls outside the boundaries of normal analytical cognition. The influential work by Polanyi on tacit knowledge is noted, which suggests a cognitive home for intuition. Later work on heuristics by Kahneman and Tversky, as well as Simon, also make contribution. The role of expertise in providing fertile ground for intuition is further supported by Simon's work on codifying expertise for artificial intelligence programs, as well as the Dreyfus brothers' fundamental critique of the limits of such attempts to "clone" human cognition and reasoning. The 1990s is notable for works by Epstein and others, while the first decade of the 21st century includes numerous works including those of Kahneman and Klein, among others.

On the management side, Akinci and Sadler-Smith (2012) trace early mention of the topic back to Chester Barnard's distinction between logical and non-logical processes. Mintzberg's (1976) seminal work on "Planning on the Left Side and Managing on the Right" reinforces the idea that the seat of intuition emanates from the right side of the brain. Throughout the 1980s and 1990s several works by Robey, Agor, Isenberg and others begin inquiry into the role of intuition in managerial decision-making and its impacts on the organization. More recent works have looked at the role of intuition in specific organizational functions and activities from entrepreneurship (e.g., Blume, Covin) to organizational learning (e.g., Crossan), to strategy (e.g., Khatri, Hodgkinson) to skill development (e.g., Hogarth).

Baldacchino et al. (2015) do an excellent job of mapping the various definitions and conceptualizations of intuition. "Broadly speaking, intuition is a source of knowledge distinct from a more logical, analytical or rational mode of reasoning…." (Baldacchino et al., 2015, p. 213). This characterization of intuition as a foil to the analytical aspects of the human mind is a common thread in the research. Baldacchino et al. (2015, p. 213–214) further outline four primary characteristics of intuition:

1. Intuition originates beyond conscious thought.
2. Intuitive processes are associative and holistic.
3. Feelings, emotions, and affect play a key role in intuitive processes.
4. Intuition is linked to domain-specific experience and expertise.

We can use these distinctions to explore the role intuition plays in the creative contexts described in this chapter.

Another useful distinction regarding the conceptualization of intuition is from a theory construct perspective. Several works (e.g., Baldacchino et al., 2015; Thompson, 2014; Sinclair and Ashkanasy, 2005) articulate the emergence of competing concepts of intuition from a unitary or dual-processing view. The unitary processing view posits that people perceive information and make decisions by relying on a single psychological process as noted by Allinson and Hayes in 1996 (appearing in Baldacchino et al., 2015).

Dual-processing theories on the other hand, "share the assumption that individuals rely on two distinct but complementary cognitive systems to process information (Evans, 2010)"(Baldacchino et al., 2015, p. 217). We adopt the latter point of view that there are two distinct means of processing information available to the brain: one for analytical decision-making and one for intuitive decision-making (Sinclair and Ashkanasy, 2005). See Figure 11.2.

Figure 11.2   Dual-processing view of human decision-making.

Table 11.1   Scorecard to Assess the Degree to Which a Context Is "Intuition-Rich"

Factor	Score (Y, N, p > 0)	Analysis
Analytical Processing Requirements		
Supplemental Processing Capabilities		
Linked to domain-specific experience and expertise		
Feelings, emotions, and affect play a key role in processes		
Knowledge originates beyond conscious thought		
Processes are associative and holistic		

In the following sections, we will use these distinctions to examine the role of intuition in the four areas of creativity denoted by IDEAS. Toward that end, I have constructed the following tabular "scorecard" that can be applied to assess the degree to which the creative context is "intuition-rich." We can use this tool to illustrate the overlap each creative area has with intuition and to pinpoint subjects for future research (Table 11.1).

The Improviser: Real-Time Decision-Making Using Improvisation (I)

About 20 years ago, management scholars became very interested in the role of improvisation in managerial decision-making. In 1998, a whole issue of the *Academy of Management Review* (Volume 23, Issue 4, 1998) was devoted to papers on improvisation. Around the same time period, placements on the topic in *Organization Science* (e.g., Peplowski, 1998) and even earlier in *Information Systems Research* (Orlikowski, 1996) appeared. Much of the work on improvisation rests on reflections on the nature of improvisation in other contexts such as jazz music. According to Berliner (1994):

> Improvisation involves reworking pre-composed material and designs in relation to unanticipated ideas conceived shaped and transformed under the special conditions of performance, thereby adding unique features to every creation.
>
> **(Berliner, 1994, p. 241)**

Berliner later refined this understanding in the following way, which emphasizes the expertise and deep knowledge required to be an effective improviser:

> The popular definitions of improvisation that emphasize only its spontaneous, intuitive nature ... are astonishingly incomplete. This simplistic understanding belies the discipline and experience on which improvisers depend, and it obscures the actual practices and processes that engage them. Improvisation depends ... on thinkers having absorbed a broad base of ... knowledge, including myriad conventions that contribute to formulating ideas logically, cogently, and expressively.
>
> **(Berliner, 1994, p. 492 as noted by Weick, 1998)**

Another aspect of improvisation, especially in a group setting, is the ability to engage in mindful introspection: "Making effective decisions in real-time group contexts requires that the decision maker make sense of what is being communicated by others in the moment and to self-reflect (or hear) the words and behaviors uttered by him or herself" (Stein, 2014a, p. 35). In the parlance of Karl Weick, improvisation requires the ability to engage in retrospective sense-making (Weick, 1998).

As a working proposition, I define improvisation in the following way:

> Improvisation is the ability to make effective real-time decisions in new and complex situations using current information and appropriately chosen (or modified) routines, scripts, and patterns.
>
> **(Stein, 2014a, p. 36)**

Let's unpack this definition. First, unlike the common notions of improvisation, which suggest making things up in the moment (e.g., bricolage), improvisation depends on agents having developed deep expertise in one or more bodies of knowledge (Stein, 2014a). For the jazz improviser, it is the scale and chord patterns that overlay shifting harmonies and rhythms that must be first internalized. Mastery takes years if not decades to achieve. As that knowledge becomes integrated into the player's repertoire, she or he is able to invoke appropriate patterns of information in real-time decision-making contexts such as a live performance in a club or on stage. The player must selectively and coherently "converse" with other members of the band as conditions change. Going too far astray will result in confusion by the listeners; sticking too close to the script will be met with a degree of ho-hum by the audience. Great solos incorporate well-worn patterns intermixed with surprises along the way.

If we were to apply the distinctions about intuition to the jazz player, this is what we would find (see Table 11.2).

Table 11.2   Intuition Context Scorecard for Jazz Musician

Factor	Score	Analysis
Analytical Processing Requirements	Yes	While earlier players in the 20th century relied on rote memorization and oral history, since the 1960s there has been an attempt to codify and transmit jazz knowledge to younger players. Numerous schools, camps, and workshops exist that leverage a plethora of books on the subject, each with its own "system" of analysis. Jazz studies programs at the college level emphasize analysis of harmony, composition and rhythm. What was formerly tacit knowledge has been converted to explicit knowledge (e.g., Nonaka, 2007).
Supplemental Processing Capabilities		
Linked to domain-specific experience and expertise	Yes	Mastery takes years of practice at both the experiential and cognitive levels.
Feelings, emotions, and affect play a key role in processes	Yes	Emotions play a key role in the expressions that come from jazz players, from soft heart-touching solos to fiery blasts of machismo and power.
Knowledge originates beyond conscious thought	Likely $p>0$	Most likely. Players will report being "out of mind" or in a state of wide-eyed bewilderment after a performance.
Processes are associative and holistic	Yes	Given the length of time required to gain mastery and the integration of biomechanical, cognitive, and emotional structures, it is likely that intuitive processes are holistic and associative.

Of course there are multiple contexts within which improvisation takes place; jazz is only one instance. I have categorized these contexts by the degree of structure of the problem space and by the magnitude of consequences (Stein, 2014a). Magnitude of Consequences (MoC) is defined by Jones (1991, p. 374) as the "sum of the harms (or benefits) done to victims (or beneficiaries) of the moral act in question." This approach yields four key contexts within which improvisers (and designers and others) operate. See Figure 11.3.

Managers, like jazz musicians, engage in frequent episodes of improvisation to handle unforeseen problems, changing goals, and changes in the environment. Like jazz players, effective managers and leaders develop deep knowledge in key areas of industry or organizational functions. Scripts and routines are followed … until they are not. Feelings play a key role along with analysis. Trusting your "gut" or more recently, your heart, has become a mantra. Interviews with top executives suggest moments during crisis when things became "clear," as solutions break through beyond conscious thought or directed analysis. Leaders, like jazz musicians, are performers. They make real-time decisions based on the analytical parts of their brain, but when overwhelmed with complexity or shortened timeframes, will improvise as necessary. I believe these episodes should be the target for the fruitful study of the role intuition plays in management decision-making. The question becomes: how do we identify frequent improvisers as subjects for our studies? I address that in a later section of the chapter.

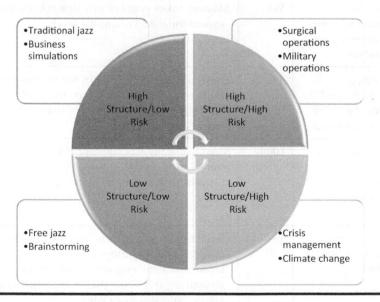

Figure 11.3 Contexts for improvisation.

The Designer: Creative Problem-Solving Using Design (D)

The ability to effectively design new products and services has become a key differentiating factor for businesses. One need only attend a conference such as the Consumer Electronics Show (CES) to revel in the power of design and its impact on society. In 2019, CES showcased more than 4,500 exhibiting companies, including manufacturers, developers, and suppliers of consumer technology hardware, content, and technology-delivery systems. The conference program included more than 250 conference sessions and more than 180,000 attendees from 150 countries (About CES, 2019). Hundreds of thousands of attendees were treated to smart toilets, loveable robots, new laptops, smart watches, and immense monitors. All of these innovations are possible because each company has developed the necessary expertise in design.

We can define this capability in the following way: "Design is the ability to envision and construct an object or process that meets the goals and requirements of a particular user" (Stein, 2014a, p. 51). Like improvisation, design operates in different contexts, based on the problem space structure and the magnitude of consequences. High-structure/low-risk projects include designing a print advertisement or a variation of an existing computer program. High-structure/high-risk projects include designing roadways, bridges, and power plants. Low-structure/low-risk projects include novel innovations such a new iPhone app or that smart toilet; we can live with or without them. Finally, low-structure/high-risk projects include designing transportation to the moon or Mars or a new healthcare system. Designers are the hidden, but vital and often unseen, assets of modern business organizations.

Throughout history designers have had a huge impact on our built world. From the works of Leonardo da Vinci to Edison to great architects such as Gehry to the designers at Tesla, Apple, or OXO, each has changed the way we interact with the world. One of the most potentially impactful contexts for design includes sustainable design, i.e., the massive redesign of products and services required to produce more sustainable recovery and reuse of what we build. These efforts are best articulated by McDonough and Braungart (2002).

Designers share certain characteristics. According to Tim Brown (2007), CEO of Ideo, designers have a unique skill and personality profile. On one hand, they develop deep knowledge and expertise in a particular domain of knowledge such as computer programing, aeronautics, or fashion. They ascend from novice to competency to mastery after years of immersion in a domain. In addition to their core expertise, another unique aspect of designers, however, is an ability and even a desire to work across disciplines. They embrace other disciplines and try to learn from them. Brown designates this dual profile as "T-shaped." The vertical leg of the T represents deep knowledge, while the horizontal part represents an ability to work across disciplines. Another critical characteristic of designers is empathy, i.e., the ability to appreciate and anticipate the needs of another person. Without empathy, all design is simply an exercise in hollow invention.

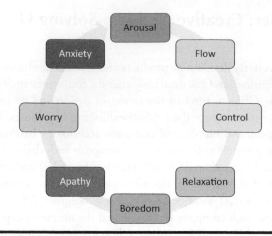

Figure 11.4   Internal states of test subjects based on relationship between skills and challenges.

Another interesting aspect of designers is the degree to which they engage in *flow* when in the process of designing and creating. Insights on the flow state come to us from decades of work by Mihaly Csikszentmihalyi, an organizational psychologist. Csikszentmihalyi (1996, 2004) has studied the internal states of athletes, leaders, designers, and artists using novel techniques for data collection. For example, a smartphone app might trigger at random intervals over the day by asking the participant to identify the current state he or she is in based on the relationship between that individual's skill level (high/low) and the task at hand (high/low). The choice of affective states includes those indicated in Figure 11.4.

Csikszentmihalyi's work focuses on and illuminates the experience of the flow state. His work finds a unique set of characteristics define this state, which are identified in Table 11.3.

It seems to me that designers (and anyone frequently in flow) are ideal candidates for intuition research. Table 11.4 applies our scorecard to designers.

Table 11.3   The Characteristics of Flow[a]

1. There are clear goals every step of the way. 2. There is immediate feedback to your actions. 3. There is a balance between challenges and skills. 4. Action and awareness are merged. 5. Distractions are excluded from consciousness. 6. There is no worry of failure. 7. Self-consciousness disappears. 8. The sense of time becomes distorted. 9. The activity becomes 'autotelic'—meaning it is an end in itself.

[a] Csikszentmihalyi (1996, 2004).

Table 11.4 Intuition Context "Scorecard" for Designers

Factor	Score	Analysis
Analytical Processing Requirements	Yes	Although design is oftentimes considered an "art," it also has become increasingly distilled into codified knowledge. For example, there now exist design templates especially in software development. Numerous books have been written on "design science," which tries to codify design into theories and principles.
Supplemental Processing Capabilities		
Linked to domain-specific experience and expertise	Yes	To become an expert designer takes years of practice at both the experiential and cognitive levels. Designers practice in the domain by taking on projects of increasing complexity and difficulty. Designers in one field are not likely to be proficient in other fields; e.g., we would not expect an architect to be able to design software apps or robots.
Feelings, emotions, and affect play a key role in processes	Yes	Emotions play a key role in the design of products and services. As noted earlier, having empathy, self-awareness, enthusiasm, and connection are all key attributes of good designers. It is not uncommon for designers to describe their works based on feelings and emotions.
Knowledge originates beyond conscious thought	Yes	It seems as if some parts of design lie outside of consciousness. It is not unusual for designers to solve problems in their sleep or while taking a walk.
Processes are associative and holistic	Yes	Descriptions of the flow state suggest that designers are in synch and pursue holistic thinking. They look for solutions outside of the confines of the reference domain, i.e., by leveraging associative thinking and methods.

The Scientist: Knowledge Creation Using Scientific Methods and Experimentation (E)

Einstein was decidedly clear on the dominant role that intuition plays in scientific discovery and knowledge creation:

> The supreme task of the physicist is to arrive at those universal elementary laws from which the cosmos can be built up by pure deduction. There is no logical path to these laws; only intuition, resting on sympathetic understanding of experience can reach them. ... The state of mind which enables a man to do work of this kind ... is akin to that of the religious worshipper or the lover; the daily effort comes from no deliberate intention or program, but straight from the heart.

> **(in Culham, 2015, p. 294)**

Einstein believed that intuition lead rational thinking and analysis and not the other way around. Einstein saw all great discovery as resulting from intuition and not through the application of logic or prior knowledge.

The great historian of scientific discovery Thomas Kuhn distinguishes between normal science and science that results in monumental shifts in paradigms or scientific revolutions (Kuhn, 1996), the kind that Einstein revered. Normal science is incremental and cumulative. It serves to refine and articulate the current domain of knowledge. Scientists who participate in these efforts are identified as *Masters* by Howard Gardner, the well-known developmental psychologist from Harvard. Gardner defines a Master as one who fully exhausts the knowledge domain in which he or she toils (Gardner, 1994). Masters explore all aspects of the domain and extend their boundaries, but without altering their fundamental assumptions or foundations. Mozart (classical music) was an example of a Master, as were the Rolling Stones (pop music).

In counter-position to Masters are Makers. Gardner (1994) defines a Maker as one who *re-makes* the domain by changing its rules and shifting the paradigm as noted by Kuhn. Einstein himself was a Maker. Makers in other fields include Charlie Parker (jazz music), The Beatles (pop music), Beethoven (classical music), Picasso (art), and Niels Bohr (quantum physics). Both Masters and Makers are deeply grounded in domain-specific knowledge. This is consistent with Herbert Simon's work on expertise that confirms that people need to accumulate at least 50,000 "chunks" of learning episodes to really master a domain, e.g., about 5 to 10 years (Simon, 1969). Malcolm Gladwell (2008) also suggests that 10,000 hours is the period of time required to reach critical mass in terms of expertise and insight. Gardner further observes that the average interval of time between major creative works is about 10 years. In short, Masters and Makers are not born overnight. Long intervals of time may elapse between dramatic contributions to knowledge. They are both deeply invested in the domain of knowledge, and vice versa. One can see from Einstein's quote that he favors the mind of the Maker as being grounded in intuition and that he cared less for Masters doing "normal science" as defined by Kuhn (1996).

However, we know that both are equally important to the process of discovery. The field of science is populated by both theoreticians and experimentalists, Makers and Masters. Theorists, like Einstein, prepare hypotheses using the language of mathematics and offer them up for testing by experimentalists. Both are creative and essential to scientific inquiry. For every Einstein there is a Rutherford or Curie. Formal scientific inquiry may be parsed into five distinct phases:

■ Craft theory and frame hypotheses.
■ Design experiment to collect data to test hypotheses.
■ Execute experiment.
■ Evaluate hypotheses.
■ Revise theory.

In its essence, scientific inquiry can be boiled down to *theory-test-revise*. Experimentation is thus fundamental to the knowledge creation process. An experiment is an opportunity to observe an event or object under certain conditions framed by the design. The context includes an observer and some object or process. Scientists collect sensory input (i.e., data) to test certain hypotheses and assumptions. Once the data is collected, it is analyzed for patterns and regularities, and referred back to theory.

> Experimentation is the ability of an observer to decide between two competing goals, courses of action, or viewpoints by designing a process that yields sufficient information to rank each choice according to certain criteria. This process is referred to as an experiment.
>
> **(Stein, 2014a, p. 86)**

Of course, not all forms of learning and knowledge creation are the result of formal experiments. Experimentation in normal life may be described more aptly as "tinkering." Brown (2008) argues that we produce new knowledge and learn by informal testing, i.e., tinkering. Kolb's (1984) model of experiential learning builds on the work of the pragmatists such as Dewey, and makes testing of mental models and theories to be fundamental to the knowledge production process. He refers to this stage as "active experimentation."

While scientific inquiry may be formal and structured, at least on paper, scientists often report bursts of insight or "hunches" in all fields. For example, Varma (2012) reports how "an intuitive guess—hunch—in relation to a system of charged particles in a magnetic field pursued over four decades, has led to the discovery of an entirely new set of phenomena, which could not have been conceived in view of the prevailing conceptions" (p. 497). This outcome was reported in the arcane world of macro-scale quantum phenomena and charged particle dynamics. Hunches are also prevalent in medical science as noted in the *Archives of Disease in Childhood* (1997):

> It's not only Hollywood detectives who have hunches; most, if not all, experienced clinicians must be familiar with the situation in which they feel sure that a certain course of action is the right one but are unable to explain why. Much as we may strive towards evidence-based medicine clinical intuition can not be ignored. Now research neuropsychologists in Iowa (Antoine Bechara and colleagues, *Science* 1997;275:1293–5) have given scientific respectability to the concept of valid but non-rational decision making.
>
> **(p. 85)**

The role of hunches has been documented in chemistry (e.g., Platt and Baker, 1931), bio-chemistry (e.g., Singh, 1998), social psychology (Smith et al., 1991), physics (e.g., Benford, 2005), and many other sub-fields. Intuition is as much a part of science as its methods of analysis. See Table 11.5.

The Artist: Perception and Flow as Part of the Aesthetic (A)

Gardner (1998) defines a creator as someone who creates on a regular basis, fashioning ideas, concepts and objects in a given domain in new and novel ways that are ultimately accepted by the community of which they are a part. Unlike leaders who influence people through the stories they tell, creators lead others indirectly through symbol creation, artifact construction, and experience creation. Creators include artists, designers, and experience architects.

I refer to anyone who deals with the aesthetic dimensions of the world as artists. Artists not only populate our academies and city lofts, but also reside in modern business organizations. While seldom used in the context of business, aesthetics is very much a critical success factor for companies in order to grow and flourish. All consumers of goods and services exercise aesthetic judgment in the evaluation of how much they like, or dislike, a particular item or experience. Information coming directly from our senses to our emotions is just as important knowledge from logical analysis. Consider the impact of a well-planned occasion at a top-rated restaurant. The food, the ambiance, the service, the music, the people, the linens, and all the other details combine to create a

Table 11.5   Intuition Context "Scorecard" for Scientists

Factor	Score	Analysis
Analytical Processing Requirements	Yes	Scientific inquiry provides one of the most effective means to create new knowledge and to codify it. Much of normal science is based on rigorous analytical methods.
Supplemental Processing Capabilities		
Linked to domain-specific experience and expertise	Yes	Scientists are deeply grounded in their domains of knowledge, and to such a degree that it may be nearly impossible to read and comprehend works outside of one's own field of study. Deep knowing, hunches, and intuition arise out of each field of inquiry.
Feelings, emotions, and affect play a key role in processes	Yes	Emotions play a role in science, especially as new paradigms are evolved. Breakthroughs elicit jubilation while setbacks can lead to dark periods. For example, documentaries on the evolution of *string theory* in physics (e.g., Greene, 2003) recount the human emotional challenges and frustrations of being on the wrong side of mainstream science.
Knowledge originates beyond conscious thought	Yes	The extensive descriptions of hunches in scientific discovery suggest that knowledge originates beyond conscious understanding and problem-solving.
Processes are associative and holistic	$p > 0$	The processes of discovery appear to be holistic and associative.

lasting impression, deeply embedded in the sights, smells, sounds, tactile sensations, and of course, tastes of the time slice. The participants may describe the experience as *beautiful*, perhaps the highest praise a business might hope for. This is aesthetics in action.

Aesthetics finds its roots in the Greek words *aisthetikos*, which means "sensitive, perceptive," and *aisthanesthai*, which means, "to perceive (by the senses or by the mind), to feel" (Harper, 2010). Gibb (2004, p. 67) defines aesthetics as "the simultaneous, and unified, engagement of the mind, body, and sensibilities." Aesthetic experiences present themselves as holistic and highly integrative. Interestingly, they appear in both the creator of the experience or the artifact as well as the recipients of those experiences or constructions. The designers at Apple or Tesla appreciate the role of aesthetics and incorporate those elements into the structures, forms, and functions of their objects of creation. They know the reaction of a buyer's hands to smooth impervious glass and anodized aluminum; the metal and glass evoke strength and signal status, perhaps prestige. The creators at Cirque du Soleil similarly know well in advance the impact the music, colors, costumes, and movements will trigger in the audience in terms of sensations, emotions, and thoughts. In this way, the unveiling of new creations is a sensory experiment. It includes the creator, his or her designs, and an observer. "The outcome of an aesthetic experiment is a complex cognitive and emotional reaction to the sensory data. The 'experiment' may produce happiness, sadness, revulsion, or some other emotion" (Stein, 2014a, p. 93). It will result in thoughts and an evaluation in terms of its beauty (or lack therein). Each time we interact with new structures, experiences, products, services, art, or nature results in new experimental outcomes that reinforce existing schemas and mental models. Kant characterized interactions between the observer and nature to be "pure" in his *Critique of Judgment*, whereas those between the observer and human produced objects such as art to be "impure" (Stanford University, 2005).

Aesthetic awareness can be defined as "the ability to discriminate between various sensory inputs (e.g., visual, auditory, etc.), recognize the feelings and thoughts invoked, and to rank the object of reflection in terms of certain criteria such as beauty" (Stein, 2014a, p. 93). Aesthetics is thus a process that begins with sensations and perceptions that trigger emotions resulting in thoughts and evaluations. See Figure 11.5.

Artists (of all types) engineer these sensory experiments for their audiences, sometimes while in flow. It is expected that intuition plays a key role in designing these episodes (Table 11.6).

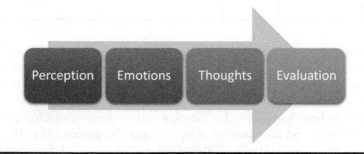

Perception   Emotions   Thoughts   Evaluation

Figure 11.5   The aesthetic experience as process.

Table 11.6 Intuition Context "Scorecard" for Artists

Factor	Score	Analysis
Analytical Processing Requirements	Yes	Artists train for years and even decades in order to perfect techniques and methods that enable them to speak in the vocabulary of their chosen métier. For the visual artist it is internalizing the knowledge of colors, lines, shapes, hues, perspective, and shading. For the industrial artist it is the bio-mechanics of materials, lighting, textures, and forms.
Supplemental Processing Capabilities		
Linked to domain-specific experience and expertise	Yes	There is no question that all art, both applied and pure, is deeply embedded in a domain of knowledge.
Feelings, emotions and affect play a key role in processes	Yes	Feelings and emotions are essential to the aesthetic experience and define it.
Knowledge originates beyond conscious thought	Yes	Sensory experiences and perception themselves precede thoughts. Artists therefore operate in this area beyond conscious thought. Many artists are considered "mad" by the standards of their day because their works oftentimes are accompanied by chaotic thoughts and ideas as they stretch the boundaries of existing convention.
Processes are associative and holistic	Yes	By their very nature, aesthetic experiences are holistic and freely associative and likely include frequent episodes of intuitive processing.

Identifying Candidates for Intuition Research

While inventors, designers, business leaders, and artists of all types have already been the subject for intuition research, in many cases, researchers work with exemplars in these domains, i.e., experts. There is no question that working with these samples is critical to intuition research. On the other hand, it seems to me that we also need to look at the rest of us, more average, folks as Gardner would say. Research should be extended to include all types of designers at a variety of organizations. We also should include improvisers of all types (especially leaders and managers), those who leverage science or scientific thinking, as well as anyone who dwells in the aesthetic dimensions of work. The question is: how do we identify these candidates for study?

Over the past year, I have developed an online assessment tool that scores people according to the four creative strengths identified in this chapter:

- Real-time decision-making using improvisation (I)
- Creative problem-solving using design (D)
- Knowledge creation using scientific methods and experimentation (E)
- Perception and flow as part of the aesthetic (A)

Here is a brief overview of the sub-components of the assessment. The assessment has been taken by over 500 subjects and has produced reliability scores of 0.8 or better (e.g., Cronbach's alpha > 0.80). A more complete paper on the instrument and its efficacy is targeted for future publication (Table 11.7).

The survey is easy to administer, takes less than 25 minutes to complete, and provides results immediately, both to the researcher and the respondent; i.e., the respondent gets immediate feedback on his or her strengths, which incentivizes participation. I encourage researchers in this field to use it. Access to the survey is available at http://ideasmethod.com/creative-strengths-survey/. I believe that this assessment can serve as a useful additional means of selecting candidates working in a modern organization for the study of intuition and creativity.

Summary and Conclusions

The study of intuition is an important addition to the management literature and helps to fill a gap in our understanding of how people process in parallel ways. On one hand, humans exercise their rational-logical minds to arrive at conclusions through analysis and goal-directed problem-solving. On the other hand, research suggests an alternative pathway to knowledge, one that is beyond consciousness, associative and holistic yet grounded in deep knowledge within a domain. In this mode, emotions and feelings play a significant role. While still a black box, intuition confers evolutionary advantage by providing a means of making decisions, especially when the problem space becomes computationally intractable. Some people, especially creative types, have come to rely on intuition to a greater degree than perhaps the general population. This outcome makes sense because creation by its very nature involves the solution of ill-structured problems. In many cases, creatives deal with precedents of $N = 0$. Creative people are forced to take cognitive leaps in order to solve the problems with which they are tasked. I argue that for artists, scientists, designers, and managerial improvisers, this ability is a well-worn muscle. Trusting one's gut is an acquired skill; the more you do it the more likely

Table 11.7 IDEAS Creative Strengths Assessment

Area	Description
Real-Time Decision-Making Using Improvisation (I)	
Planning Score	Degree to which you use plans
Improvisation Score	Degree to which you modify plans
Unconstrained Score	Degree to which take action but you do not use plans
Response P Score	Degree to which you are responsive to others in decision-making
Response T Score	Degree to which you respond to real-time conditions, i.e., quickly
Creative Problem-Solving Using Design (D)	
Design Behavior Score	How you currently use design to solve problems at work
Design Task Score	The degree to which you perform tasks associated with design
Design Preference Score	Your preference for design-type activities
Design Skills Score	The degree to which you have skills associated with designers
Knowledge Creation Using Scientific Methods and Experimentation (E)	
Experimental Behavior Score	How you currently implement scientific methods in your work
Experimental Attitudes Score	Attitudes toward scientific methods
Experimental Preference Score	Preferences for scientific methods
Experimental Knowledge Score	Knowledge of scientific methods
Experimental Tinkering Score	Degree of structure when learning and using scientific principles
Perception and Flow as Part of the Aesthetic (A)	
Aesthetic Preference Score	Your preference for aesthetic activities
Aesthetic Behavior Score	Degree to which you engage in aesthetic behaviors

(*Continued*)

Table 11.7 (Continued)   IDEAS Creative Strengths Assessment

Area	Description
Aesthetic Cognition Score	Degree to which your thoughts are triggered by aesthetic experiences
Aesthetic Emotion Score	Degree to which your emotions are triggered by aesthetic experiences
Aesthetic Judgment Score	Degree to which you exercise aesthetic judgment
Aesthetic Perception Score	Degree to which you are sensitive to sensory and perceptual experiences

you are to do it. It involves a tolerance for risk and ambiguity. Creative people in all fields learn to trust that inner voice, that feeling, that vague image, that dream-like state of inner knowing. In short, they trust their intuition. It is my hope that continued study of this population will yield new insights into the nature of both creativity and intuition, and pave the way for new methods of learning to encourage us to exercise this side of our brains.

References

"About CES." (2019) Consumer Technology Association. Retrieved from: www.ces.tech/About-CES.aspx

Akinci, C. and Sadler-Smith, E. (2012). Intuition in management research: A historical review. *International Journal of Management Reviews*, 14, 104–122.

Allinson, C.W. and Hayes, J. (1996). The Cognitive Style Index: A measure of intuition analysis for organizational research. *Journal of Management Studies*, 33, 119–135.

Baldacchino, Leonie, Ucbasaran, D., Cabantous, L. and Lockett, A. (2015). Entrepreneurship research on intuition: A critical analysis and research agenda. *International Journal of Management Reviews*, 17, 212–231.

Benford, G. (2005). Being true to our own imaginatons. *Physics Today*, 58(11), 48.

Berliner, P. (1994). *Thinking in Jazz: The Infinite Art of Improvisation*. Chicago, IL: University of Chicago.

Brown, T. (2007, December 19). Strategy by design. Retrieved February 1, 2011, from FastCompany.com: www.fastcompany.com/magazine/95/design-strategy.html

Brown, J.S. (2008). John Seely Brown: Tinkering as a mode of knowledge production. Retrieved from Youtube.com: http://youtu.be/9u-MczVpkUA

Csikszentmihalyi, M. (1996). *Creativity*. New York, NY: Harper Collins.

Csikszentmihalyi, M. (2004). TED Talks: Mihaly Csikszentmihalyi: Creativity, fulfillment and flow. Retrieved 2011, from YouTube: www.youtube.com/watch?v=fXIeFJCqsPsplaynext=1list=PL5EE8EAA551ED6420

Culham, T. (2015). Reuniting virtue and knowledge. *Journal of Philosophy of Education*, 49(2), 294–310.

Epstein, S. (2008). Intuition from the perspective of Cognitive–Experiential Self-Theory. In Plessner, H., Betsch, C. and Betsch, T. (eds), *Intuition in Judgement and Decision Making*. New York, NY: Taylor & Francis Group, pp. 23–37.

Gardner, H. (1994). *Creating minds: An Anatomy of Creativity as Seen through the Lives of Freud, Einstein, Picasso, Stravinsky, Eliot, Graham, and Gandhi*. New York, NY: Basic Books.

Gladwell, M. (2008). *Outliers: The Story of Success*. New York, NY: Little, Brown and Company.

Greene, B. (2003). *The Elegant Universe: Superstrings, Hidden Dimensions, and the Quest for the Ultimate Theory*. New York: W.W. Norton Company.

Hornett, A. and Stein, E.W. 2007. Mapping the knowledge management domain of ideas: Evidence from a practice group. *International Journal of Knowledge Management*, 3(3), 1–25 (Recipient of Innovation Award from Idea Publishing).

Hunch theory. (1997). *Archives of Disease in Childhood*, 77(1), 85.

Jones, T.M. (1991). Ethical decision making by individuals in organizations. *The Academy of Management Review*, 16(2), 366–395.

Kolb, D.A. (1984). *Experiential Learning: Experience as the Source of Learning and Development* (Vol. 1). Englewood Cliffs, NJ: Prentice Hall.

Kuhn, T.S. 1996. *The Structure of Scientific Revolutions*. 3rd ed. Chicago, IL: University of Chicago Press.

McDonough, M. and Braungart, W. (2002). *Cradle to Cradle: Remaking the Way We Make Things*. New York: North Point Press.

Mintzberg, H. (1976). Planning on the left side and managing on the right. *Harvard Business Review*, July 1976.

Nonaka, I. (2007). The knowledge creating company. *Harvard Business Review*, July-August 2007.

Orlikowski, W. (1996). Improvising organizational transformation over time: A situated change perspective. *Information Systems Research*, 7(1).

Peplowski, K. (1998). The process of improvisation. *Organization Science*, 9(5), 560–561

Platt, W. and Baker, R.A. (1931). The relation of the scientific "hunch" to research. *Journal of Chemistry Education*, 8(10), 1969

Shah, A. (August 2, 2018) Apple hits $1 trillion, but it's still not the most valuable company in the world. *Forbes*. Retrieved from: www.forbes.com/sites/alapshah/2018/08/02/apple-hits-1-trillion-but-its-still-not-the-most-valuable-company-in-the-world/#6fff3f512175

Simon, H. (1969). *The Sciences of the Artificial*. Cambridge, MA: MIT Press.

Sinclair, M. and Ashkanasy, N.M. (2005). Intuition: Myth or a decision-making tool? *Management Learning*, 36, 353–370.

Singh, N.J. (1998) Decisions, premonitions and hunches: Is there any rationality? *Journal of Biosciences*, 23(5), 542–543.

Smith, H.J., Archer, D. and Costanzo, M. (1991). 'Just a hunch: Accuracy and awareness in person perception. *Journal of Nonverbal Behavior*, 15(1), 3–18.

Stanford University. (2005). *Kant's Aesthetics and Teleology*. Retrieved December 7, 2010, from Stanford Encyclopedia of Philosophy: http://plato.stanford.edu/entries/kant-aesthetics/#2

Stein, E.W. (1995a). Social and individual characteristics of organizational experts. *International Journal of Expert Systems: Research & Applications*, 8(2), 121–143.

Stein, E.W. (1995b). Organizational memory: Review of concepts and recommendations for management. *International Journal of Information Management*, 15(1), 17–32.

Stein, E.W. (2005). A qualitative study of the characteristics of a community of practice for knowledge management (KM) and its success factors. *International Journal of Knowledge Management*, 1(3), 1–24.

Stein, E.W. (2007). Factors that contribute to the success of knowledge management communities of practice. Appearing in *Knowledge Management in Modern Organizations*. Hershey, PA: IGI Global Publishing, pp. 142–170.

Stein, E.W. (2011). Improvisation as model for real-time decision-making. Appearing in the *Annals of Information Systems, Special Volume in Decision Support Systems: Supporting real time decision-making: The role of context in decision support on the move*. Edited by F. Burstein, P. Brezillon, and A. Zaslavsky. Berlin/Heidelberg: Springer.

Stein, E.W. (2014a) *Fostering Creativity in Self and the Organization: Your Professional Edge*, Jean Philips and Stan Gully, Series Editors. New York: Business Expert Press.

Stein, E.W. (2014b). *Designing Creative High Power Teams and Organizations*, Jean Philips and Stan Gully, Series Editors. New York: Business Expert Press.

Stein, E.W. and Vandenbosch, B. (1996). (Case Western Reserve University). Opportunities for and obstacles to organizational learning during advanced system development. *Journal of Management Information Systems*, 13(2), 115–136.

Stein, E.W. and Zwass, V. (1995). Actualizing organizational memory with information systems. *Information Systems Research*, 6(2), 85–117.

Stein, E.W., Manco, M. and Manco, S. (2001). A knowledge-based system to assist administrators in meeting disability act requirements. *Expert Systems with Applications*, 21, 65–74.

Stein, E.W., Pauster, M. and May, D. (2003). A knowledge-based system to improve the quality of titanium melting. *Expert Systems with Applications*, 24(2), 239–246.

Thompson, V. (2014). What intuitions are … and are not. *Psychology of Learning and Motivation*, 60, 35–75.

Varma, R.K. (2012). From hunches to surprises—Discovering macro-scale quantum phenomena in charged particle dynamics. *Current Science*, 103(5).

Weick, K. (1998). Improvisation as a mindset for organizational analysis. *Organization Science* 9(5), 543–555.

Index

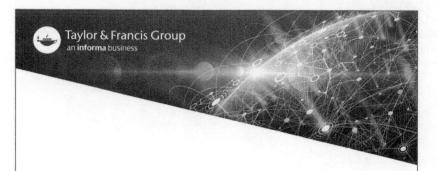

Taylor & Francis eBooks

www.taylorfrancis.com

A single destination for eBooks from Taylor & Francis
with increased functionality and an improved user
experience to meet the needs of our customers.

90,000+ eBooks of award-winning academic content in
Humanities, Social Science, Science, Technology, Engineering,
and Medical written by a global network of editors and authors.

TAYLOR & FRANCIS EBOOKS OFFERS:

A streamlined
experience for
our library
customers

A single point
of discovery
for all of our
eBook content

Improved
search and
discovery of
content at both
book and
chapter level

REQUEST A FREE TRIAL
support@taylorfrancis.com

 Routledge
Taylor & Francis Group

 CRC Press
Taylor & Francis Group